PELICAN BOOKS

A470

LANGUAGE IN THE MODERN WORLD

Simeon Potter was born in London in 1898, and was educated at Kilburn Grammar School, at the University of London, and at St John's College, Oxford. In the First World War he served with the Royal Navy. He travelled widely and for many years he taught English abroad in Czechoslovakia in the University of Brno, and in Denmark in the University of Aarhus. His keen interest in the problems of language was greatly stimulated by his close association with the Prague Linguistic Circle in its early days, and later with the London Philological Society, of which he has long been a life member. He has broadcast frequently for Prague Radio and occasionally for the BBC. For many years he kept in personal touch with several living tongues in his capacity as Adviser to Overseas Students in the University of Southampton. His Pelican book *Our Language*, and his volume on *Modern Linguistics* in Eric Partridge's Language Library, are now well known. For twenty years (1945–65) Dr Potter held the Baines Chair of English in the University of Liverpool, where he is now Professor Emeritus.

LANGUAGE IN
THE MODERN WORLD

BY

SIMEON POTTER

...language, the most valuable
single possession of the human race.

C. F. HOCKETT
Cornell University

PENGUIN BOOKS

Penguin Books Ltd, Harmondsworth, Middlesex, England
Penguin Books Inc., 3300 Clipper Mill Road, Baltimore 11, Md, U.S.A.
Penguin Books Pty Ltd, Ringwood, Victoria, Australia

—

First published 1960
Reprinted with revisions 1961, 1964, 1966

—

Copyright © Simeon Potter, 1960

—

Made and printed in Great Britain
by Hazell Watson & Viney Ltd
Aylesbury, Bucks
Set in Monotype Baskerville

CONTENTS

SYMBOLS

<   'changed from' or 'derived from'

>   'changed to' or 'becomes'

[ ]   enclose *phonetic symbols*

/ /   enclose *phonemic symbols*

:   after phonetic symbols denotes *length*

:   between forms denotes *contrast* or *opposition*

/   between forms denotes *alternation*

*   indicates a *reconstructed* or *hypothetical form*

PHONETIC SYMBOLS

The consonant-letters p, b, t, d, k, g; l, r, m, n; f, v, s, z, h, w have their usual English values. Below are given the key-words for other sounds appearing occasionally in this book:

CONSONANTS

tʃ	*church*	ʃ	*ship*
dʒ	*judge*	ʒ	*measure*
ŋ	*sing*	x	Scots *loch*
θ	*thin*	ɥ	French *huit*
ð	*then*	j	*yes*

VOWELS

i:	*see*	ã	French *blanc*
i	*sit*	u:	*moon*
e	French *thé*	u	*put*
ɛ	*set*	ʌ	*but*
a	*cat*	ə:	*bird*
ɑ:	*father*	ə	*father*
ɔ	*hot*	y	French *pur*
ɔ:	*for*	ø	,, *creux*
œ̃	French *un*	œ	,, *seul*
ɔ̃	,, *bon*	o	,, *mot*
ɛ̃	,, *vin*		

DIPHTHONGS

ei	*day*	ɔi	*boy*
ou	*go*	iə	*here*
ai	*fly*	ɛə	*there*
au	*now*	uə	*gourd*

CHAPTER I

INTRODUCTORY

LANGUAGE plays such a prominent part in the daily lives of all of us that we should do our best to understand its first principles. Those principles are now better known than ever before. New life has been given to the study of language in our day, and anyone who has had time and opportunity to follow the progress made in general linguistics in recent years cannot help feeling elated and exhilarated at the prospects that now unfold themselves before the eyes of the imaginative observer. What, then, has happened? Linguistics has at last cast off its chains and has gone far on the way to becoming an exact empirical science. Structure, not grammar, is the key word to the new linguistics, just as, in a different way, it is the key word to modern mathematics and to nuclear physics. The scientific revolution of our time, in relativity, in quantum physics, and in biological statistics, has led to the reorganization of the logical structure of thought itself. At last the student of language has succeeded in developing a technique more nearly perfect than that of any other science concerned with man and man's institutions.

Today we are living in a time of hope for the future of mankind, and of fear; of great hope, and of great fear. (Can hope and expectation ever dwell conspicuously in the minds of men without some fear and apprehension lurking beneath?) Our hope for the future of language is that by greatly improved linguistic techniques all educated people may master at least one of the great living languages of the world other than their own, and that thus all men of good will may be able to communicate freely and fully with one another. Our fear is that people who now speak one and the same birth tongue may, in fact, become so highly specialized and departmentalized in all their words and ways that they will no longer be able to understand one another from sheer lack of a common basis of discourse, and that they will find themselves quite incapable of understanding workers in other fields of investigation or of communicating the fruits of their labours to mankind at large in lucid, intelligible words. Philosophers and psychologists, statisticians and economists, have evolved such elaborately technical languages, or metalanguages as we may perhaps call them, that they are in danger of forgetting how to talk simply and naturally to others outside their own particular circle. Even the poets, the inspired voices of contemporary society, have become more and more specialized and obscure. Too often they seem to prefer to speak darkly and obliquely to sophisticated coteries rather than clearly and straightforwardly to all men.

Effective language is ever two-way. It is, first of all, an instrument of communication. It consists of an arbitrary system or pattern of speech-sounds by means of which man imparts to others, and shares with others, his thoughts, emotions, and desires. Inasmuch as language is human and non-instinctive, it is raised above the noises made by animals, birds, and insects: such instinctive forms of self-expression as the neighing of a horse, the barking of a dog, the croaking of a frog, the hooting of an owl, or the stridulation of a cricket. Language is a series of sounds or air-vibrations produced by the articulating organs of the speaker and received by the auditory organ or ear of the hearer, and implying a highly complex network of adjustments in the nervous systems and the brains of both speaker and hearer. Such arbitrary series of sounds are theoretically infinite in number. No one will ever know how many languages have been devised by man in the course of his long history. Many have disappeared without a trace. In the modern world their number is between two and three thousand.

The linguist of today is concerned, first of all, with the objective analysis of the pattern or structure of the sounds, syllables, words, phrases, and sentences of any language or languages in the world. He may include many languages in his survey or he may limit his observation to just one or two. Naturally he may begin with a careful analysis of the structure of the language he knows best, namely his mother tongue, and thence he may proceed to the next language with which he happens to be acquainted. It is doubtful whether any man could accomplish a complete analysis of a speech-system without some basis of comparison, and this applies with equal force to the beginner. That is why it is so important in the modern world that all our children in the British Commonwealth and in the United States should be encouraged to acquire a sound knowledge of the mechanism of at least one language other than their own, because, in the end, this is the quickest way of understanding the structure of English, of getting into the habit of thinking straight in English, and of detecting, as in a flash, pretentious, slovenly, inadequate expressions which are the outcome of vain, lazy, or crooked thoughts. Students, to be sure, will be attracted most by the great living tongues of western civilization – French, German, Spanish, Portuguese, Italian, and Swedish – with their rich literature and cultures, but in order to establish their standard of comparison they might choose any language under the sun, the more unlike English the better. Alternatively, of course, they might choose any one of the great languages of antiquity. Have you ever tried translating an untidy sentence into Latin or Greek? There is probably no surer way of demonstrating the emptiness of loose verbiage arising from muddled thinking.

In emancipating himself from prejudice and from preconceived theory the modern linguist is really beginning all over again. He is putting himself back into the position of Pāṇini who gave a completely objective analysis of Old Indian or Sanskrit in the fourth or third century before Christ and thus produced a linguistic document which has been well described as 'one of the greatest monuments of human intelligence'. On the whole the leading languages of the older civilizations were remarkably well served by their chief grammarians: Yāska and Pāṇini for Sanskrit, Dionysius Thrax and Apollonius Dyscolus for Greek, Aelius Donatus and Priscian for Latin, Sībawayhi and Al Khalīl for Arabic. These grammarians were reliable because they were independent: they based their conclusions upon observation unhampered by dogma. Donatus and Priscian, it is true, followed their Greek predecessors closely, even slavishly, but they did no great harm so far as their own language was concerned. Latin was near enough to Greek in its structural pattern, in the cases of its nouns and the tenses of its verbs, for the adopted framework to fit fairly well. Both Greek and Latin were highly inflected languages. In many ways Latin was simpler than Greek. It had no dual number, for example, and it had no aorist tense. A regular Greek verb had no fewer than ten participles: Latin three only. Like Greek, Latin had an architectonic sentence pattern, but it was more rigid. All this meant that no serious consequences arose from the fact that Latin grammarians took their framework from Greek. Later, however, the grammarians of the Middle Ages came to regard their Latin precursors, especially Donatus and Priscian, as unimpeachable and impeccable authorities whose rules and prescriptions might be applied indiscriminately to all tongues. Grammar meant primarily Latin grammar and somehow Latin grammar was thought to embody universally valid canons of logic. This notion persisted in Western Europe for many decades after the Renaissance and it is by no means dead today. Even Antoine Arnauld, Claude Lancelot, and the other advanced and enlightened scholars who were responsible for the famous Port Royal Grammar of A.D. 1660, *Grammaire générale et raisonnée*, could not free themselves entirely from Latin domination, and the writers of the most popular text-books of English Grammar in the eighteenth century, able men like Joseph Priestley, Robert Lowth, and, above all, Lindley Murray, followed Dr Samuel Johnson in their veneration for classical traditions. It was largely due to the rediscovery of Sanskrit by Sir William Jones and others towards the close of the century that this Latin domination was shaken, that the ancient Indo-European languages were reconstructed, and that the modern science of linguistics was initiated. Friedrich von Schlegel, whose notable treatise *On the Language and Wisdom of the Indians* (1808) heralded this century of 'comparative grammar', had learnt Sanskrit from Alexander Hamilton (1762–1824), that enterprising Scot and orientalist who had seen long service with the East India Company in Bengal and who had used his leisure time so profitably as to make himself the leading Sanskrit scholar of his day. Eight years later came Franz Bopp's great book *On the Conjugation-System of Sanskrit* (1816) which appeared exactly one hundred years before Ferdinand de Saussure's *Cours de linguistique générale* (1916), which, as we shall see later, inaugurated the present era of 'structural linguistics'.

Bopp and his followers, more especially August Friedrich Pott, Jakob Grimm, August Schleicher, Karl Brugmann, and Hermann Paul, built up an imposing picture of the Germanic languages on their Indo-European foundations, and their achievements were supplemented by those of pioneers in other fields, Friedrich Diez in Romance, Franz von Miklosich in Slavonic, and Johann Kaspar Zeuss in Celtic. Together they were able to show the broad relations existing between the tongues of Europe and Western Asia. They made bold and fairly convincing attempts at reconstructing the parent Indo-European language of five thousand years ago, the forms of the words, the precise shapes of their elaborate inflexions, and the structures of the main types of sentences. They went so far as to establish 'sound laws' by which sounds changed in one way and not in another, and they went so far as to determine the precise periods of time over which these particular changes were operative.

How exciting it was, for instance, to discover that English *tooth*, French *dent*, and German *Zahn* all derived by normal sound developments from the present participle of the verb 'to eat' *(e)dent-*, *(e)dont-*, *(e)dṇt-* in the parent language, and then to be able to show further that Sanskrit *dán*, *dántam* and Greek *odoús*, *odónta* are related by gradation or

13

ablaut to Latin *dens*, *dentem*, from which Italian *dente*, French *dent*, and Spanish *diente* manifestly derive! The English form *tooth* comes from older *tanth as may be clearly seen by comparing it with Modern Dutch, Danish, and Swedish *tand*. Notice, by the way, that we use both Greek-derived *odontology* and Latin-derived *dentistry* to discriminate between the scientific study of the structure and development of the teeth on the one hand, and the practical art of tending them on the other. A *dandelion* (French *dent de lion* 'lion's tooth') is so named from its widely toothed leaves. The opening word of this paragraph is *indented* or inset, as by a tooth-shaped space.

Is it surprising that nineteenth-century comparative philologists were fascinated by such discoveries? Their intellectual output was certainly most impressive and meritorious, and yet, according to present-day standards, their work fell short of perfection in two respects. First, they did not always free themselves from the error of confusing written letters with spoken sounds; and, secondly, they were too prone in their exuberance to indulge in dreamy speculation instead of exercising observation at every step. To illustrate the first point I may perhaps be allowed to refer to a trivial incident in my own recent experience. Last week I happened to be strolling along a side-street near St Patrick's Cathedral in Dublin when I heard a boy telling his playmate that he had just found his lost ball for he had 'come acrost it' by chance in so-and-so's garden. Now this Irish lad's *acrost*, I said to myself, for normal *across*, is such a natural *lapsus linguae* that it might be both readily explained and easily paralleled. It actually appears in seventeenth-century letters. It is like dialectal *oncet* for *once*; or archaic *hest* from Old English *hæs*; or standard *against*, *amidst*, *amongst*, and *whilst* from older adverbial genitive terminations in -(*e*)*s*; or countless other forms in many different languages. The boy's tongue quite naturally touched or flicked his gum or teeth-ridge ever so slightly in passing from the position of fricative or sibilant *s* to that of nearby high-front vowel *i*, and, as a result, I distinctly heard a plosive sound. I might say that 'the boy put in an excrescent *t*', or that 'a *t* came creeping in', but such expressions would not describe the facts of speech scientifically. Changes in ways of speaking take place on the lips of men and not in the pages of books. I should therefore think, not of printed letters, but of spoken sounds, first and always. To illustrate the second point concerning excessive speculation, I may perhaps revert for a moment to that etymology of *tooth* which I mentioned in the preceding paragraph. Today we feel just as certain as August Friedrich Pott, who first explained their relationships, that English *tooth*, French *dent*, and German *Zahn* are cognate forms, but we are not so downright in our conclusion that they derive directly and simply from the Indo-European present participle of the verb 'to eat', and that, having tracked *tooth* and its cognates down to their root *eating* (*thing*) or *eater*, we have reached rock-bottom, and there is nothing more for us to do. There is evidence to show that the ancient word for *tooth* was not completely identical with *eater* after all, but that, by a kind of primitive folk etymology, it was *associated* with the verb *to eat* by the Indo-European people themselves. In any case the modern linguist refuses to regard the Indo-European language as simply primordial. Like Common Germanic, Anglo-Saxon, or Tudor English, it was merely one stage in the long development of human speech.

The scientific observer must, of course, show imagination and enterprise, but he should be careful to differentiate between surmise and fact at every step. When evidence is inadequate, he must say so. In their over-confidence and enthusiasm, nineteenth-century 'comparatists' thought that they could explain everything, with sometimes disastrous results, especially in the field of etymology. They certainly laid themselves open to criticism in their venturesome reconstruction of the parent language. Georg von der Gabelentz laconically observed that Proto-Indo-European 'had changed beyond recognition in the short time between Schleicher and Brugmann'. There are still, however, plenty of highly intelligent and well-informed persons who think

that it is the plain duty of the editor of any sort of etymological dictionary to present a neat history of every word in
a language and that, if he does not, he has failed in his task.

Many famous American and English philologists were
trained in Germany in the nineteenth century, including
William Dwight Whitney (1827–94) of Yale, and Henry
Sweet (1845–1912) of Oxford. Whitney, who studied at
Berlin under Bopp, placed the scientific study of language
in America upon sure foundations: Sweet, who studied at
Heidelberg under Holzmann, insisted throughout his life
on the supreme importance of the minute observation of
living speech. Insistence on first-hand observation was also
emphasized by Ferdinand de Saussure (1857–1913) who
taught with brilliant originality at Paris and Geneva, who
wrote remarkably little during his lifetime, but whose
lectures were published posthumously in 1916 by his pupils
Charles Bally and Albert Sechehaye under the title *Cours de
linguistique générale*. It would be no exaggeration to say
that de Saussure was the founder of present-day linguistics.
In this course, or strictly three courses, of lectures, he
wrestled with four main problems: the relationship between language and speech, between the inherited resources of language or *langue* and the particular uses made
of those more permanent resources in speech or *parole*;
the analysis of linguistic symbols; the differentiation between
the descriptive or *synchronic* and the historical or *diachronic*
methods of study; and the ways of examining the general
structure of a linguistic system. His teachings have since
been accepted and extended by his illustrious pupil Antoine
Meillet (1866–1936) of the Sorbonne, by Nikolai Trubetzkoy (1890–1938) of Vienna, and by many distinguished
linguists in the United States, notably Edward Sapir
(1884–1939) and Leonard Bloomfield (1887–1949). Both
Sapir and Bloomfield derived great profit from their first-
hand observation of American Indian languages whose
structural patterns are quite unlike those of English and
other Indo-European languages, and also unlike one another. Sapir studied Athapaskan: Bloomfield worked on

Central Algonquian. In this way they trained themselves for their more general investigations. Some of these aboriginal forms of speech are described synchronically, to use de Saussure's term, in the pages of *Language*, the Journal of the Linguistic Society of America, which was founded in 1925. It was to the second volume of this periodical that Bloomfield contributed his remarkable *Set of Postulates for the Science of Language* (1926), a daring attempt to apply mathematical principles to human speech on the assumption that 'the postulational method can further the study of language, because it forces us to state explicitly whatever we assume, to define our terms, and to decide what things may exist independently and what things are interdependent'. Bloomfield's handbook *Language* (1933) served as a convenient starting-point and guide to the many aspects of linguistic study discussed and ventilated at debates and conferences, especially at the International Congresses of Linguists now held quinquennially.

Some languages are spoken by quite small communities and they are hardly likely to survive. Before the end of the twentieth century many languages in Africa, Asia, and America will have passed into complete oblivion unless some competent linguist has found time to record them. The languages that remain are constantly changing with the changing needs and circumstances of the people who speak them. Change is the manifestation of life in language. The great languages of the world, such as English, Russian, Chinese, Japanese, German, Spanish, French, Italian, Portuguese, Dutch, and Arabic, are just as liable to change as Swahili, Tamil, or Choctaw. Change may, it is true, be artificially retarded in special conditions: for example, in the great liturgical languages of mankind, such as Sanskrit, the language of the orthodox Hindu religion of India; or Pali, the sacred language of Buddhism; or Latin, the liturgical language of the Roman Church. By arduous schooling a man may train himself to read, write, and converse in these crystallized forms of speech. Sanskrit, Pali, and Latin are magnificent and awe-inspiring exceptions to the otherwise universal principle of change. Their immutability depends upon two main factors or conditions: first, that they are not normally used in everyday conversation, but are entrusted instead to the care of a privileged class of priests and scholars; and, secondly, that they possess memorable recorded literatures and liturgies which are constantly read and recited in acts of religious devotion and worship.

It is just because these two conditions do not apply to artificial languages like Volapük, Esperanto, and Ido, that they, however carefully devised and constructed, cannot come alive and then escape from the law of change. Over one hundred artificial languages have been framed by men in recent times, but the three just named are far more widely known and used than any others. Volapük, or 'World's Speech', was created by a Bavarian pastor named Johan Martin Schleyer, in 1879, when it was acclaimed with enthusiasm as the future universal speech of mankind. Only eight years later, however, many of Volapük's most ardent supporters abandoned it in favour of the system invented by the 'hopeful doctor', Doktoro Esperanto, a Polish Jew named Lazarus Zamenhof (1859–1917). Esperanto is certainly an improvement upon Volapük in that it is both more flexible and more regular. To Latin roots (*okulo* 'eye', *dento* 'tooth') are added adaptations from French (*arbo* 'tree'), English (*lando* 'land'), and German (*jaro* 'year'). Compounds and derivatives are freely formed. Substantives, adjectives, adverbs, infinitives, and imperatives end in -*o*, -*a*, -*e*, -*i*, and -*u*, respectively (*homo* 'man', *bona* 'good', *bone* 'well', *esti* 'to be', *estu* 'be'), and all plurals end in -*j* (*bonaj homoj* 'good men'). Verbs show present tense forms in -*as*, past in -*is*, and future in -*os*, with corresponding active participles in -*anta*, -*inta*, -*onta*, and passive participles in -*ata*, -*ita*, and -*ota*. Even within Zamenhof's lifetime, however, the mechanism of Esperanto was improved in various ways, and in 1907 Ido (a made-up name consisting of the initials of International Delegation + substantival suffix -*o*) was formulated. This Delegation included scholars prominent in various branches of learning, but its recommendations were not accepted by the main body of Esperantists who were reluctant to admit that all their well-established text-books might now be out of date. Today Esperanto, and not its more advanced form Ido, is easily the first constructed language in the world and it has proved its worth at numerous international gatherings. It no longer aspires to supplant ethnic languages. Like those other artificial languages created in the twentieth century – Giuseppe Peano's *Latino Sine Flexione* (1903), Otto Jespersen's *Novial* (1928), Lancelot Hogben's *Interglossa* (1943), and the International Auxiliary Language Association's *Interlingua* (1951) – Esperanto can be regarded as a valuable bridge-language which any man may find unexpectedly useful in unforeseen contingencies. Learning Esperanto is a pleasant pastime, and manipulating its regularized affixes and inflexions may become a healthy form of mental gymnastics. Nevertheless, even loyal Esperantists have been known to chafe and strain under the necessary bonds of orthodoxy. However much society may desire and demand that it should remain constant, 'language changes always and everywhere'. In the New World, where opportunities are limitless and enthusiasms boundless, and where whole families have been reputed to adopt Esperanto as their everyday language, it has become modified considerably within the space of one year to suit the special circumstances and way of life of that particular community. The worlds in which different social communities live are separate worlds, not just one world with different linguistic labels attached. An American and a Russian may converse pleasantly in Esperanto about travel, food, dress, and sport, but they may be quite incapable of talking seriously in Esperanto about religion, science, or philosophy. 'Men imagine', as Francis Bacon said long ago, 'that their minds have command of language; but it often happens that language bears rule over their minds.' Whether we like it or not, we are all very much under the spell of that particular form of speech which has become the medium of discourse for our society.

Let us recognize this truth, and the truth shall make us free. As our world draws more closely together, and as the need for understanding the motives of human conduct grows ever more pressing, so it becomes increasingly necessary for us English-speaking people to reconsider that all too facile notion that we need not bother our heads very seriously about language-learning because all the rest of the world will be able and willing to talk to us in bad English before the dawn of the twenty-first century. We should surely be better advised to extend the range of our studies to include the great languages of the east, to be more realistic and energetic in perfecting our teaching techniques, and, above all, to search more deeply into the nature and essence of language itself.

CHAPTER 2

LANGUAGE AND NATIONALITY

FIVE main factors may be said to divide mankind in the modern world: race, religion, culture, language, and nationality. Obviously these factors are not mutually exclusive. For example, there may be wide and deep associations between race and religion; and also between religion and culture, both of which may include art, law, institutions, morals, customs, and taboos. For our present purpose, however, it may be profitable to keep these five factors separate in our minds and to focus our attention on each one in turn before proceeding to examine current conceptions and misconceptions concerning language and nationality.

By *race* I mean the grouping together of people sprung from the same *stock* or *breed* and therefore possessing certain physical characteristics in common, as when I allude to the Jewish race, or as when I say that we Europeans today are all of mixed race, every one of us; that racial purity can no longer be determined anywhere in the west; and that Nordic, Mediterranean, and Alpine, once discernible races, are now intermingled everywhere to a greater or less degree. Race is not a scientific term at all and it therefore finds no place in the nomenclature of that taxonomy, or system of classification of living creatures, which has now won universal acceptance. The world of nature has its three realms or kingdoms: animal, vegetable, and mineral. Each of these is arranged in a sevenfold hierarchy of sub-kingdoms or phyla, classes, orders, families, genera, species, and varieties. Man belongs to the genus *Homo*, which includes lemurs, monkeys, and apes: the anthropoid apes consist of orang-utans, chimpanzees, and gorillas. Man comprises the biological species *Homo sapiens*. My binomial designation is thus composed of the capitalized name of the genus, immediately followed by the epithet (with small initial) denoting the species, just as that of the cat sitting on my hearth-rug is *Felis domestica*, and that of the song-thrush hopping about on my lawn is *Turdus musicus*. How neat and convenient it would be if we could still follow Johann Friedrich Blumenbach (1752–1840) and subdivide this species *Homo sapiens* into five varieties according to easily observable skin pigmentation called white Caucasian, yellow Mongolian, black Ethiopian, red American, and tawny Malay; and then proceed to describe them all with reference to their skeletons or bony structures, the shape of the skull (whether long, medium, or broad – dolicho-, meso-, or brachy-cephalic), the straightness and width of the nose, the projection or prognathism of the jaw, the curliness of the hair, the colour of the eyes, the presence or otherwise of the eye-fold, the degree of skin-coloration, and so on. Such classifications have indeed been attempted from time to time by eminent anthropometrists, but the conclusions they have reached have proved both confusing and uncertain. They have discovered beyond a doubt that the distribution of races throughout the world varies unpredictably according to the particular features, or combinations of features (stature, skull, nose, jaw, eyes, hair, or skin), selected as criteria. Whatever races they choose to distinguish are found to be arbitrary and elusive.

Meantime the geneticists, students of heredity and environment, have been more successful. Although the pioneer discoveries of Gregor Johann Mendel (1822–84) never became known to Charles Darwin and were little used until after the turn of the century, progress has since then been rapid. It is now well attested that inheritance operates through genes contained in chromosomes, and not through blood. That blood is inherited is a venerable misconception as old as Aristotle, who taught that a woman's menstruation, which ceases during pregnancy, contributes to the substance of the child's body she is bearing. In fact, there is no such menstrual flow between mother and offspring because not a single drop of blood normally passes from the mother to the babe in her womb. The nucleus of every cell in the child's body contains twenty-three pairs of chromosomes, one of each pair deriving from the father and one from the mother. Inasmuch as a child has this number of paired chromosomes in each cell, the number of possible combinations is $2^{23} = 8,388,608$. All children inherit twenty-three chromosomes from each of their two parents, but it is highly probable that they receive variable numbers from their four grandparents, their eight great-grand-parents, and (if no inbreeding) their sixteen great-great-grandparents. It may well occur that a child has not obtained chromosomes from every one of these sixteen forebears. Indeed, if we go back only two generations more to his sixty-four ancestors (if no inbreeding) in the sixth generation, we reach a state where there are actually more individual parents than inherited chromosomes, so that it is physically impossible for the child to derive genes from them all. What disconcerting facts to tell a person whose proud boast rests solely on the assumption that he is descended in a direct line from the Plantagenet Kings!

Biologically it may be found that there are few differences between an African negro and a white Scandinavian. On analysis their blood-groups may prove to be identical. Even their gene differences may be assumed to reside in only six pairs or less. Truly, though in a different sense from that intended by him, Blumenbach's main hypothesis that *Homo sapiens* constitutes one species throughout the world retains its validity.

Race, as hitherto conceived, is thus largely a delusion. The word itself came into Tudor English from Arabic *ra's* 'head' by way of Spanish *raza* or Portuguese *raça* and French *race*. It contains an altogether different etymon from the *race* in *racehorse* (from Old Norse *rás*) or the race in *race of ginger* (from Latin *rādix, rādicem*). It was first used of animals to denote the offspring of a single sire as in 'a stud or race of mares' (*Privy Council Acts*, 1547), the earliest instance of its use recorded in *The Oxford English Dictionary*, or as in Shakespeare's 'wild and wanton herd or race of youthful and unhandled colts' (*The Merchant of Venice*, v.i.71–2); or 'Duncan's horses ... beauteous and swift, the minions of their race' (Macbeth, II.iv.14–15). It was also applied by Shakespeare to human beings as in 'a happy race of kings' (*King Richard the Third*, v.iii.159) or 'the whole race of mankind' (*Timon of Athens*, IV.i.40). Although the word occurs about a dozen times in Shakespeare, it does not appear at all in the King James Bible where its meaning is expressed by *seed, kindred, people,* or *generation.* Milton spoke of the 'race of Satan' in *Paradise Lost,* and later the term acquired a vagueness that it has never entirely lost. It was most unfortunate that Friedrich Max Müller, a young German scholar who came to England in 1848 and made Oxford his home for the rest of his life, should have applied the epithet *Aryan* to people as well as to language, and should have come to the conclusion that the *Ariana* of the ancients in Central Asia was the cradle of mankind. The epithet *Aryan* had previously been used correctly by Sir William Jones as a name for the speakers of a group of Indian languages, but Max Müller alluded not only to an Aryan language and its descendants but also to a corresponding Aryan race. His conception of an idealized Aryan race, long-headed, tall, and fair, was adopted by many British writers, who should have known better, like Thomas Carlyle, James Anthony Froude, Charles Kingsley, and John Richard Green; by the French Count Joseph de Gobineau; and, much later, by Nazi propagandists in Germany. Max Müller was subsequently convinced of the stupidity of his hypothesis and he recanted in no uncertain terms. 'I have declared again and again', he wrote in 1888 (in *Biographies of Words and the Home of the Aryas*) 'that if I say Aryas, I mean neither blood nor bones, nor hair, nor skull; I mean simply those who speak an Aryan language ... When I speak of them I commit myself to no anatomical characteristics. The blue-eyed and fair-haired Scandinavians may have been conquerors or conquered. They may have adopted the language of their darker lords or vice versa ... To me an ethnologist who speaks of Aryan race,

Aryan blood, Aryan eyes and hair, is as great a sinner as a linguist who speaks of a dolichocephalic dictionary or a brachycephalic grammar.' Today we do just the opposite. We apply *Aryan* to race and we use the unambiguous term *Indo-European* when referring to language. Sometimes, however, it may prove impossible to find two mutually exclusive terms for race and language. We have to use *Celtic*, for example, in both senses, because no other term is available. We speak of Celtic art and the Celtic fringe, that is, the fringe of Celtic-speaking people – Scottish Gaelic, Manx, Irish, Welsh, and Breton – round the coasts and islands of north-west Europe. The context must show clearly which meaning is intended. The important thing for us to do is to keep breed and speech clearly differentiated in our minds and not to allow ourselves to be misled by ill-informed persons who cling to fallacious notions about race and who will persist in talking arrant nonsense about 'racial purity' and 'racial superiority'.

By *religion* I mean *spiritual allegiance*, as when I say that now, since China has spurned Confucius, and since Brahminism and Judaism are restricted to chosen peoples, there remain only three universal religions, claiming the loyalty and devotion of all mankind, namely Buddhism, Christianity, and Islam. Inasmuch as these are truly universal and timeless, they rise above all limitations of race and nationality, all orders of society, all classes and castes, and all temporal laws and institutions. They all insist upon the reality of an immaterial, intangible, and invisible world, and they all proclaim the eternal changelessness of the absolute values of goodness and beauty and truth. To mankind they all offer 'plenteous redemption' and 'that peace which the world cannot give'. An individual may assume such spiritual allegiance quite suddenly, in the twinkling of an eye, as Saul of Tarsus did when he 'was not disobedient unto the heavenly vision' which he saw on his way to Damascus in the year of grace 33; or as Aurelius Augustine did when he came to read the latter's epistles to the young churches in a garden in Milan three and a half centuries later. A whole nation may adopt a new religion within a short space of time as Scandinavia did when it was won over to Christianity in the late tenth century under the impetuous leadership of King Olaf Tryggvason. For these northern lands this meant a change not only of religion but also of culture. It also meant a great enrichment of language. Lettered clerks and teachers found themselves driven to create fresh terms to express concepts relating to the new doctrine and discipline.

The imprint of religion on language may take other forms. Thus Croatian and Serbian are essentially one and the same language today, but, only because they have their origins in different Christian traditions, they are recorded in different alphabets, the former in Latin letters, and the latter in the Cyrillic characters of the Greek Orthodox Church.

By *culture* I mean *inherited way of life*, as when I speak of the traditional civilization, say, of the Aztecs of Mexico, their arts and crafts reaching back into a remote antiquity, their code of law, their idea of organized society, their elegance of manners and refinement of taste, their view of toleration, and their sense of humour. Civilization, as opposed to barbarism, implies living as a *civis* 'citizen, city-dweller' in an orderly, law-abiding society. It indicates a stage in social evolution and it may be the outcome of long and arduous development. The earliest centres of civilization and culture lay on navigable rivers – the Nile, the Tigris, the Indus, and the Hwang Ho. They arose independently as the products of wise and prosperous husbandry in wide valleys where interchange of things and ideas was easy. The impact of one culture upon another is unpredictable and imponderable. From time to time great peoples have bestowed various gifts upon the world, enriching it inestimably. The Egyptians gave it that particular kind of pictography which subsequently developed into the Phoenician syllabary and the Greek alphabet; the Hebrews gave a code of ethics and the concept of One God; the Greeks gave sculpture, drama, music, and philosophy; the Romans gave law and administration; the Arabs extended the knowledge of mathematics and astronomy. The Normans excelled in architecture. They built the west front of Wells Cathedral, which, with its medieval colours restored, now vies with its majestic counterpart across the sea at Chartres – a Te Deum in stone.

A people's culture may be unstable. It may advance steadily for generations and then unexpectedly and inexplicably recede. What, we may profitably ask, is the simplest measure of culture in the modern world? Can we estimate it from a close study of art, or literature, or law? Or does it depend in the first place upon the general standard of literacy and education? Doubtless it depends to some extent upon all of these things, but it reflects most clearly the degree of liberality and tolerance exercised by men in their ordinary intercourse day by day, and the extent of their willingness to allow freedom of opinion and choice to others. If we look around us and find that forbearance and latitude are everywhere apparent in the community in which we happen to find ourselves, we may fairly conclude that the standard of culture in that particular society is high. If, on the other hand, we observe that these same qualities are on the decline and that regimentation and intolerance are increasing, no impressive manifestations of art and architecture, no efficient organization of education and government, can compensate us for the loss of culture itself. The unmistakable hallmarks of culture are liberality and tolerance.

By *nationality* I mean *political adherence* to a particular State, or membership of that State, whether by birth or by naturalization, as when I say that William Shakespeare, who was born at Stratford-upon-Avon in the county of Warwick in the very heart of England, remained a loyal subject of Queen Elizabeth and King James all his days; whereas Thomas Stearns Eliot, who was born at St Louis in the State of Missouri in the very heart of North America, crossed the Atlantic as a mature citizen and sought British nationality. It is necessary to emphasize that nationality in its present passport sense is a relatively recent notion. Indeed, the conception of a nation as a completely independent political unity, possessing sovereign power to do just what it likes, is not older than the Renaissance. By one of history's tragic ironies it was also at this time that interbreeding between white and coloured peoples first took place on any considerable scale with the initiation of that iniquitous transatlantic Slave Trade in which Portuguese, Spaniards, French, Dutch, Swedes, and English all had some share.

The most casual perusal of a newspaper now published anywhere in the world would suffice to convince us that journalists join with politicians in regarding race, culture, and language as different facets of a single social unity, which they then proceed to identify with nationality. However loudly ethnographers and biologists may protest, people continue to confuse language with nationality and to associate race and culture with both. Unscrupulous demagogues exploit this popular confusion to further their selfish ends. Man's well-being in the future will rest more than ever upon his speed and courage to detect and expose such palpable fallacies at the outset and, like Socrates of old, to warn his fellow-citizens against the corrupting influences of slogans and propaganda.

Not one of the great languages of the world follows ethnic geography at all closely. French, for example, is spoken by a very mixed population which is largely Nordic in the north, Alpine in the centre, and Mediterranean in the south, and all these ethnic stocks are freely represented elsewhere in Europe. Standard German, which arose mainly from the movement for religious freedom guided by Martin Luther in the sixteenth century, is now spoken by a no less heterogeneous group of peoples. In Germany, even more than elsewhere, exaggerated notions of sovereign nationhood have been closely tied up with language in recent times. In the ancient world, and throughout medieval Europe, numerous cultural and linguistic diversities persisted side by side without violent conflict. Political adherence to the

Roman Empire or, later, spiritual allegiance to the Christian Church, carried far greater significance as the symbol of a man's place in the community than the language that he happened to speak. To assert, therefore, that linguistic differences in twentieth-century Europe are responsible for national antagonisms is to misinterpret the evidence of history. It would be more reasonable to deduce from this same evidence that a national unit, when once it has been created and consolidated by political forces, finds in language the clearest and most obvious token of its identity. Thence arises the peculiarly modern notion that every language should properly function as the acknowledged expression of a distinctive nationality.

Language is, after all, the most easily measurable and the most readily ascertainable of all the factors that divide mankind. Each of us has one *mother tongue* (where *mother* comes from the Old English *s*-less genitive feminine form like the *lady* in *Lady Day* 'Our Lady's Day'). We may, if we are truly bilingual, know one other tongue equally well, but even then we probably give subconscious priority to the one or the other in our 'interior monologues' and especially when we 'talk to ourselves' in moments of anxiety and stress. On the assumption, then, that every man has one and only one *langue maternelle*, the numbers of speakers of various languages can be counted. Inevitably some countings are approximations, since accurate statistics are not always available. According to recent computations, there are just one dozen languages, apart from Chinese, which are used by over fifty million speakers each, namely English, spoken by 265 millions; Hindi-Urdu 185; Russian 180; Spanish 145; German 100; Japanese 95; Arabic 90; Bengali 85; Portuguese 85; French 65; Malay 60; Italian 55. Then, after a fairly wide gap, follow Javanese 45, Telugu 42, Korean 39, Punjabi 38, Tamil 37, Marathi 35, Polish 33, Vietnamese 31, and Turkish 27.

It will be observed that nine out of these first twelve languages, all except Japanese, Malay, and Arabic, belong to the Indo-European family. From the early Middle Ages until the time of Napoleon Bonaparte, French, now holding tenth place, was the leading European tongue. Old French was the *lingua franca* of the Crusaders. Quite correctly Sir Winston Churchill headed the sixth chapter of the first volume of his *History of the English-Speaking Peoples* plain *Cœur de Lion*, for thus was Richard I called by his contemporaries. Like all the Plantagenet Kings before Henry Bolingbroke, Richard's mother tongue was French. In his day French was the most widely spoken of all the Latin-derived languages, descended from the common speech of the provincial administrators and legionaries manning the western outposts of the Roman Empire, and it was destined to remain the first means of communication in the west for the greater part of a millennium. It moved further away than any other Romance tongue from the speech of Cicero and Ovid, developing highly individualistic features, and assimilating hundreds of everyday words from contiguous Germanic dialects; but later it became thoroughly disciplined and organized as the medium of expression for a superabundant literature and as the vehicle of international diplomacy. We are, of course, guessing when we put the leading languages of Europe in their order in the sixteenth century according to numbers of speakers: French 14 millions; German 12; Italian 10; Spanish 9; English 5; and Muscovite Russian 3.

The population of England had probably reached four millions by the first half of the fourteenth century, but during Chaucer's lifetime these four millions were reduced to two by the mortal ravages of the bubonic plague. In his own day Shakespeare addressed a potential audience of only five and a half millions. English was then fifth among the languages of Europe, and not long afterwards, by the time of Napoleon, it had sunk to sixth place in consequence of the rise of Russian, which then vied with German for second place after French, the order then being: French 32 millions; Russian 31; German 30; Spanish 26; Italian 25; and English 20. Already, however, while holding sixth place in Europe, English had assumed a high position outside it during the era of vigorous expansion in the eighteenth century. It goes without saying that the secession of the thirteen New England colonies made no difference at all to the sum total of speakers of English. Soon after the fall of Napoleon, English surpassed French as the first language in the western world. Many inhabitants of Britain, it is true, continued to speak a Celtic tongue – Scottish Gaelic, Manx, Irish, Welsh, or Cornish; and some dwellers in the remote Highlands and Western Isles of Scotland still spoke Norse. Owing to the small area of the British Isles, English could obviously never become the first language of Europe. At the time of Christ the first language was Hellenistic Greek, or *koinè diálektos*; then Latin until the threshold of the Dark Ages; and later Gallo-Roman passing into French, which, as already observed, remained the first language until after Napoleon, when it was exceeded by German, which in its turn has recently been surpassed by Russian.

Meanwhile, what has been happening to Chinese? In many ways Chinese is unique, and on that account we have omitted it from our list of leading languages. Since it is still confined to China and Manchuria and south-east Asia, it differs from western tongues like English and French, which are in use in widely spread regions of the world; and from Spanish and Portuguese, which, far from being limited to their home countries, share the greater part of Central and South America between them; and it differs even from Arabic, which, though seventh in our list of twelve, is easily the first language of Africa, since it is the means of communication used over an exceptionally extensive area reaching for thousands of miles across the coastal plain all the way from Agadir to Aqaba, and beyond into Syria, Iraq, and Arabia. Moreover, as the sacred language of the 'reading' or Qur'an, the Bible of Islam, it is understood by the literate in all Moslem lands. Chinese is now made up of many mutually unintelligible dialects, but everyone who reads at all can interpret the ancient characters with equal facility. One needs to know only two thousand characters to be able to read the daily newspapers, though, sad to relate, some four thousand more to be able to enjoy the exuberant wealth of China's literary inheritance. To appreciate the simple fact that speakers of different dialects may pronounce the same character in widely divergent ways, one has only to observe the various reactions of Europeans when they see the same Arabic numeral 5. An Englishman at once says *five* when he sees it, a Dutchman *vijf*, a German *fünf*, a Swede *fem*, a Frenchman *cinq*, an Italian *cinque*, a Spaniard *cinco*, a Russian *pjat'*, a Czech *pět*, and so on. Hitherto Chinese has possessed no alphabet, but now, under the direction of Mao Tse Tung, it has acquired one. Mandarin Chinese, the Peiping variety in a standardized form created by Hu Shih and his helpers, is now printed in a newly devised Latin alphabet generally known as *putonghua* 'universal speech'. These normalized and westernized forms are being made compulsory by presidential edict. By commanding them to be taught to all schoolchildren, Mao intends to make them generally intelligible and thus to construct and stabilize one great language uniformly written and pronounced throughout the People's Republic. By these methods he is doing his best to promote universal literacy throughout that vast community which may number 800 millions in the foreseeable future. He intends, in fact, to do for China far more than ever Mustafa Kemal Atatürk had occasion to do for Turkey in 1928, when he issued a presidential decree to all teachers to substitute Latin for Arabic letters in the writing of the national speech. Kemal's task was certainly more manageable than Mao's, since Turkish, although a Ural-Altaic language, had long been written in Arabic letters. He just substituted one alphabet for another. In a remarkably short space of time he was successful in this particular reform because he wielded dictatorial powers and because he made it an integral part of a wider scheme of westernization. Kemal was notably less successful, however, in his efforts to eliminate Arabic loanwords from the living vocabulary, because not even a dictator can prevent people from speaking as they please. Linguistic necessity outweighs irrelevant considerations of national prestige. Before his death in 1938, the 'father of the Turks' had nevertheless raised the standard of education among his people to a level previously unattained and, since then, that level has been steadily preserved. The struggle to maintain a national literacy once achieved is inevitably arduous and incessant. Literacy is precarious: there is no guarantee that it will survive in a community without constant vigilance and toil.

As the modern world becomes more highly industrialized and mechanized, and as men choose in ever greater numbers to leave the countryside and dwell in cities, so language becomes a more definite and tangible mark of nationality than race, religion, or culture. The great languages tend to increase of themselves, more from social necessity than as the outcome of direct political pressure. Since its foundation in 1917, the Soviet Union has shown some hesitation and inconsistency in its attitude towards the languages and dialects of the minorities within its borders, but on the whole its policy has been more tolerant and perspicacious than that of other totalitarian governments. By exercising a certain cynical indifference towards the languages of its small ethnic groups, it has probably jeopardized their survival far more seriously than by any acts of overt hostility and persecution. Ambitious youth leaders, who aspire to make their counsels heard not only in local committees but also in higher assemblies through which they may hope to work their way up the pyramid to its apex in the supreme soviet or praesidium, surely need no other or stronger urge than this to make themselves fully proficient in their command of Muscovite Russian. Enterprising and enthusiastic students likewise discover that they can make little headway in their chosen courses of study unless they can assimilate with ease the information they find in the text-books, periodicals, dictionaries, and encyclopedias published by the State-owned presses in Moscow.

As striking contrasts to such tendencies towards linguistic centralization so manifest in the Chinese People's Republic and the Soviet Union, we encounter stimulating examples of speech survival in smaller countries like Belgium and Switzerland, where law and government are still administered in more than one officially recognized language. Over half the people of Belgium speak Flemish, but French is everywhere current, whether in its Parisian dress or in its dialectal variety called Walloon. Switzerland has twenty-two cantons, four recognized languages (German, French, Italian, and Rumansch), and one federal government. In some measure, therefore, the Swiss Confederation (Confoederatio Helvetica) may be regarded as a prefiguring or prototype of a possible world administration, based on universal law, and transcending both national and linguistic frontiers.

CHAPTER 3

LANGUAGE AS COMMUNICATION

WE naturally think of the organs of speech as those of the articulatory tract extending from the larynx to the lips, but in fact the whole of the upper part of the body plays some part in the act of speaking. The primary impulse comes from the diaphragm or midriff, that dome-shaped muscular wall which separates the thorax from the abdomen and is fastened to the breastbone in front, to the spinal column behind, and to the cartilages of the lower six ribs on either side. As its muscles contract, the concave vault of this tendinous partition is drawn downwards and the lungs become filled with air. When these same muscles again expand, the air is forced upwards from the lungs into the bronchial tubes and windpipe into the mouth. In this last movement, of course, the thoracic muscles also participate to a greater or less degree. Try timing yourself with a watch and you will find that normally you breathe out more quickly than you breathe in, although the difference is small, in the ratio, perhaps, of 1 to 1·1, or 1 to 1·25. In speaking, however, the breathing-in speed is increased and the breathing-out speed is reduced so that the ratio may become 1 to 3, 1 to 10, or even, in very excited utterance, 1 to 30. You have so much to say, and so little time to say it in, that you find yourself literally gasping for breath!

As this outgoing breath stream is forced upwards by pressure from the diaphragm, it may be checked at various points on its way from the larynx to the lips. Four organs are movable: vocal cords, soft palate or velum, tongue, and lips. The vocal cords are, in fact, more like bands or lips than cords. They are horizontal folds of elastic tissue which may behave in much the same manner as the lips of the mouth. They may be held wide apart so that they remain motionless, or they may be kept close together so that they vibrate when the air is forced through them. When these elastic folds are held wide apart and the air passes between them without any vibration at all, the sounds produced are said to be *voiceless*; but when the folds vibrate, the resultant sounds are said to be *voiced*. This gives us the first broad dichotomy of sounds into voiceless and voiced. By definition all vowels are voiced: consonants may be either voiced or voiceless. You will readily observe that when you utter the voiceless consonants *p*, *t*, *k*, *f*, and *s*, the vocal cords are open and motionless, whereas when you enunciate their voiced counterparts *b*, *d*, *g*, *v*, and *z*, or any vowel, the cords vibrate. Should you find yourself in any doubt about this, you may try two quite simple tests. Place forefinger and thumb firmly on your Adam's apple and you will feel nothing when you pronounce the first group, but a distinct throbbing movement when you change over to the second. Next, put your thumbs firmly in both ears and you will feel and hear nothing when you pronounce the first group, but a distinct buzzing noise when you change over to the second. Say 'Very good indeed!' and you will realize at once by either method that all the twelve phones in the utterance are voiced.

With the aid of a *laryngoscope* you can see your vocal cords quite clearly in a good and well-adjusted light. You can examine your soft palate with or without a laryngoscope, not to mention that curious dangling appendage known as the uvula. Look in the glass as you yawn, and you will see the arch of the soft palate raised high with the uvula almost disappearing behind it into the pharynx or cavity above the larynx at the back of the nose where channels (or meatuses) and recesses (or sinuses) serve as resonance chambers for the voice. Stand in front of the looking-glass again, breathe normally through nose and mouth, and then open your throat and make a clear long low back *a* sound as in *are* or *ah*! You will see your velum rise and you will find yourself no longer breathing out through the nose. This demonstrates the second broad division or dichotomy of sounds into *buccal* and *nasal*. In articulating the sounds of the first class, the breath passes through the mouth alone: in pronouncing those of the second, the breath passes through both nose and mouth. Most sounds are buccal, but *m, n,* and *ng* are nasal consonants in English as in all other languages, and the four vowels in the French expression *un bon vin blanc* 'a good white wine' are nasal. Polish also has two nasal vowels as in *sąsiad* 'neighbour' and *mięso* 'meat', and Portuguese has nasal diphthongs as, for example, in *sermão* 'sermon'. English has no such distinctive nasal vowel sounds, but some people naturally use slight nasalization of the vowel in such a word as *man* where it is both preceded and followed by a nasal consonant. Some Americans pronounce all their words with varying degrees of nasalization. This means that they habitually speak with the velum drooping a little and not held close to the rear wall of the pharynx. Thus the breath passes partly through the nose all the time, giving their speech that nasal resonance which, if we wish, we can easily mimic. Indeed, we may amuse ourselves by uttering a sentence with an open throat and therefore high velum in the English fashion, and then saying it again with drooping velum and consequent nasal twang.

The tongue is obviously the most important and at the same time the most supple and flexible of all the speech organs. Among many nations the word *tongue,* as in English, indicates both the fleshy organ in the mouth and the spoken language (Latin and Italian *lingua,* French *langue,* Spanish *lengua,* Czech *jazyk,* and Russian *yazyk*). You can move your tongue about in all directions by reason of its highly elastic and pliable structure. With the tip of your tongue you can touch any part of the upper mouth as far back as the middle of the velum. You can make it concave or convex from back to front and from side to side. By modifying the size and shape of the buccal resonance chamber, the tongue plays the main part in the pronunciation of vowels; and by partially or completely checking the breath stream in such a way as to produce plosion or friction, it plays a prominent part also in the articulation of many consonants. This gives the third dichotomy of sounds into *vowels* and *consonants.* The former are articulated without check or occlusion: the latter are always accompanied by audible plosion or friction.

Are you blessed with a complete set of teeth? If so, you have eight incisors, four canines, eight bicuspids, and twelve molars. Without incisors, whether natural or artificial, you cannot enunciate some sounds properly: the labio-dentals, for example, [f] and [v] – square brackets henceforth denote phonetic symbols – are made by upper teeth and lower lip; and the interdentals, [θ] as in *thin* and [ð] as in *then*, are made by upper teeth and tongue-blade. You might manage to enunciate [t] and [d] fairly well without teeth because in English these sounds are normally postdental, made by the tongue touching the gums or teeth-ridge, whereas in French, Spanish, and Italian they are true dentals, made by the tongue actually touching the incisors.

Other sounds in which the lips participate are the buccal plosives [p] and [b], the nasal plosive [m], and the semi-vowels [ʍ], as in *where*, and [w], as in *were*. The lips may also affect the qualities of vowel-sounds according to their position and shape, whether spread out, neutral, open-rounded, or close-rounded.

The number of potential vowels and consonants is infinite, although the human ear can distinguish far fewer sounds than the speech organs are capable of producing. The articulation of a particular sound will often vary according to the context. Say 'Keep calm and cool!' [ki:p kɑ:m ənd ku:l], and observe carefully how your tongue recedes slightly in passing from the initial sound of *keep* to that of *calm*, and yet again in passing from *calm* to *cool*. If you doubt this, try again. It is essential in all linguistic study to follow empirical methods, to take nothing for granted, and, whenever practicable, to base conclusions upon direct observation and experiment. The sound [k] is made by raising the back of the tongue until it touches the soft palate or velum, which is itself lifted so high as to shut off the nose passage completely. The air stream is momentarily compressed as the tongue makes contact with the velum, and then, when it is released, it suddenly escapes with a mild explosion through the open mouth. The vocal cords are still. We therefore call this [k] a *voiceless velar plosive* and we may proceed to define most sounds in terms of these three variables answering the simple questions *whether?*, *where?*, and *how?*, referring to the activity of the vocal cords, and the place and manner of articulation respectively.

With these facts in mind, pronounce this alliterative injunction 'Keep calm and cool!' once more, and now try hard to locate yet more precisely the three points of contact between the tongue and the roof of the mouth which produce the three varieties of the sound [k], or, in technical language, the three *allophones* of the *phoneme* /k/. (Henceforth oblique strokes denote phonemic symbols.)

A phoneme may be defined as a class or bundle of sounds or phones, no two of which can ever take each other's place in the same environment. Such phones are said to be in *complementary distribution*: they are *positional variants* or *allophones* of one and the same phoneme.

It is worth while to observe that phonemes are limited to particular languages. There is no such thing, for example, as a general or universal phoneme designated /k/. There is, however, an English /k/, an Arabic /k/, and so on. Each is a feature peculiar to its own language and therefore not relevant to any other language. That is why an ordinary Arabic speaker, unacquainted with phonemic theory, thinks that the initial sounds in *keep* and *calm* are quite different (as indeed they are), whereas an Englishman remains blissfully unaware of this difference and consequently has no small difficulty in differentiating between the initial sounds in, say, Arabic *kateb* 'clerk', and *qara* 'to read'. This simple fact, by the way, is reflected in our vacillating transliterations of many Arabic proper names, *Aqaba* alternating with *Akaba*, and *Al Qur'an* 'the reading' also appearing as the Koran.

It is, moreover, important to observe that linguists habitually use the term *phoneme* in two senses: as a feature of language structure, and as a concrete example of that feature. Every language may be said to have its phonemic or phonological structure, acquired and built up by long use as the means of communication among members of a social group. It is not an assemblage of unconnected patterns, but a system showing a high degree of integration. A so-called primitive language, even one that has never been committed to writing, may show a most surprising and interesting structure at all three levels: phonological, morphological, and syntactic. Experienced linguists find no evidence for the naïve assumption that unsophisticated peoples are less capable than we are of wielding highly elaborate forms of speech.

Although the phonemes of English and Russian differ considerably in their qualities, their number is about the same, namely 44. The number of phonemes has been found to range from little more than 20 in some Polynesian languages to about 75 in certain Caucasian dialects. In French and German, although the qualities of phonemes differ widely, their quantity is about the same, namely 36.

A useful method differentiating phonemes in a language is to apply the *substitution* or *commutation test*, since, according to the principle of complementary distribution, no two allophones of one and the same phoneme will ever occur in a word in the same phonetic environment. It follows, therefore, that if, in the same context, sound A can be substituted for sound B to form a different word, then A and B are two phonemes. Thus the presence in English of such a *binary opposition* as [n:ŋ] is proved by the use of such pairs of words as *kin* and *king*, *sun* and *sung*, *tan* and *tang*. Clearly [n] and [ŋ] are two phonemes in English because one can be thus substituted for the other to form a different word. In Spanish and Italian, however, although both [n] and [ŋ] are heard in speech, they can never be interchanged in this fashion. The sound [ŋ] is used as an allophone of /n/ before the velar plosives [k] and [g] in such words as Sp. *cinco* [θiŋko] 'five' and *venga* [βeŋga] 'revenges', or Ital. *banca* [baŋkɑ] 'bank and *lungo* [luŋgo] 'long'. In French [ŋ] is heard only occasionally as a dialectal allophone of /g/ in [lãŋ] 'tongue, language', where, however, the standard

Parisian pronunciation is [lãg]. So, too, [k] and [g] are demonstrably two phonemes in English since these two sounds stand in binary opposition in such pairs of words as *come* and *gum*, *could* and *good*, *sack* and *sag*. In Dutch, on the other hand, [g] is a mere positional variant or allophone of /k/, occurring only before voiced consonants as in *zakdoek* [zagduk] 'pocket-cloth, handkerchief'. This [g] must not be confused with the fricative [x] heard in such a word as *groot* [xrout] 'great'. Similarly, just as Dutch [g] is an allophone of /k/ so is Spanish [z] an allophone of /s/ in that language. In English [z] may be commuted for [s] with functional significance in such pairs as *seal* and *zeal*, *sip* and *zip*, *sink* and *zinc*; but [z] occurs in Spanish to the exclusion of [s] only before voiced consonants and in no other environment, as in *mismo* [mizmo] 'self, same'. Many varieties of laterals are heard in English, and yet clear [l], used when a vowel follows, and dark [ł], employed finally and before consonants, comprise one phoneme. In Polish, on the contrary, clear and dark laterals occur in the same phonetic situation in the words *laska* 'cane' and *łaska* 'grace', and they therefore count as two phonemes in that language. Finally it may be observed that many kinds of vibrants are heard in English and that they are all allophones of one comprehensive phoneme. In Czech, however, that strongly fricative alveolar vibrant (as in Polish and Swedish) and that normally trilled vibrant (as in Scottish and Northern English) appear in the same environment, for example, in *řada* 'row' and *rada* 'council, counsel'. They therefore function as two separate phonemes.

Such facts have manifest significance for the teacher of modern languages. They remind him that every learner of a new tongue is preconditioned by the nature of the structure of his native speech and, to a lesser degree, by the linguistic patterns of all the other languages he may have studied. The most learned philologists can never fully escape from the effects of this preconditioning, however far they may advance along the road that leads to a one-hundred-per-cent objective attitude.

Phonemic distribution varies from language to language. It is interesting to observe, for instance, that the syllables in Japanese nearly all end in vowels: Fuji Yama, Hiroshima, Nagasaki, Osaka, and Tokijo. Since French has shed so many of its final consonants in pronunciation, this is partly true of that language also. In English /ŋ/ and /ʒ/ never stand at the beginning of a word, unless we are prepared to admit the French loan *genre* [ʒãr] to our lexicon. Some sounds – /v, ð, z, tʃ, dʒ/ – occur only alone at the beginnings of words, although English people have no difficulty whatever in saying Russian *Vladivostok* 'rule the east'. Other sounds occur both alone and in clusters, but whereas some of these are used only as first members of these initial clusters – /b, d, g, s, ʃ, h, θ/ – others occur only as last members – /j, w, r, m, n/. Others again appear as first, middle, or last members of clusters – /p, t, k, f/. On the whole, English speakers are not fond of tongue-twisters at the beginnings of words. They have nothing to compete with Czech *čtvrt* 'quarter', or even *džban* 'jug'. Nevertheless, partly as the result of developments in flexion, they seem to raise no objection to quite complex consonantal clusters at the end, like *glimpsed* /-mpst/ and *sixths* /-ksθs/.

All these facts illustrate certain minor aspects of phonemic structure. They form part of *descriptive* or *synchronic linguistics*, the study of the entire system of a language at any one point in time; if unqualified, then now at the present moment, regardless of past developments. Such study has its complement in *historical* or *diachronic linguistics*, which is concerned with the evolution of language in the course of time. In a later chapter we shall concern ourselves with *comparative linguistics*, or the study of related languages with particular reference to similarities and differences.

We may pursue all three themes – description, history, and comparison – on three different levels or planes: *phonological* (as in this chapter), *morphological* (as in Chapter 5), and *syntactic* (as in Chapter 6); and let us not forget that all the time we are concerned not only with the analysis of forms but also with the scientific exposition of systems. It is now customary to dispense with the term *grammar* altogether, though we may sometimes find it a quite useful term to denote both morphology and syntax taken together.

So far in this chapter we have been mainly concerned with articulatory phonetics and the theory of phonemics. It is now time to turn our attention to acoustic phonetics and the theory of communication. We pass from the speaker to the hearer. After all, communication in all its diverse forms is always reciprocal. The vibrations set in motion by the human voice may express 'interior monologue' and may merely help the speaker to 'order his experience'. Normally, to be sure, they will utter a message. As the vocal cords move rhythmically to and fro, they set the contiguous particles of air into similar motion and this in turn is conveyed to the next set of particles, and so on. The resulting disturbance takes the form of a pressure wave which spreads outwards in all directions, at the same time diminishing in intensity both from the spreading and from the effect of friction in the medium itself. Sound is pressure-wave motion through air. The speed of sound through calm air of average humidity at freezing point is 1120 feet a second, or approximately twelve miles a minute. If you happen to live two miles from Westminster, you will hear Big Ben strike the hour from your radio set on a still night just ten seconds before you hear those same airborne chimes through your open window.

The speed of vibration of the vocal cords may be measured in cycles per second (abbreviated *cps*). A cycle is one complete movement forwards, backwards, and forwards again to the original position. The greater the number of cycles, the higher is the musical tone. You may easily test your own vocal range on the pianoforte, whose keyboard extends from A to A with seven octaves between. If you bear in mind that the frequency of top A but one is exactly the same as the number of yards in a mile, you may quickly calculate the range of your singing voice in terms of cps. With this infallible mnemonic (1760) as guide, you will readily calculate the frequency of top A as 3520 and the frequencies of the other A's in descending order as 880, 440 (A above middle C), 220 (A below middle C), 110, 55, and 27·5 cps. You will probably find that your singing voice extends over two octaves or more. No human voice has ever exceeded the range of the pianoforte at either end. Gaspard Foster went as low as 44 cps and Ellen Beach Yaw as high as 2048 cps. Indeed, it is interesting to observe that a true A below the bottom A on the pianoforte with a frequency of only 13·75 would only be detected by persons of exceptional acuity of hearing. It would, in fact, sink beneath the 'threshold of audibility'. A man with normal hearing can hear high tones better than low ones. Somewhere in the highest octave of the pianoforte lies a tone at which the sensitivity of the human ear functions best and at which a very small amount of sound energy can make itself heard. As this particular tone (which may vary slightly, but not greatly, among normal individuals) is raised or lowered, so the sound sinks beneath the threshold of audibility, and 'the rest is silence'. Dogs hear higher frequencies than men. This enables police detectives to communicate with sleuth-hounds by means of high-pitched whistle-blasts that are inaudible to the wretched lawbreaker they are pursuing. Bats can hear ultrasonic frequencies up to 60,000 cps, whereas man's average reaches little above 20,000 cps.

Having ascertained the approximate range of your singing voice, you may then test the compass of your voice in speech and you may be agreeably surprised to find that this is slightly wider. Speech has varying cadence and gliding pitch, whereas song is made up of a series of tones, each of which has a determined pitch and is held for an appreciable period until a change is made to a higher or lower frequency. A good singer exercises a precise control learnt from long years of practice. We may liken speaking to a rising and falling gradient and singing to a series of regular steps ascending and descending. The human voice never produces a pure tone like a tuning fork. In both speech and song it has complex harmonies based upon fundamental tones. The harmonies and tones produced by the vocal cords are wonderfully varied. No two individuals have precisely the same qualities of voice. After long years of separation you may recognize an old friend by his voice alone.

As you speak, you produce a series of air waves which strike upon the tympanic membrane or ear drum of any person within earshot. As these air vibrations hit the drum they set in motion the ossicles of the middle ear which transmit them to the inner ear or labyrinth. The latter contains the end-fibres of the auditory nerves along which sensations of sound are carried to the brain. The labyrinth comprises small twisted but inter-connected channels in the bone, consisting of the vestibule, the three semi-circular canals, and the cochlea (so called from its resemblance to a snail-shell) which is the organ of hearing proper. The canals are filled with a fluid and their primary function is to control balance or equilibrium. Biologically, therefore, they are much older than the cochlea. Even as the human mouth was first the organ of nourishment and only later evolved into that of speech, so the ear was first the instrument of equilibrium and only later developed into its present form as the all-too-elaborate mechanism of audition.

Across the open cochlea extends the basilar membrane with its 24,000 hair cells which carry direct to the brain the vibrations it receives from the ear drum by way of the ossicles (malleus, incus, and stapes) of the middle ear. Hearing may also be stimulated and reinforced by bone conduction direct. Vibrations are transmitted to the cochlea through the skull itself. Partly by bone conduction you hear the sound of your own voice as you speak. That is why you never hear your words precisely as others do, and that is why you may be agreeably surprised or somewhat disappointed when you hear your recorded utterances played back by disk, tape, or radio for the first time.

The unit of sound intensity is the *decibel* (abbreviated *db*), which is one tenth of a *bel*, so named from Alexander Graham Bell (1847–1922), inventor of the magnetic telephone, son of Alexander Melville Bell, author of *Visible*

Speech. The decibel is not an absolute unit like a degree of temperature measured by a thermometer, but a logarithmic unit recording the minimum difference in power perceptible to the human ear. The range of a man's voice in terms of power will cover about 60 decibels, extending from $+$ 20 db when he shouts most loudly to $-$ 40 db when he faintly whispers.

Some sounds have greater inherent sonority than others and acousticians have corroborated such data relating to resonance as have been obtained by other methods. They have demonstrated, for example, that the phoneme /ɔ:/ as in *born* has greater sonority than any other vowel, closely followed by the phoneme /ɑ:/ as in *barn*. The sounds of English in particular, and of those Indo-European languages in general which happen to have a phonemic pattern generally similar, may thus be arranged in order of increasing sonority: voiceless plosives /p, t, k/, voiceless fricatives /f, θ, s, ʃ/, and voiceless affricate /tʃ/ as in *church* [tʃə:tʃ]; voiced plosives /b, d, g/, voiced fricatives /v, ð, z, ʒ, h/, and voiced affricate /dʒ/ as in *judge* [dʒʌdʒ]; nasals /m, n, ŋ/; vibrant /r/ and lateral /l/; high vowels /u, i/, and semi-vowels /w, j/; middle vowels, low front vowels, and diphthongs; long back vowels /ɑ:/ and /ɔ:/.

In telephone messages and sound broadcasts the voiceless plosives are seldom heard, but the listener will supply them unconsciously or subconsciously from the context. If he hears no sound at all, he nevertheless cannot fail to detect a split-second gap in the chain of utterance which he will automatically fill from his linguistic experience. The simple facts of acoustic reality are scientifically verifiable by means of the *spectrograph* which makes an objective record of speech sounds at the moment of utterance. We may distinguish two kinds of spectrograph according to the nature of the recording, whether temporary or permanent. The first variety has been constructed in the Bell Telephone Laboratories in New York. Sound-waves are translated into patterned striations on a moving belt of phosphor which may be deciphered by the observer direct. After suitable training a deaf person can interpret this complex design of light and shade (called a *spectrogram*) and catch the meanings of utterances while they are actually being spoken. The second variety of spectrograph makes a permanent record of the sound frequencies present at every instant of a short sample of speech. This record can be then inspected by linguists at their leisure in order to ascertain the range of variation for any given phoneme, and to determine the acoustic implications of syllabic junctures and pauses, and other relevant features.

Many systems of communication in the modern world involve the use of a *code*, or arbitrary and pre-arranged set of symbols, and the employment of a *channel* or *medium* through which these code signals are transmitted. The process by which certain signals are selected and put into the channel is known as *encoding* and that by which they are identified and interpreted into action is known as *decoding*. Most methods of signalling make use of these two processes. Even television involves similar principles. The basic factors are an instrument at the sending end for the conversion of the optical properties of original images into equivalent electrical forms and at the receiving end an agent (the cathode-ray tube) for the reconversion of these forms (400 to one square foot) into picture-patterns of light and shade. An entirely new and extensive branch of science, which we may call *communication theory*, now claims the attention of linguists.

CHAPTER 4

SOUNDS AND SYMBOLS

IF you say to me 'Keep calm!', you are using six sounds or phonemes to tell me something. These sounds are themselves vocal symbols. They are conventional signs uttered with a purpose and communicating a meaning. They form part of a language. A language may be defined as a system of arbitrary or conventional vocal symbols by means of which human beings communicate and cooperate with one another.

If in the course of an epistle to me you write 'Keep calm!', you are then using eight letters to tell me something. These letters are written symbols and, inasmuch as they stand for vocal ones, they may rightly be regarded as symbols of symbols, or symbols twice removed. The double *e* in *keep* indicates a long vowel and the *l* in *calm* is mute.

If you send me a message in the Morse code and tap out —·—|·|·|·———|—·—·|·—|·—··|——, you are using a sequence of dots and dashes to tell me something. These dots and dashes are telegraphic symbols and, inasmuch as they stand for the letters and not for the sounds, they may rightly be regarded as symbols of symbols of symbols, or symbols three times removed.

What is a symbol? A symbol is a sign that stands for something else. It is always a substitute or surrogate for some other sign with which it is made synonymous. All signs not symbols are signals: all signs not signals are symbols. The essential act of thought is symbolization. Our minds transform experiences into symbols. There is nothing in experience that cannot be transformed into a symbol by the mind: nothing that cannot be made to signify something else.

A sign is any mark or gesture conveying information to the beholder. A sign-symbol is a special kind of sign selected or devised to represent something else. A sign-signal is a special kind of sign that conveys a message or gives immediate information. It is important to keep these simple distinctions before us if we wish to understand how language works, and if we wish to get some insight into that fascinating realm of study known as *semiotics* or the science of signs.

Traffic lights at crossroads are obviously sign-signals. If you are motoring through a village and catch sight of a red triangle far ahead, you take it at once as a warning sign, and if then you discern the figure of a flaming torch beneath it, you know that you are approaching the village school. Yes, sure enough, the children are pouring out of the main gate and the traffic warden (or lollipop-man as the children affectionately call him) in his white overall makes himself prominent by raising his red disk on high: 'Stop, children crossing'. As you think of the warning signs of the Highway Code – a St Andrew's cross for crossroads, three circumferential arrows for a roundabout, a picture of a gate for a level crossing, a black triangle for a steep hill, and so on – you realize that there are degrees of symbolization. In some ways the silhouetted torch is the most symbolic of all these signs in the Code for the simple reason that it is no immediate or necessary substitute for the school building or for the children who gaily chatter as they cross in front of you. Most appropriately this symbol stands for the 'light of light', the light of learning and civilization and spiritual enlightenment. As you wait patiently for the warden to invert his monitory disk, you may find yourself ruminating on light and darkness, on learning and ignorance, on the relay of torch-bearers running hundreds of miles from Athens to the chosen venue of the next Olympic games, the final torch igniting the flame which burns in a spacious brazier throughout the festival.

Sign-signals may point to past, present, or future events. A wet roof is a signal that it has been raining; a rainbow is a signal that somewhere in the landscape rain is falling; a red sky in the morning is a signal that it will probably rain later in the day.

Symbols are timeless. They always call for some kind of interpretation of which *Homo sapiens* alone is capable. The most intelligent of all sheep dogs could never be trained to interpret the torch of learning as the symbol for the village school, however skilful he might be in obeying the most intricate signals of his master. The anthropoid apes – orang-utans, chimpanzees, and gorillas – may be trained to perform an increasing number of marvellous tricks, but they all stop dead at anything approaching symbolization. It is this faculty that raises man above beast. It is this, above all else, that raises man's intelligence above that of the animals. It is his ability to use symbols that has made man master of the world of nature, but man's world is nevertheless circumscribed by his language. The circumscription of that world marks the limits of human understanding.

Although words are symbols for things or ideas, there is no direct connexion between symbol and thing. Why, for instance, do you call your home *a house* and not *ein Haus* or *une maison*? An Italian and a Spaniard agree in calling it *casa*, but a Russian speaks of *dom*. Of course, you may look at a house from more points of view than one. English *house* and German *Haus*, almost identical in pronunciation, formerly expressed the notion of 'hide-out' or 'cover'; French *maison*, cognate with our *mansion* (from Latin *mansio*, *mansiōnem* related to *manēre* 'to remain') denoted 'staying, stopping place, lodging'; the idea behind Italian and Spanish *casa* was that of a lowly 'wicker-work cottage'; Russian *dom* meant just 'building', cognate with the first syllable of our *domicile*, which comes from Latin *domicilium* (a derivative of *domus*) and which still indicates in legal parlance 'the place where one has his home or permanent residence, to which, if absent, he has the intention of returning'. It has often been said that the idea of the English *home*, with all its evocative and emotive associations, is untranslatable. That is true, but most languages have neat adverbs or adverb phrases answering to our *at home*, like Latin *domī* or *domuī*, French *chez moi* (where *chez* is actually cognate with the Italian and Spanish *casa* just mentioned) or *à la maison*, Italian *a casa*, Spanish *en casa*, German *zu Hause*, Dutch *te huis*, Swedish *hemma*, Russian and Czech *doma*, and so on.

Between word and thing, or symbol and referend, there is no direct connexion other than through the image in the mind. We might illustrate this fact more fully by considering other examples, but we should probably not proceed very far in our examination before discovering that there are scores of little words – articles, conjunctions, conjunctive adverbs, and prepositions – like *between, and, or, than, through, the*, and *in* in the previous sentence, which may be described as operators, whose function is mainly syntactic, showing the relationship between substantive and substantive, between substantives and verbs, or between phrases and clauses within the sentence. *Operators* (a term borrowed from mathematics) are sometimes called *functors* or *structure-words* to distinguish them from the others which may be called *full-words*. Exclamations like *Aha! Alas! Oh!* and *Hurrah!* have no conceivable referends and may therefore be defined as meaningless. They are just emotive noises expressing outbursts of joy, sorrow, surprise, or exhilaration according to circumstance.

There is one important class of word, however, quite apart from operators, to which this complete denial of symbol-referend connexion does not apply, namely those words whose sounds echo the sense and which may therefore be designated as echoic, imitative, or onomatopoetic words. Such are *bang, boom, clack, clang, clank, clash, clatter, clink, hum, mutter, rattle, roar, splash, swish, tinkle, whisper*, and *whiz*. Enterprising poets, dramatists, and novelists may invent them as nonce-words for their special effects. Many other words like our *laugh*, German and Dutch *lachen*, and Danish *le* no longer echo the sense so fully and effectively as they once did in their older forms (Indo-European *klok- klōk-* ⟩ Common Germanic *hlah- hlōh-*) before they followed the regular trend of sound changes in the course of linguistic history. Indeed, the number of words which have their ulterior origins in some kind of sound-sense echo will vary notably from language to language and will certainly prove a most rewarding object of investigation. Nevertheless, because language is always and everywhere a system of arbitrary symbols, even echoic words must fall into line if they are to survive, and so they are sure to become more or less conventionalized in any one language. In an English nursery a dog becomes a *bow-wow*, because that is our customary representation of a friendly bark. But in French this is *toutou*, in Italian *bau-bau*, and in German *Wau-wau*. In Shakespeare's day the cock crew *cock-a-diddle-dow* (*The Tempest* 1.ii.386), today he crows *cock-a-doodle-doo* with slightly more sonorous vowel-sounds in the tail end, but in France *cocorico*, in Germany *kikeriki*, in Denmark *kykeliky*, in Sweden *kukeliku*, and so forth. As we might expect, 'to whisper' is expressed in most languages by an imitative verb, but that verb may assume diverse shapes: French *chuchoter*, Spanish *susurrar*, and German *flüstern* and *wispern*. The ringing of bells is generally depicted by echoic antiphonies, but even these may vary from our *ding-dong* to German *bimbam* and Spanish *dindan*. Many other examples might be adduced to show that such words are usually standardized in any one language both in their spoken and in their recorded forms.

Every language is first of all a system or code of vocal symbols. Indeed, some of the two thousand and more languages still spoken in the world have never yet been consigned to writing. Elaborate and extensive as they sometimes are, they remain systems of inherited symbols by means of which their speakers communicate adequately with one another. Even such an important European language as Finnish, now spoken by some three million persons, went unrecorded until the middle of the sixteenth century when a translation of the Bible was first made. As for the *Kalevala*, or 'Land of Heroes', the historic epic of Finland, composed in trochaic tetrameters like Longfellow's *Hiawatha*, it was not printed until the nineteenth century. The history of recorded Finnish has therefore been short in comparison with that of English, French, Spanish, Italian, and German whose written symbols have persisted unchanged for long periods of time, or have been only slightly modified by usage or decree, but whose sounds have drifted and changed from century to century. That is why Finnish approaches more closely than any other European tongue to the principles that 'each spoken sound should be represented by one and the same corresponding written symbol'. Long vowels and double consonants are written twice. All vowels have their proper phonetic qualities. There are no ambiguities and no ambivalencies.

Like Estonian and Magyar (or Hungarian), Finnish belongs to the Finno-Ugrian group of languages: it is non-Indo-European. Portuguese, Spanish, Italian, and Czech are the languages with the most phonetic spellings in the Indo-European family, and those with the least phonetic spellings are undoubtedly English and French. The latter shows wide divergencies between sounds and symbols because its orthographic history may be traced back continuously to its beginnings in the famous Strasbourg Oaths of 14 February 842, as recorded in a manuscript of about A.D. 1000 now preserved in the Bibliothèque Nationale at Paris. In sounds French has changed most and Italian has changed least from antecedent Latin. Italian might be called Modern Latin, not, of course, to be confused with Church Latin, the living liturgical language of Western Christianity. Dante regarded the speech of Florence as Latin even in the thirteenth century. French moved away from Latin earlier. For over a thousand years it has served as the means of expression for an exceptionally intellectual people. From time to time, it is true, the illustrious Académie Française, founded by Cardinal Richelieu in 1635, has affected reforms especially in the third (1740) and fourth (1762) editions of its Dictionary. Later, however, it assumed a more conservative attitude. Apart from a few minor reforms in the seventh edition of 1878, it clearly intended to stabilize traditional orthography. French vies with English in the possession of a deplorably unphonetic spelling. The ten letters of *souhaitent* '(they) wish' and the eleven letters of *changeaient* '(they) used to change' register only four sounds each. Latin *aqua* 'water', with its four sounds so pronounced, has become [o] in Modern French, but the present spelling *eau* still records the pronunciation of the twelfth century. It lags eight centuries behind the times.

If we so desire, we may amuse ourselves by tracing the changes from Latin *aqua* [ɑkwɑ] to French *eau* [o] down the ages, for we have long, though not unbroken, chains of evidence to guide us. We have longer chains of written evidence for the Romance languages than for any other group of languages in the world. We can trace the ascertainable and easily explicable articulatory changes from Latin *aqua* to *eau* in Old French with its low vocal glide, to *e'au* in Middle French with its shift of stress, to *e'o* in early Modern French with its monophthongization of the second element, and so finally to [o] in the seventeenth century.

Meantime in Italian, Spanish, and Portuguese the only changes were those that affected the voiceless plosive consonant. In Italian it was doubled to *acqua*: in Spanish and Portuguese alike it was voiced to *agua*. That was all.

In spelling, German is not so phonetic as these last mentioned Romance languages, but it is reasonably consistent according to the principles laid down in the sixteenth century by Martin Luther, whose vigorous personality dominated both religion and language. The literary forms of the Lutheran Bible (1534) were subsequently taken over by Klopstock and Lessing and they were duly expanded and modified by Goethe and Schiller, since whose time many minor reforms have been effected. Some inconsistencies remain. If, say, you would like to know why the high back vowel of *Nuss* 'nut' is short, whereas that of *Fuss* is long, you must take these forms back to Old High German and Common Germanic and you will then discover that *Nuss* and *Fuss* have never made a good rhyme throughout all their known history. If, again, you would like to know why the vowel sounds in *Tage* 'days', *Rede* 'speech', and *leben* 'to live' are long, although there is no indication of this in the spelling, you must take account of that phonetic principle by which short vowels were lengthened when stressed in the open syllables (i.e. syllables ending in a vowel) of disyllabic words in Middle High German just as they were in contemporaneous Middle English and just as they had been in fourth-century Latin. Contrariwise, when *h* was no longer sounded between vowels in Middle High German, it was retained in writing and, since the preceding short vowel was naturally lengthened in compensation, *h* itself came to be regarded as a symbol of length. Not only, therefore, has *sta-hel* 'steel' come to be spelled *Stahl*, but also *zal* 'tale, number' and *zan* 'tooth' are now written *Zahl* and *Zahn*. Further, when initial *s-* was shifted to *sh-* before all following consonants, it was written *sch-* except before *p* and *t*. Hence today we have *schlafen* 'to sleep' and *schneiden* 'to cut', but *speisen* 'to eat' and *stehen* 'to stand', although these words all have the same pre-palatal sibilant (English *sh*). If we had time to extend this list of discrepancies, we should probably conclude that German orthography is far more systematic and consistent than English and French, but considerably less phonetic than Spanish, Portuguese, and Italian.

The Russian alphabet or *azbuka* now comprises thirty-two letters (or thirty-three if we count the two *e*'s, *ye*, and *yo*, as separate symbols). The consonants record sounds with remarkable fidelity, but the vowels fail signally to do so because they vary with changing stress. Just as the qualities of our vowels vary with changing stress in *family*, *familiar*, and *familiarity* or in *period*, *periodical*, and *periodicity*, so are the qualities of Russian vowels largely dependent upon word stress and sentence rhythm. The main stress in a word, which is not marked in ordinary orthography, may fall on a quite unimportant syllable. If we compare the Russian farewell which in one of its forms is *Do svi'danya* 'To the seeing again' with its counterparts in other languages, French *Au revoir*, Italian *Arrivederla*, or German *Auf Wiedersehen*, we observe how very much more obscured the notion of 'seeing' becomes in Russian than in other languages because such a strong stress falls on the insignificant -*dan*-. It is a misfortune that Moscow has not adopted the western alphabet, and yet it must be admitted that Russian shows closer sound-symbol correspondence when recorded in its proper Cyrillic orthography than when it is transliterated into Roman characters, whether in the American style as used for bibliographical purposes by the Library of Congress, in the British fashion as favoured by the London School of Slavonic Studies, or in the European system which has recourse to diacritical marks as introduced into Czech in the early fifteenth century by Jan Hus. Meantime, Russia's great eastern neighbour has decided in favour of Romanization. The Chinese People's Republic will regularize the new spelling of the standard language through mass instruction in teachers' training colleges and schools. This, as we have already seen (in Chapter 2), was the means adopted with such signal success by Mustafa Kemal Atatürk in 1928 when by presidential edict he commanded all teachers henceforth to substitute Latin for Arabic letters in the writing of Turkish. Such decrees become effective only in compact communities with totalitarian governments. All published books at once become inaccessible to children bred to the new orthography, but not to mature students who will gladly pay the price and master the old script in order to read the national literature of the past. The value and importance of recording all the great languages of the world in similar sets of symbols can hardly be exaggerated.

Even advanced students are prone to forget that Old English literature was not written as it now appears in modern editions of texts. Moreover, before their conversion to Christianity, the Anglo-Saxons used the runic alphabet or *futhorc*, so named after its first six letters, *th* being one letter and not two. This runic futhorc was itself an adaptation of Greek and Latin letters straightened and so made suitable for engraving in wood and stone. Unfortunately, it was by no means uniform. It originally comprised just two dozen letters, but in England this number was afterwards extended, first to 28, and later to 33. Would it be feasible to enlarge the present English alphabet from 26 letters to 45 so that the number of letters might tally exactly with that number of phonemes in the southern variety of Standard English? Yes, it would be possible to do this. In some measure it has already been achieved in the transcription of our language into the conventional symbols of the International Phonetic Association but, when we come to examine closely successive editions of British and American pronouncing dictionaries, we find surprising, if not startling, instability. 'Language changes always and everywhere.' In order to fix sound-symbol correspondence it would be necessary to decide categorically on one received standard pronunciation, to insist that all members of that speech community should not change their articulatory habits, and, most difficult of all, to ignore variations of sound that arise from the operation of the prosodic factors of length, stress, pitch, and juncture.

It is indeed surprising that a language can function efficiently as a means of communication even when it carries a heavy burden of homophones, words like *rite*, *write*, *right*, and *wright*; or *raise*, *raze*, and *rays*, in which sounds are identical but spellings are not. Thus French *vert* 'green' is homophonous with *ver* 'worm', *vair* 'squirrel's fur', *verre* 'glass', *vers* 'verse', and *vers* 'towards'. Etymologically, of course, these last two words are the same, both deriving from the Latin past participle *versus* meaning 'turned'. A *verse* implies 'turning' to begin a fresh line: *towards* signifies 'turned towards'. Other French homophones include *pain* 'bread', *pin* 'pine', and *peint* '(he) paints'; *soi* 'self', *soie* 'silk', and *soit* 'so be it'; *or* 'gold', and *hors* 'outside'; *Jean* 'John', and *gens* 'people'. Homophones may arise from recent sound-changes. Consider, for instance, all those pairs of words like *bean* and *been*, *beat* and *beet*, *heal* and *heel*, *meat* and *meet*, *read* and *reed*, *sea* and *see*, *seam* and *seem*, *steal* and *steel*, *team* and *teem*, uttered with a long close *e* and a long *i* respectively by the men of Shakespeare's day, but which fell together later in the seventeenth century when long close *e* was itself raised to long *i* in these and in scores of other words.

Today they remain fully homophonous but, because the constituents of each pair belong to separate grammatical categories (or parts of speech) and thus fulfil different syntactic functions within the sentence, there is small danger of misapprehension. In pairs of substantives like *beach* and *beech*, *breach* and *breech*, *mead* and *meed*, *peace* and *piece*, *peal* and *peel*, this danger is inevitably increased, although the contexts in which these particular words might be confused is hardly conceivable. Even in this brief list, however, it may be observed that *breech*, if not a term in gunnery, is generally used in its plural form *breeches* (historically a double plural since Old English *brēc* was itself a mutated plural of *brōc*); that *meed* is now archaic for 'reward', and that *mead* in the sense of 'meadow' is restricted to poetry, since it already has a homonym in *mead* 'honey wine'. These last two forms are called *homonyms* since they are identical in sound and spelling, but different in origin and meaning, whereas *homophones* are identical in sound alone.

When an obsolescent or rarely used word finds itself in homophonic clash with another word in frequent use, it naturally stands in danger of being completely ousted from the speech of everyday conversation. Robert Bridges (in the second Society for Pure English Tract of 1919) went so far as to predict the eventual disappearance of the verb *know* because in its infinitive and present-tense forms it is homophonous with *no* and *nose*, and in its past-tense forms with *new*. 'The whole inconvenience', he avowed, 'is too radical and perpetual to be received all over the world'. The poet laureate was commendably solicitous for the efficiency of English as a world language, but he probably underestimated the wide differences in function and meaning in the words concerned. After all, both French *sais* and German *weiss* '(I) know' may be said to suffer a comparable 'inconvenience': *sais* has a homophone in *c'est* 'this is', whereas *weiss* has a homonym in the epithet *weiss* 'white'. Both English and French have many one-vowel and one-diphthong homophones: *are*, *ah*; *awe*, *oar*, *or*, *ore*; *aye* 'ever', *eh*; *owe*, *o(h)*; *ay* 'yes', *eye*, *I*; *air*, *ere* 'before', *eyre* (in the legal title 'justices in eyre'), *heir*: *où* 'where', *ou* 'or'; *au(x)* 'to the', *eau* 'water', *os* 'bones'; *eux* 'to them', *œufs* 'eggs'; *ai* '(I) have', *est* 'is', *et* 'and'; *aie* 'have!', *ais* 'board, plank', *hait* '(he) hates'; *an* 'year', and *en* 'in, of it'.

If English and French are burdened with a plethora of homophones and homonyms, Arabic abounds in *homographs* or *heteronyms*, words identical in spelling, but different in sound, origin, and meaning. Such anomalies may seem to present a yet more 'radical and perpetual inconvenience' to the users of a language. English, too, carries far more homographs than the casual inquirer might at first suppose. First, there are many monosyllabic forms like *sow* 'to scatter seed' and *sow* 'female pig', which have no historical connexion whatsoever and which have coincided in spelling quite fortuitously; and so also *bow* 'weapon for shooting arrows' and *bow* 'to incline, bend', deriving ultimately but not immediately from related forms; *mow* 'to cut grass' and *mow* as in *mop and mow* 'to make grimaces'; *row* 'number of things in line' or 'to propel a boat with oars' and *row* 'brawl, disturbance'; *bass* 'lowest part in music' and *bass* 'common perch'; *lead* 'to guide' and *lead* 'base metal'; *read* present tense and *read* past tense; *live* 'to be alive' and *live* (as in *live wire*) aphetized form of the adjective *alive* 'living', now used attributively; *lives* third person singular present indicative of the verb *live* and *lives* plural of the substantive *life*; *slough* 'quagmire' and *slough* 'snake's cast skin'; *tear* 'drop of moisture from the eye' and *tear* 'to rend'; *wind* 'breeze' and *wind* 'to coil'; *wound* 'injury' and *wound* 'coiled'. Secondly, we find various derivatives that have fallen together in spelling like *'entrance* 'entering, way in' and *en-'trance* 'to throw into a trance, delight'; *hinder* 'more behind' and *hinder* 'to prevent'; *prayer* 'one who prays' and *prayer* 'act of praying, supplication'; *sewer* 'one who sews' and *sewer* 'public drain'; *singer* 'one who sings' and *singer* 'one who singes'; *tarry* 'covered or smeared with tar' and *tarry* 'to wait'. Thirdly, there are scores of homographs differentiated by stress and resultant modifications of vowel qualities according to syntactic function, like *'perfect* adjective but *per'fect* verb, and like *'compact* substantive but *com'pact* verb, and so also *'conduct* and *con'duct*, *'contact* and *con'tact*, *'contest* and *con'test*, *'contrast* and *con'trast*, *'increase* and *in'crease*, *'object* and *ob'ject*, *'record* and *re'cord*, *'subject* and *sub'ject*, and many more. We may observe that the substantive *'refuse* 'what is rejected as worthless or left over after use' and so 'rubbish' differs from the verb *re'fuse* not only in stress and in vowel modifications as in all the other examples just cited, but also in the unvoicing of the consonant z to s, and in this respect we may compare the verbs *close*, *house*, and *use*, and also *mouth*, with their corresponding substantives. Moreover, if we compare the electrician's *re-fuse* 'to supply with a new set of fuses' with its unhyphenated homograph *refuse* 'to deny, say no', we find that it differs from the latter in three properties: it has level stress, lengthened vowel in its prefix, and open internal juncture instead of close between its constituent syllables.

A full study, both descriptive and historical, of the homophones, homonyms, and homographs in any one language will disclose many interesting and even perhaps unsuspected deviations from regular sound-symbol correspondence. In all his researches the investigator will be well advised to keep spoken and recorded language separate in his mind, at no point confusing sounds with letters and at no point forgetting that spelling has only limited value as evidence. Linguistics is primarily concerned with the analysis of the structure or pattern of living speech considered as the expression of meanings by forms and series of forms which may be scrutinized under the broad and overlapping categories of phonology, morphology, and syntax. Philology, it is true, is primarily concerned, at least in its traditional application, with texts and their exact and minute interpretation. Philology is an attractive term not only because it is associated more comprehensively with humane studies but also because its very vagueness gives it a usefulness denied to more precise appellations. The shift of emphasis from comparative philology to general linguistics reflects the main change of approach and attitude to the science of language on the part of scholars in the transition from the nineteenth century to the twentieth.

Technical advances may sometimes put a language to new kinds of tests. With the invention of the telephone it was soon discovered that, of the ten ciphers 0 1 2 3 4 5 6 7 8 9, two pairs had the same vowel sounds and therefore gave rise to endless confusion: 0 (pronounced 'nought') was confused with 4, and 5 with 9. It was a fortunate coincidence that the Arabic sign for zero happened to be identical with the letter o (from Greek omicron), and so 'owe' was permanently substituted for 'nought', but the other pair – 5 and 9 – remained such a continual source of error that many people requested the Post Office not to assign them a telephone number containing either of these figures. Had not the system of automatic dialling been invented, one of these two ciphers would doubtless have been re-named, even as in Germany the dialectal *zwo* has been substituted telephonically for *zwei* in order to eliminate confusion with *drei*. The telephone, radio, and television have all contributed to greater clarity of speech in that they have demanded and encouraged the maximum differentiation of phonemes. In some measure, too, they may have encouraged 'spelling pronunciations'. Where education is widespread, the eye takes precedence of the ear and words may be pronounced in closer accord with their recorded spellings than with their traditional sounds. We should not allow ourselves to be either surprised or depressed by such changes. In English we read by syllables rather than by single letters and on that account our language is safeguarded against any rapid decline in sonority. On the whole, it seems to me, the dispassionate observer should welcome changes that bring spoken sounds and recorded symbols more into line, however reluctant he may feel to adopt such changes in his own way of speaking.

CHAPTER 5

THE MAKING OF WORDS

ALTHOUGH we naturally regard a *word* as a very important linguistic unit, we should realize that scientifically it is not a fixed and definite division like the *morpheme*. A word is merely a conventional or arbitrary segment of utterance, a minimum free form, consisting of one or more morphemes. A morpheme is the smallest significant or meaningful unit, and it may be either *bound* or *free*.

Take, for instance, the word *home*. Clearly this is a minimum free form consisting of one and only one morpheme, since it cannot be broken down into smaller elements. If, however, I use this word in its plural form and say *homes*, I then employ two morphemes, the free form *home* and the bound form *-s* (bound because it cannot be used independently or in isolation) which happens to be one of the marks of plural number in English and is called an *inflexion*. The word *homely* also comprises two morphemes, the free form *home* and the bound form *-ly*, which here serves as an adjective-forming suffix. So, too, the word *homeward* likewise consists of two morphemes, the free form *home* and the bound form *-ward*, which obviously has nothing to do with its homonym *ward* meaning 'guard, custody', but which here serves as an adverb-forming suffix. The words *homestead* and *homework* also contain two morphemes each, but both are free.

The inflected form *homes*, the derivatives *homely* and *homeward*, and the compounds *homestead* and *homework* exemplify the morphological processes known as *inflexion* (or simply *flexion*), *derivation* (or *affixation*), and *composition* (or *compounding*) respectively. *Home* is a *simple* word, *homely* and *homeward* are *complex* words, whereas *homestead* and *homework* are *compound* words.

Since *home* is a simple word of one morpheme, it may be

said to contain only one *root* or radical element. This is true of thousands of words like *man, wife, boy, son, house, room, roof, door, tree, ash, oak, beech, elm, flower, hedge, field,* and *moor*. Of some words, like *barn* and *nest*, it is true *synchronically* (descriptively for the language as it now is) but not true *diachronically* (or historically). If we go back far enough, we find that *barn* comes from two words meaning 'barley hall' and *nest* from two words meaning 'nether sit, place where a bird sits down'. *Barn* and *nest* may therefore be described as *obscured* or *latent* compounds.

The possible arrangements of sounds within syllables may vary in a most interesting manner from one language to another. Some languages, like Japanese and Malay, avoid consonant clusters altogether. Classical Greek tolerated few final consonants apart from -*n*, -*r*, and -*s*. Benjamin Lee Whorf (in his remarkable essay on *Linguistics as an Exact Science*) went so far as to devise a 'structural formula' for all words of one syllable in the English language. Even a casual observer will soon discover that the Germanic tongues favour far more consonant clusters than the Romance languages do. In English these clusters are certainly more restricted at the beginning of words than at the end.

The use of inflexions within a particular language will depend upon its *typology*. It will depend upon whether the language concerned is *analytic* or *synthetic*. An analytic language consists for the most part of free forms: a synthetic one has mostly bound forms. Chinese is highly analytic. Finnish is highly synthetic. The development of English from Indo-European to the present day shows a general drift from synthesis to analysis. Nevertheless, the distinction between these two contrasting types is relative. Any one system of speech may be in some ways more synthetic and in other respects more analytic than another language. We might, in fact, attempt to classify the languages of the world according to these two criteria – more analytic or more synthetic. At the same time we might attempt a more discriminating quadripartition of languages into *isolating, flexional, agglutinative,* and *incorporating*. An *isolating* language is one that is completely analytic, and therefore again Chinese is a very good example. Lithuanian and Lettish are excellent specimens of *flexional* languages because they have conserved the old Indo-European system almost as fully as ancient Sanskrit itself. *Agglutinative* means 'uniting as with glue' and this may seem a strange term to apply to any form of speech. It is indeed applicable to the Ural-Altaic family (Chapter 8) to which Turkish belongs. The latter is probably the most highly agglutinative of all tongues. It differs from an *incorporating* language which has a way of merging various elements into the verb and of making the verb a composite form expressing by itself a complete statement or proposition. This was pre-eminently characteristic of Nahuatl, the language of the ancient Aztec civilization of Mexico.

In general it may be said that English and German are both analytic languages, but these two related West Germanic tongues have obviously proceeded in their development at different speeds. Compare the verbs *ride* and *reiten*. The former has only five forms today (*ride, rides, rode, riding, ridden*), although in Old English it had thirteen forms (if we count the inflected participles, present and past, as one form each), but German *reiten* still possesses as many as sixteen forms. German has changed less and is therefore far less analytic than English, not only in flexion, but also in affixation and composition. In English, however, the movement is not all one way. We now witness a considerable extension in the use of Greek and Latin *living* affixes – living in the sense that educated people are conscious of their meanings as they speak. Indeed, they may have a choice between, say, *hypo-thesis* and *sup-position*, both denoting etymologically *under-setting*. Speakers of German can also choose between *Voraussetzung* and *Hypothese*, and they even possess a verb *supponieren* adapted direct from the Latin infinitive *supponere*, but they feel that *Hypothese* and *supponieren* are technical and foreign and they are therefore reluctant to incorporate them into their ethnical vocabulary or lexicon. English speakers, on the contrary, show no hesitation in admitting both Greek and Latin derivatives quite freely, even when, as in the following list, they form morphological equivalents:

dys-morph-o-sis	mal-form-at-ion
dys-troph-y	mal-nutr-it-ion
-ec-tom-y	ex-cis-ion
en-tom-on	in-sect
hyper-aesth-et-ic	super-sens-it-ive
hyper-phys-ic-al	super-n-at-ur-al
hypo-sta-sis	sub-stan-ce
hypo-the-sis	sup-pos-it-ion
meta-phor	trans-fer(-ence)
meta-the-sis	trans-pos-it-ion
meta-morph-o-sis	trans-form-at-ion
odont-o-log-y	dent-ist-ry
peri-pher-y	circum-fer-en-ce
peri-phras-is	circum-loc-ut-ion
phos-phor(-us)	luc-i-fer
sphen-oid	cun-ei-form
sym-path-y	com-pass-ion
syn-drom-e	con-curr-en-ce
syn-erg-y	co-op-er-at-ion
syn-thes-is	com-pos-it-ion

Far from being dead, the Greek and Latin languages are promised immortality in this new international language of learning: these ancient prefixes and suffixes live again in the minds of those speakers who are conscious, or subconscious, of their significations as they speak. It goes without saying that these pairs of derivatives vary considerably in their degrees of synonymity and in the ranges of their semantic spheres. Hypostasis, for instance, denotes substance only in a philosophical and theological sense. Metamorphosis is more technical and therefore more restricted than transformation: it is used to denote those astounding shape-changings displayed by metabolous creatures, when tadpoles turn into frogs, cocoons into silkworms, and chrysalids into butterflies. Odontology is concerned with the theory, but dentistry with the practice of the care of the teeth. Syndrome and synergy are primarily medical terms. Sympathy and compassion both imply 'suffering together with another, fellow-feeling', but whereas the first suggests a state of mind or mental participation, the second expresses active pity leading to the relief of distress. Because Charles Lamb felt himself to be 'a bundle of prejudices – the veriest thrall to sympathies, apathies, antipathies', he entitled his all-too-human essay *Imperfect Sympathies*; but Aldous Huxley, in *Ends and Means*, concluded after much deep thought and anguish that only one form of human progress really matters in the light of eternity, namely progress in charity and compassion.

Classical affixes live a new life in modern tongues, and that is why, it seems to me, *hybrids* are sometimes justifiable, or at least not always reprehensible, in the making of words. Hybrids – the metaphor is clearly a botanical and zoological one – are derivatives and compounds whose constituent elements come from different stocks. *Sociology*, for example, is a combination of Latin *socio-*, the linking form of *socius* 'companion', and Greek *-logia* 'branch of knowledge'. It has long been accepted as an indispensable technical term into French, Spanish, Italian, German, and Russian. As Sir Alexander Carr-Saunders has recently reminded us, *sociology* is, although a hybrid, a better term than *social science*, since that branch of study is not really a science at all. It involves the systematic investigation into the forms, institutions, and functions of human society and these are amenable neither to scientific definition nor to precise measurement. *Automobile* 'self-movable', a hybrid of Greek *auto* 'self' and Latin *-mōbile* from older *movibile* 'that can be moved', is now shared as an international word by both east and west. *Television* is a notorious hybrid, deliberately created in recent times from Greek *tēle-* 'far' and Latin *vīsio* 'seeing'. Rejected by German purists, *das Fernsehen* has taken its place, but the compound word for 'television set' has to be a hybrid all the same and not an attractive one either – *der Fernsehapparat*!

Compound words, as we have already noted, differ from

derivatives in that they are made up of free forms only: *home-land*, *home-stead*, and *home-work*. These are primary compounds: each consists of two simple free forms. Both components are substantives, the first determining and qualifying the second. This type of compound occurs in all Indo-European languages, although, as we shall see in a moment, in some languages it is very rare. In English it is certainly prolific: *airman*, *beehive*, *bookcase*, *daybreak*, *flowerpot*, *landmark*, *lifeline*, *network*, *notebook*, *pathway*, *rainbow*, *seashore*, *snowflake*, *thunderbolt*, *vineyard*, *waterfall*, and countless others. You will observe that the precise relationship between the two component substantives may vary considerably. An *airman* is a man who flies in an aircraft, but a *beehive* is a hive in which bees are housed, and so on. The signification of a particular compound is arbitrary, determined by custom and use. Having once become settled in its use by the speech community, a newly-formed compound henceforth functions as one morphological unit and it then acquires lexical status. Because in English the determinant (*air*) always precedes the determinatum (*man*), we may create reversible compounds in our language like *boathouse* 'shed at the water's edge for storing boats' and *houseboat* 'boat adequately equipped for living in'; *bookcase* 'case containing shelves for books' and *casebook* 'book in which legal or medical cases are recorded'; *workbasket* 'receptacle for sewing implements and materials', and *basketwork* 'work consisting of plaited osiers or twigs'. In using such compounds the speaker runs no risk of ambiguity because it is characteristic of the inherited structure of English that the determinant comes first. In French, however, with its different structure, this no longer holds. There the determinant generally, though not rigidly, follows the determinatum. That is why combinations like *montre-bracelet* 'watch-armlet' 'wrist-watch' are comparatively rare. A Frenchman prefers to use either a verb-object compound like *tire-bouchon* 'corkscrew' or a phrase like *chute d'eau* 'waterfall'. English has plenty of verb-object compounds too. Indeed, it probably has far more than French because the latter makes small use of composition in general, preferring phrases of the substantive-preposition-substantive type like *chute d'eau* just mentioned, *arc-en-ciel* 'rainbow', *moulin à vent* 'windmill', *salle de bain* 'bathroom', *brosse à cheveux* 'hairbrush', *coucher du soleil* 'sunset', and *clair de lune* 'moonlight'; or phrases of the substantive-preposition-infinitive type like *brosse à peindre* 'paint-brush', *salle à manger* 'dining room', and *chambre à coucher* 'bedroom'.

Compare English *breakwater* with French *brise-lames* 'break-waves', Spanish *rompeolas*, and Italian *frangiflutti*. Such verb-object compounds were quite unknown in English before the fourteenth century, when, however, they quickly grew in number under French influence: *crackjaw* 'word difficult to articulate', *cutthroat*, *daredevil*, *holdall*, *makeweight*, *scapegrace* (older *escape-grace* 'one who gets no grace'), *scarecrow*, *skinflint*, *spitfire*, *spoilsport*, *stopgap*, *telltale*; not to mention family names like *Shakespeare*, *Drinkwater* (French *Boileau*), *Makepeace*, and *Lovejoy*. If we now reverse the process and put the object of the verb first, we find ourselves compelled to conform to the inherent structure of our language and to use *parasynthesis*, or composition and affixation combined, as in *housekeeper*, *landowner*, *metalworker*, *nutcrackers*, *screwdriver*, *timeserver*, *typewriter*, and *woodpecker*. You may have observed that such parasynthetic formations are as rare in the Romance languages as those of the break-water (*brise-lames*, *rompeolas*, *frangiflutti*) type are abundant, but they are frequent in German: *Haushälterin* 'housekeeper' (with feminine suffix *-in* causing mutation or umlaut of the root vowel in *Haushalt* 'household'), *Grundbesitzer* 'landowner', (*ein*) *Nussknacker* '(pair of) nutcrackers', *Schraubenzieher* 'screwdriver', and the like.

Another notable type of compound is exemplified by such primary forms as *blackberry* and *blackbird*, which bear the main stress on the first syllable. If we show this stress by a short raised stroke before the syllable carrying it, we may then differentiate yet more clearly between the compound word '*blackberry*, denoting one particular species of bramble, and the two words '*black* '*berry*, with level stress, indicating any berry that is black; and also between '*blackbird*, denoting one particular species of bird, and the two words *'black 'bird*, again with level stress, indicating any bird that is black. *Blackberry* is a very old compound. Ælfric recorded it in a glossary one thousand years ago. As the commonest wild fruit in England, it became the proverbial symbol of abundance. Falstaff, you may recall, refused to be compelled to give any man a reason even 'if Reasons were as plentie as Black-berries' (*Henry IV*, Part I, II.iv.265). Compare other compounds of this type like *bluebell, broadsheet, freeman, gentleman, greenhouse, quicksilver*, and *shorthand* with their two-word counterparts. You will at once detect differences in stress and meaning. Each pair of forms has its own linguistic history. Take, for example, *'greenhouse* and *'green 'house*. This pair is peculiar because the adjective *green*, related etymologically to *grow* and *grass*, was early substantivized and came to denote any herb or plant. A professional gardener may well have young growth in mind, rather than green colour, when he talks about his greenhouse. He will see nothing incongruous in the irrelevant circumstance that it is painted yellow or brown! Not grand enough, perhaps, to be called a conservatory, his greenhouse is for him a garden structure in which delicate and tender plants are reared and preserved.

Parasynthetic adjectives, like *heart-breaking, labour-saving, life-giving, peace-loving, soul-stirring*, and *time-consuming*, consist of substantive as object and present participle. Unknown in the Romance tongues, this type is fairly frequent in German in such compounds as *arbeitsparend* 'labour-saving', *bahnbrechend* 'revolutionary, pioneering' literally 'track-breaking', *herzzerreissend* 'heart-rending', and *zeitraubend* 'time-robbing'. German also has true *bahuvrihi* forms, so called from this Sanskrit compound signifying '(possessing) much rice', like *barfuss* 'barefoot'. Besides the latter we use *hunchback, paperback, scatterbrain, wryneck*, and a few others. Generally, however, we prefer extended bahuvrihi combinations like *largehearted, narrowminded*, and *oldfashioned*, in which the immediate constituents are clearly adjective-substantive, to which the past participle inflexion has been added. German prefers to use adjectival suffixes in such instances: *grossherzig*, *engherzig*, and *altmodisch*.

Fashions may change in the making of words. A growing class of English compounds consists of phrasal verbs, like *break down* and *build up*, used as substantives. *Break-down* may retain its ordinary meaning of 'collapse, failure', but more often in the modern world it denotes 'distribution into categories, analysis, or classification; division of an operation into distinct processes': whereas *build-up* implies 'organization or accumulation of forces'. These verb-adverb combinations are often printed without hyphens in America to show that they are felt to be closely-knit compound substantives. They are often more picturesque and vivid than their older synonyms and at the same time they may have wider spheres of reference. In certain situations, calling for diplomacy and tact, a speaker may find it advantageous to use the less committal and more intimate and factual word. He may prefer such compounds as *climb-down* 'lowering of demands'; *get-away* 'escape'; *get-together* 'meeting'; *get-up* 'style of dress or equipment'; *hold-up* 'obstruction, delay'; *let-up* 'relaxation'; *rake-off* 'commission or profit, often illegitimate, received by a party to a transaction'; *set-back* 'reverse of fortune, unexpected check'; *set-up* 'organization, arrangement'; *show-down* 'definite disclosure of facts, intentions, or resources'; and *write-up* 'press report, elaborate account, or laudatory article'.

People may or may not be conscious of the meanings of the constituent elements of compounds as they speak. Why, for instance, do the French say *au printemps* 'in spring', but *en été*, *en automne*, and *en hiver* for the other seasons of the year? Surely it is because this phrase became stereotyped at a time when the people of France were still conscious of its literal meaning 'at the first time (of the year)'. How many Englishmen realize as they speak that *breakfast* is a substantival compound of the verb-object type, like *breakwater* discussed above? It is, of course, the first meal of the day when you *break* your *fast*. Even as late as 1665 John Evelyn wrote (*Memoirs* i, 375) quite naturally: 'I brake fast this morning with the King' instead of 'I breakfasted'. Less naturally, no doubt, and more as an intentional archaism or piece of dialect, Scott described (*Marmion* I, xxxi) how 'knight and squire had broke their fast'. How far are you aware, as you speak, of the separate components of common nouns like *boatswain*, *cupboard*, *forehead*, *shepherd*, and *waistcoat*; or of place names like *Bradley*, *Hampstead*, *Langley*, *Morton*, and *Sutton*? If you are genuinely interested in words, you may well be aware of the meanings of constituent elements when for some reason you pause to think or when you are challenged outright to proffer an elucidation. It is clear, however, that at some time ordinary folk must have ceased to associate *Bradley* with 'broad lea', *Hampstead* with 'home stead', *Langley* with 'long lea', *Morton* with 'moor town', and *Sutton* with 'south town'. Take, for instance, *Hampstead* and *home stead*. Old English *hām stede* was the common origin of both, but, whereas in speech *hām* was changed in the course of time to *home*, in the name it was shortened to *hăm* in this position before the end of the Old English period and then, by faulty timing in the adjustment of velum and lips in passing from the bilabial nasal consonant to the following sibilant, a buccal plosive was heard and actually recorded as *p* in the spelling of the name. Consequently later generations came to dissociate *home* from *Hampstead*, just as today we do not readily link together in our minds *croup* and *crupper*, *food* and *fodder*, *feet* and *fetter*, *hare* and *harrier*, *game* and *gamble*, *keel* and *kelson*, *toad* and *tadpole*.

Sometimes a word gets so worn down by a kind of phonetic attrition that it loses distinctness in speech and has to be reinforced by some therapeutic device. It may, of course, be replaced altogether, as when Old English *æ* was ousted by Scandinavian *lagu*, which became *law*; and Old English *ēa* was superseded by Old French *rivere*, which became *river*. Similarly in French the inherited form *os* 'mouth' (Latin *ōs*, *ōris*, whence our adjective *oral*) would have given [o] and would thus have become homophonous with *eau* 'water', as well as being identical in spelling with *os* 'bone' (Latin *os*, *ossis*, whence our adjective *osseous*).

French speakers have therefore discarded *os* 'mouth' altogether in favour of *bouche* from Latin *bucca* 'cheek' (as in our adjective *buccal*). As an example of a reinforced form in French, we may take the word for 'bee'. Its Latin antecedent was *apis* (as in our *apiary*) and this has survived in Italian *ape*, still pronounced as two syllables, and also in French dialects as *ep*, *ef*, and *é*. The standard French form, however, is *abeille*, which, like Spanish *abeja*, comes from the Latin diminutive or pet form *apicula* 'dear little bee', even as French *oiseau*, like Italian *uccello*, derives not from *avis* (as in our *aviary*) but from the diminutive or hypocoristic form *avicellus* which became *aucellus* in later Latin. Curiously enough, it is now Spanish, and not Italian, that preserves the simple form *ave* without any strengthening or therapeutic device to give it greater body and distinctness in everyday communication, reminding us of that plain truth that speech is a human activity and that development is sometimes capricious and unpredictable. In fact the Italians, living in the land of that renowned bird-lover St Francis, are fond of using the double diminutives *uccellino* and *uccelletto*.

Am I right in thinking that even English speakers tend to avoid leaving *bee* too much in isolation and to say *honey bee* or *bumble bee* or perhaps *busy bee*, in dialect *bee-fly*, adding another word to fortify it, to give it greater body and substance, and to distinguish it quite clearly in conversation from the substantive verb? As a fully completed process we see this in such bird-names as *jackdaw* and *magpie*, which have supplanted simple *daw* and *pie*. In the early seventeenth century Michael Drayton (in his poem on *The Owle*) sang of 'the thievish daw and the dissembling pie', but already nursery extensions with prefixed *Jack* and *Mag* (for *Margaret*) were gaining currency, as Jonathan Swift playfully observed a century later:

> Pyes and daws are often stil'd
> With Christian nicknames like a child.

Today simple *pie* is preserved in the derivative *pie-d* and the compound *pie-bald*, both now meaning not only 'black and

white like a pie' but also 'particoloured, of different colours'. Browning's Pied Piper of Hamelin, you may remember, wore a coat 'half of yellow and half of red'.

Another widespread morphological process performing a
variety of functions in the languages of the world is the
doubling of syllables or reduplication. In Malay, for instance,
reduplication may be used to make the plural of nouns:
bunga 'flower', *bunga-bunga* 'flowers'; *orang* 'man', *orang-
orang* 'men', whereas *orang-utan*, the international designation of one of the anthropoid apes, has the attribute *utan*
'wild, of the forest' as its second component. This reduplicated plural is not used with numerals since the singular form
is there felt to be unambiguous and adequate, as if we said
in English *one man*, *two man*, but *many man-man*. In Indo-
European tongues reduplication was employed to make the
past tense of verbs, as in the solitary English survival *do*: *di-d*.
In Greek this process was regular, but sporadic in Latin:
mordet 'it bites', *mo-mordit* 'it bit'. In a few languages reduplication indicates the superlative degree of comparison, as if
we said in English *great-great* instead of *greatest*. This comes
near to its general function which is to emphasize, intensify,
or produce special effects as in *goody-goody* and *pretty-pretty*;
or, with change of consonant, *hanky-panky*, *namby-pamby*,
teeny-weeny (for *tiny wee*); or again, with vocalic antiphony,
singsong, German *Singsang*, showing ablaut, apophony, or
gradation; or *ding-dong* echoic or onomatopoetic, imitating
the chime of bells, *chit-chat*, *dilly-dally*, *zigzag*; Malay
bengkang-bengkok 'zigzag, twisting', *gilang-gemilang* 'dazzling,
sparkling'.

Contradictory and opposing processes may sometimes be
seen at work together in one and the same language, such as
derivation and *back-formation* (which we may fairly regard as
regressive or negative derivation). It implies the analogical
creation of a new simple word from an existing word that is
wrongly assumed to be complex. The verb *to grovel*, for
example, is back-formed from *grovelling* on the assumption
that this is a present participle, whereas in fact it is an
adverb signifying 'face downwards', since *-ling* is the same

bound suffix as that found in *headlong* for older *headling* 'head-first'. So, too, the verb *to edit* 'to prepare for publication', first recorded in 1791, was back-formed, or derived in reverse, from the agent-substantive *editor*, first used in 1649, from Latin *ēditor* 'out-giver', French *éditeur*, German *Herausgeber*. In the seventeenth century the English *editor*, just like the French *éditeur* of today, was actually the publisher. The editor of a French periodical or newspaper is *le rédacteur*. The German *Herausgeber*, on the other hand, remains the man who prepares the work for the publisher or *Verleger*, who in his turn supervises the *Verlag* or 'press'. Among other verbs created by this reversed derivative process we may first mention those which have won general acceptance like *diagnose* from *diagnosis*, *liaise* 'to perform the functions of a *liaison* officer', *partake* from *partaker* or *part-taker*, and *reminisce* from *reminiscence*; and then, secondly, those which are not yet quite at home in good speech, like *enthuse* from *enthusiasm*, *laze* from *lazy*, *orate* from *oration*, and *peeve* from *peevish*. It may seem somewhat surprising that *greed* has arisen by this process from *greedy*, and *difficult* (replacing older *difficile*) from *difficulty*. Back-formation inevitably results from some kind of faulty analysis of complex words. If people make a verb *housekeep* from the agent-substantive *housekeeper*, they do so on the assumption that the immediate constituents of this trimorphemic noun are *house* and *keep* to which *-er* has been added and from which it may therefore now be subtracted. But this is not true. The immediate constituents are obviously *house* and *keeper*. Facetiously, of course, we may disregard all such morphological niceties and ask tersely 'Shall we mote?' which is shorter than 'Shall we go by motor-car?' by four syllables.

If *mote* is a sportive back-formation, *motel* is a *blend*, *portmanteau word*, or *telescoped form* for 'motorists' hotel'. A blend may be defined as the coalescence of two free forms resulting in the creation of a new word which shares or combines their meanings. Many languages have been enriched abundantly by this irregular process, though the precise measure of that enrichment might not easily be assessed. It is generally accepted, for example, that French *rendre* 'to give back' results from a blend in popular Latin of the two classical verbs *red-dere* 'to give back' and *prendere* from older *pre-hendere* 'to seize'. The verb *render* came into English before Chaucer, and the useful noun *rendezvous* from the French reflexive imperative *rendez vous* 'betake yourselves' has been well established in naval and military parlance since Tudor days. We have strong reasons for assuming that *bash* is a blend of *bang* and *smash*; *clash* of *clang* and *crash*; *blotch* of *blot* and *botch* (or *patch*); *knoll* of *knell* and *toll*; and *flurry* of *fluster* and *hurry*; but we cannot prove these to be blends outright and we have inadequate evidence for their times of formation. We may rightly regard blending as a continuous possibility in the making of words, likely to occur at any time and in any language. *Amerindian* for 'American Indian' appears later in this book, and *Eurasian* 'belonging to Europe and Asia as one whole' expresses a useful and potent geographical concept. Two jocular attributes, *slithy* and *mimsy*, were concocted by Lewis Carroll in Chapter 6 of *Through the Looking-Glass*: 'Well, *slithy* means "lithe and slimy" ... You see it's like a portmanteau – there are two meanings packed up into one word ... *Mimsy* is "flimsy and miserable" (there's another portmanteau for you).' The verbs *chortle* (from *ch*uckle and sn*ort*) and *galumph* (from *gal*lop and tri*umph*) have also found places in the English lexicon. *Smog* '*f*og intensified by *smo*ke' (1905) hit the headlines at the time of the memorable pea-souper of just half a century later (1955), but *smaze* 'mixture of *sm*oke and h*aze* (1953) is hardly likely to prove itself necessary. *Spam* is *sp*iced h*am*. An *escalator*, or *esca*lade eleva*tor* (Spanish *escalada* 'act of scaling with ladders'), began as a trade name before becoming (1904) a generic term. Is the day coming when southern England will consist of one vast *sub*urban u*topia* or *subtopia*? A *telecast* is a *tele*vised broad*cast*. Do you wish to in*sure* your *tele*vision set against damage or failure? Then, if you are prudent, you take out a *tele*vision in*surance* or *telesurance* policy, or (using back-formation and blend together in one word) you *telesure* it. Finding the general public well conditioned to these verbal novelties, another advertiser comes forward with *lubritection*, the synthetic oil that both *lubri*cates and offers pro*tection* at the same time.

Two other processes, aphesis and apocope, play an important part in the making of words. *Aphesis* implies the 'sending away' or suppression of an initial unstressed syllable, as when Latin *illa ecclesia* 'that church' becomes Italian *la chiesa*, but Spanish *la iglesia* and French *l'église*. The *fence* round your garden serves as a *defence* against the outside world, while the *fender* round your open fire serves as a *defender* against errant sparks. Your *drawing*-room is the *withdrawing* room, to which the ladies retire after dinner. So *sample* comes from *example*, *size* from *assize*, and *squire* from *esquire*. Losing two initial syllables, *periwig* (from French *perruque*) gives *wig*, *caravan* becomes *van*, and *omnibus* (from the Latin dative 'for all', formerly used in Parisian *voiture omnibus*, which was just schoolboy slang for *voiture pour tous*) is reduced to plain *bus*. So also the verb *mend* is the aphetic form of *amend*, *peal* of *appeal*, *ply* of *apply*, and *spy* of *espy*. The adjective *cute* comes from *acute*, *live* from *alive*, *lone* from *alone*, and *pert* from *apert*. In words like *sport* and *stain*, from *disport* and *distain* respectively, aphesis obscures etymology. In Tudor England to *dis-port* oneself meant 'to *carry* oneself *away* or *apart* from one's ordinary employment' and to *dis-tain* meant 'to tinge apart from the natural colour', and so 'to discolour or defile'.

Apocope implies the 'cutting off' or suppression of the final unstressed syllable or syllables of a word, as when Old English (*ic*) *helpe* becomes (*I*) *help*, or *grēne hnutu* becomes *green nut*. Indeed, the steady drift from synthesis to analysis in the long history of our language has resulted from a continuous sequence of such changes. Prehistoric '*bheronom* 'to bear', or, more precisely, 'act of bearing', became Germanic '*beranan* (showing change of *bh* to *b* by Grimm's Law, regular lowering of *o* to *a* during this period, and shift of point of plosion from lips to teeth-ridge in the articulation of the final nasal) and this in its turn gave Old English *beran*, whence Chaucerian *bere*(*n*) and modern *bear*. To such general morphological reduction most inflected forms were liable, but there were other occasions when final weak-stressed syllables were shed more drastically. For instance, *chapman* 'merchant, barterer, customer' was reduced to *chap* in colloquial speech because the second component *-man* bore weak stress. Today *chap* stands with English *fellow* and American *guy* as a term of friendly intimacy. No such apocope, however, has occurred in German and Dutch, where *Kaufmann* and *koopman* are quite serious expressions for 'business man'. Although *chap* was in common use in Dr Johnson's time, he refused to admit it to his Dictionary (1755), but the first reviser, Archdeacon Henry John Todd, inserted it in the 1818 edition with a warning that 'it usually designates a person of whom a contemptuous opinion is entertained'. Since then *chap* has certainly risen in status. It is no more disparaging than other apocopated forms like *hack* from *hackney* (Old French *haquenée* 'ambling horse'), *van* from *vanguard*, *pram* from *perambulator*, and *whip* from *whipper-in*. Many others, such as *ad* for *advertisement*, *cyke* for *cyclorama*, *deb* for *débutante*, *mike* for *microphone*, and *op* for surgical *operation*, remain on the level of slang and may perhaps sink into desuetude with passing fashion. Others again, though long used, like *caf*, *cert*, *digs*, *dip*, *gym*, *lab*, and *vac*, are usually confined to school and university circles.

The making of words proceeds intermittently and unpredictably at various levels, national and international, literary and scientific, dramatic and poetic, serious and comic, rhetorical and colloquial. The mind of a scientist 'voyaging through strange seas of thought alone' may create the word of the moment: Dr Norbert Wiener in-invented *cybernetics*. A learned committee may decide once and for all that fractions of metric units shall be indicated by Latin stems (*decimetre*, *centimetre*, *millimetre*) but multiples by Greek ones (*decametre*, *hectometre*, *kilometre*). Imaginative speakers entertain their hearers by inventing novel and attractive turns of phrase, which, speedily taken up by the young, may ultimately win permanent acceptance by the community.

CHAPTER 6

THE SHAPING OF SENTENCES

THE sentence is the chief unit of speech. It may be defined quite simply as a *minimum complete utterance* and it may be described as that part of a chain of discourse which occurs between two pauses and which inevitably shows some kind of arrangement, construction, or *syntax*. Whereas morphology (Chapter 5) deals with morphemes that are either free or bound, syntax is concerned with free forms only. The *ultimate constituents*, or smallest units into which speech can be analysed, are morphemes on the morphological level and words on the syntactic plane. It follows that the distinction between these two levels is not always sharp. Since a word is a *minimum free form*, it is obvious that a sentence may consist of one word only: *Fire! Time! Sunshine!* These words form complete sentences if they are spoken between two *pauses* and they form complete utterances if they fall between two *silences*, but they express no formal predication like their fuller counterparts *There's a fire! Time's up! The sun is shining!* In that last sentence the more thing-like constituent (*the sun*) is called the *subject* and the other part (*is shining*) the *predicate*. These two parts may be regarded as the *immediate constituents* of this simple *actor-action* type of sentence. If we extend it and say *The bright sun has been shining all day long in a cloudless sky*, we see that *the bright sun* forms the subject and all the rest of the sentence comprises the predicate. We must constantly bear in mind that in the shaping of sentences we are concerned with relative values and functions and that this notion of relativity applies essentially to the immediate constituent which may be defined as one of the two or three components of which any given construction is directly formed. In the simple sentence just quoted, *the bright sun* and *has been shining all day long in a cloudless sky* are the immediate constituents, the first of which can be profitably analysed only into its ultimate constituents or words, but the second of which can be readily broken down into *has been shining* (compound tense-form of the verb) and *all day long in a cloudless sky* (adverb adjunct). The first of these can now be analysed only into its ultimate constituents, but the second can obviously be divided into *all day long* (adverb phrase of time) and *in a cloudless sky* (adverb phrase of place) and these may therefore be taken as the immediate constituents of the whole adverb phrase.

If we are in doubt about the validity of any expression to be regarded as an integral constituent of a larger construction, we have only to apply the operation known as *substitution*. Indeed, in all linear analysis we rely mainly upon two operations: *segmentation* and *substitution*. Why, for instance, do we assert that the immediate constituents of *all day long in a cloudless sky* are *all day long* and *in a cloudless sky* and not, say, *all day* and *long in a cloudless sky*, or perhaps *all day long in* and *a cloudless sky*? You might well retort that the words *all day long* and *in a cloudless sky* obviously hang together, and that no test is required to prove it; or you might proceed to *parse* the words one by one – a form of segmentation – and show convincingly that they hold together in this way. Nevertheless, especially in more complicated sentences, the scientific proof which substitution offers may be of service. Quite simply, then, we submit that these are the immediate constituents because we can substitute a single adverb for the first, such as *continuously, uninterruptedly*, or *steadily*, or another phrase like *throughout the day, from sunrise to sunset, from dawn to dusk*, or *from rosy morn to dewy eve*; and for the second we can also substitute a single adverb, such as *serenely, calmly*, or *majestically*, or another phrase like *without a trace of cloud, above our heads*, and so on.

The investigation of syntactic relationships by determining successive layers of immediate constituents has the inestimable advantage that it may be applied to any language in the world, even to those (Chapter 8) which do not belong to the Indo-European family. It should not necessarily lead us to abandon altogether the time-honoured *parts of speech* (*word-classes* or *grammatical categories*) which we have inherited from the Alexandrian grammarians of classical antiquity. Let us admit that the Greeks cared only for Greek (and what a wonderful language theirs was!), that the Romans were content to take over the whole Greek system and apply it to Latin, and that the first English grammarians, beginning with Ælfric, regarded grammar as primarily Latin grammar whose rules and categories might be applied to modern tongues. These early grammarians did no great harm because English was and is a related Indo-European language, but confusion arose when they took the categories of Latin grammar to represent universal features of human expression applicable to all language anywhere or at any time. The eight parts of speech are little more than convenient labels. Parsing is just one form of segmentation. If you say *O, and how the sun shines above us*! you surely use each of these conventional word-classes once. You may well call them interjection, conjunction, adverb, adjective, noun, verb, preposition, and pronoun, and, in so doing, you doubtless give some useful information about their syntactic functions. But this kind of information is limited and inadequate: to many languages it has no conceivable relevance. In Tagalog, for example, the official language of the Philippine Islands, subject and predicate are not distinguished: noun and verb overlap in their functions. In English, too, I may say quite naturally 'A lovely tree, that!' using a pattern without formal predication. Verbless expressions like *The more the merrier* and *More haste, less speed* can be paralleled in many tongues. Instead of saying outright that 'No two individuals think the same', you may prefer to cite the Latin aphorism *Quot homines, tot sententiae* 'As many men, so many opinions'. As a possible alternative to Shakespeare's 'All's well that ends well', you may take it into your head to quote German *Ende gut, alles gut* 'End good, all good'. These are genuine binary types reflecting man's innate love of alternating rhythm and his constant awareness of the two sides, left and right, of his own body, which finds satisfactory expression in the balanced sentence.

We need not assume that the verb 'to be' has at some time been omitted and must therefore be understood. Such a statement as Latin *omnia praeclāra rāra* 'all distinguished things (are) rare' is a nominal sentence in its own right. There is no need to supply any substantive verb or copula.

Order of words is so important as a syntactic process in present-day Indo-European languages that some linguists give us the impression that they regard word order and syntax as interchangeable terms, but, as we have already noted, syntax is primarily concerned not only with order itself – as if words were like beads on a string – but also with the relationships involved in that order, especially those obtaining between immediate constituents and the larger constructions of which they form parts. Moreover, syntax is concerned with those other important processes known as *government* and *concord*.

In determining word order, the position of the verb may first be observed. It normally follows the subject in English as in the simple actor-action construction *The sun shines*, and it precedes the object in the actor-action-goal construction *The sun warms the earth*. This order is inverted in yes-no questions. *Warms the sun the earth?* would be the normal interrogative sequence in languages with inflected substantives. By using the auxiliary *do* (or some other anomalous finite – *be, have, shall, will, can, may, must, ought, need, dare,* or *used*) we now contrive to make inversion less prominent and, by a characteristic compromise, we establish the pattern: anomalous finite – subject – infinitive or participle – object: *Does the sun warm the earth? Has the sun warmed the earth?* Inversion may also occur after an initial negation or its equivalent: *Seldom does the sun warm the earth thoroughly on these northern slopes*. It may also be used in conditional clauses: *Had I time, I would go*. In French word order may seem to be unduly capricious. The position of the personal pronoun is fixed by convention in relation to the negative *ne* and the adverb-pronouns *y* and *en*. You are bound to say *Je le lui ai donné* 'I have given it to him', but *Je lui en ai donné* 'I have given him some', and *Il n'y en a pas* 'There isn't (aren't) any'. When speaking German you must bear in mind at least three main principles. In the first place, you must remember that in simple sentences and main clauses you can put one and only one expression, whether word or phrase or clause, before a finite verb, which therefore takes second place. You can say the equivalent of 'I feel glad' or 'Glad feel I': 'I go gladly' or 'Gladly go I'. Secondly, you must not forget to relegate the past participle, infinitive, or separable prefix, to the end of the sentence: 'The boy has not the book read' (past participle at the end); 'I can him not understand' (infinitive of verb with inseparable prefix at the end); and 'Usually rise I at half-seven up' (separable prefix at the end). Thirdly, you must not fail to place the finite verb last in subordinate clauses: 'If you the truth know, tell us'; 'I have no notion what it mean shall'; 'I mind not what he said', and so forth. Few languages observe more rigid principles of order than these. Theoretically, of course, word order should be more flexible in inflected tongues. Only substantives, pronouns, verbs, and the demonstrative adjectives *this*: *these* and *that*: *those* are inflected in present-day English. All simple sentences belong to one of three types: A. *The sun warms the earth*; B. *The sun is a star*; and C. *The sun is bright*. Word order is normally changeless in A and B, but not in C. Even in sober prose a man may say *Bright is the sun*.

Type A shows the simple actor-action-goal arrangement consisting of subject + finite verb active transitive + object. Its passive counterpart *The earth is warmed by the sun* shows *patient-action-agent* construction. The subject now figures as the agent and is *governed* (page 86) by the preposition *by*. In many languages this agent function is denoted not by a relation-axis construction but by a distinctive case-ending (ablative or instrumental) of the substantive.

Type B consists of subject + copula + complement. It shows equational predication substantive. Two nominative entities are joined formally by the verb 'to be', sometimes called the substantive verb, which no longer signifies 'exists', but performs the reduced function of a copula or link. The creation and development of this copula are relatively late and it still finds no place in a language like Russian: *Solnce zvezda* '(The) sun (is a) star'.

Type C consists of subject + copula + predicative adjective. The sun has the quality of luminosity and this quality is expressed by the predicative adjective which has a special form in many languages to distinguish it from the epithet adjective or attribute: Russian *Solnce jarko* 'The sun (is) bright', but *jarkoje solnce* 'bright sun'; German *Die Sonne ist hell* 'The sun is bright', but *die helle Sonne* 'bright sun'. In a completely uninflected language like Chinese these functions are differentiated by position alone: *yang² ming²* 'The sun (is) bright', but *ming² yang²* 'bright sun'.

The sun warms the earth, *The sun is a star*, and *The sun is bright* are all simple sentences of single predication. There are two other forms of sentence: *multiple*, consisting of two or more *coordinate* clauses, *The sun warms the earth and brings out the flowers*; and *complex*, consisting of one principal clause and one or more *subordinate* clauses, *The sun brings out the flowers we love*. Multiple sentences show *parataxis*: complex sentences show *hypotaxis*. The latter is generally the later development. Compare *Who knows? He can tell us* (parataxis) with *He who knows can tell us* (hypotaxis). Obviously parataxis is simpler and freer than hypotaxis and it is therefore used more abundantly in daily conversation and small talk than in literary exposition. Even in parataxis, however, clause may be made subordinate in sense to clause and phrase to phrase, but this subordination is effected by means of participles and complementary infinitives rather than through finite verbs.

When a speaker interpolates into a sentence an expression which is in no way essential for grammatical completeness, he is said to use a *parenthesis*, and its place in the flow of discourse will be shown by various marks of punctuation before and after, whether commas or dashes or round brackets (themselves technically known as *parentheses*). Such English expressions within parentheses as *it goes without saying*, *as you know very well*, and *if you come to think of it*, fulfil a useful purpose inasmuch as they give speaker and hearer a welcome break in a long and involved sentence, or they may tone down the austerity of a harsh statement, at the same time making the conversation more intimate and friendly. The infinitive may be used in such *absolute* constructions as *to be sure, so to speak, to tell you the truth, to change the subject, to cut a long story short,* and the like.

The position of the adjective in English is fairly free, but it usually comes before the substantive it qualifies: *good men, bright sun.* In the Romance and Celtic languages the reverse order prevails, as seen in place-names like Spanish *Rio Grande* (Mexico and Brazil) 'river great', *Sierra Nevada* (California) 'range snowy'; or Scots Gaelic *Ben Nevis* 'peak terrible', *Kirkcudbright* 'Church Cuthbert, i.e. St Cuthbert's Church'. This order is used in many English phrases showing French influence like *court martial, body politic, the Lords Temporal, the Princess Royal, the life immortal* (Cranmer), and *the vision splendid* (Wordsworth). Two adjectives may follow the noun, as in *men good and true, sundown serene and splendid* (Henley); or, for the sake of variety, one may precede and one follow, as in *good men and true, brave hearts and clean* (Henley). Rarely in English is the meaning changed by position, as in *linguistics proper* 'the study of language strictly so called' as against *proper behaviour* 'correct deportment'. This is, however, a fairly important feature of French: *de ses propres mains* 'with his own hands', but *venir les mains propres* 'to come with clean hands'.

Most languages show flexibility in the placing of the adverb: *Brightly the sun shines* (front-position); *The sun brightly shines* (mid-position); *The sun shines brightly* (end-position). Subject and verb may be inverted after an adverb in front-position: *Brightly shines the sun, sweetly sing the birds, gently flows the stream.* More frequently it is the anomalous finite verb that is inverted: *Brightly does the sun shine; Well do we realize this; Seldom have I heard lovelier music.* Otherwise adverbs of frequency usually precede the verb: *I often get up early; People rarely ask questions; Our friends never visit us on Sundays.* An adverb may modify one word or phrase, but it may apply to the whole sentence together. This difference is shown not only by the syntactic process of word order but also by the prosodic features of intonation and juncture: *Our guests make themselves generally useful* (They help in a general way with any domestic task that has to be done: the adverb *generally* directly modifies the adjective *useful*). *Our guests generally make themselves useful* (As a rule, on most occasions they help: the adverb *generally* modifies the statement as a whole).

The syntactic process of *government, rection,* or *regimen* is closely associated with that of word order. In the statement *The sun warms the earth* the verb *warms* is said to be *transitive* because the action 'passes over or across' (Latin *transit*) from the subject to the direct object. In the Old English period when subject and object still preserved the case-inflexions of nominative and accusative, word order might be varied without the slightest risk of ambiguity. It so happened that the earlier forms of *sun* and *earth* both belonged to a morphological category known as weak feminine *n*-stems, which had nominative in -*e* and accusative in -*an*. A man would normally say *Sunne wiermð eorðan*, observing the usual order for affirmations as in later English; or perhaps *Sunne eorðan wiermð*, putting the verb last. However he might otherwise arrange the words – *Eorðan wiermð sunne, Eorðan sunne wiermð, Wiermð sunne eorðan,* or *Wiermð eorðan sunne* – he would all the time be saying the same thing, though, by changes in word order and by variations in intonation, he might achieve different degrees of emphasis. Even before the end of the Old English period, however, inflexions became so weakened in the northern dialect that these serial changes by every conceivable permutation and combination were no longer possible; and this weakening subsequently extended to midland and southern speech in early Middle English. Thus, as so often in the growth and development of a language, one change in the system affects the entire structure. Each language at any period of its history is all of a piece, a coherent and homogeneous system in which changes are not isolable but always interdependent.

It is a notable feature of Modern English that not only the direct but also the indirect object may be promoted to the subject when an affirmation is expressed in the passive voice. Suppose, instead of *The sun warms the earth*, we say, in order to get three substantival entities, *The sun gives the earth warmth*. This sentence may then be made passive in construction as either A. *Warmth is given (to) the earth by the sun*, or B. *The earth is given warmth by the sun*. Sentences of Type A are common to most Indo-European languages, but those of Type B are limited to English and to certain dialects of German and Scandinavian. Occasionally, too, Type B was employed in ancient Greek and was even introduced as a literary embellishment into Latin poetry. It may certainly be regarded as an exceptional example of flexible syntax. Here are three entities – *the sun*, *the earth*, and *warmth* – and any one of them may be made the grammatical subject. In fact, any one of these three *referends* (See Chapter 13) may be uppermost in the speaker's mind when he makes the statement. Any one of the three may therefore constitute the *psychological subject*. It might reasonably be claimed that it is an advantage to the speaker if he is enabled by the structure of the language he is using to make psychological and grammatical subjects one and the same. Nevertheless, such extensive flexibility probably weakens the feeling for government in the minds of English speakers, who show this all too flagrantly in their defective manipulation of prepositional or *relation-axis* constructions. In earlier periods of our language certain prepositions governed, or were constructed with, the accusative case as in the phrase *geond worulde* 'throughout the world' or *ofer land* 'across country'. Others took the genitive as in *andlang weges* 'along the road', or the dative as in *mid mīnum suna* 'with my son'. In Old English this relation-axis construction was robust and steady, but in current speech it is less secure. No one would dream of saying *between I and you*, but many do say *between you and I* following Antonio's bad example long ago in his letter to Bassanio in Shakespeare's *Merchant of Venice* (III.ii.318). In other words, the feeling that this preposition governs the objective form in the pronoun has become so feeble that it cannot stand the slight shock of separation imparted by *you and* intervening. In substantives these subject-object case-forms have gone for ever and even in pronouns we are confronted with only five such oppositions – *I*: *me, he*: *him, she*: *her, we*: *us,* and *they*: *them.* Moreover, many people who are over-anxious to speak well, have vague recollections of hearing *you and me* corrected as a nominative phrase.

The third syntactic process or device common to all Indo-European tongues is known as *concord, agreement,* or *congruence,* by which harmonious relationships are observed between the flexions of substantives and adjectives in respect of number, gender, and case (*nominal concord*), and between those of verbs and substantives in respect of number and person (*verbal concord*). Nominal concord has extremely limited functions in present-day English since the definite determiners (*this*: *these* and *that*: *those*) are the sole surviving adjectival forms that show concord with the number-class of the substantive. We say *the white house* singular and *the white houses* plural with no flexional change in the adjective, but our ancestors distinguished between *þæt hwīte hūs* singular and *þā hwītan hūs* plural. Both article and adjective show modification in French and German – *la maison blanche*: *les maisons blanches* (only the article, of course, changing in speech); *das weisse Haus*: *die weissen Häuser* (all three forms changing in both speech and writing). In English we say *It's a good evening* and *Good evening* (*I wish you*) without flexional change, but in the so much more conservative German language we must not forget to change the adjectival ending: *Es ist ein guter Abend* but *Guten Abend* (*wünsche ich Ihnen*). Verbal concord is restricted to number and person. Singular goes with singular, dual with dual, and plural with plural. Dual forms are used in many languages to denote living creatures that go in pairs, or parts of the human body like eyes, ears, arms, elbows, hands, legs, knees, and feet. The pronominal dual forms *wit* 'we two' and *git* 'you two' appear in English poetry as late as the thirteenth century. Of the three persons the first refers to the speaker, the second to the hearer or person addressed, and the third to the person or thing spoken about. English now retains verbal flexion only in the third person singular of the present tense, as in *give: gives*. The auxiliaries *shall, will, can, may, must, ought, need,* and *dare* show no change; and either *give* or *gives* serves all persons alike in some dialects. In Danish this is true of the standard language, since *giver* is common to all persons. Thus the number of present-tense forms is one in Danish compared with two in English, three in Dutch, four in German, five in French, and six in Spanish, Italian, and Russian. The number in French, to be sure, is less than five in pronunciation where it will vary somewhat from verb to verb.

In unfolding the structure of involved sentences many languages use various kinds of correlative words which act as sign-posts or markers and help the hearer or reader to anticipate what is to follow. The Greek particles performed this function both delicately and efficiently. The *men* and *de* of contrasted clauses – 'The spirit (*men*) willing: the flesh (*de*) weak' (Matt. xxvi:41) – must needs be translated clumsily into English by *indeed* and *but*; or, worse still, by *on the one hand* and *on the other* (German *einerseits* and *anderseits*); or perhaps omitted altogether. Languages vary considerably in the extent of their correlatives and in the uses they make of them. English has a limited number: *both ... and ..., as well ... as ..., not only ... but also ..., either ... or ..., neither ... nor ..., (even)as ... so ..., so ... as ...,* and others. Orderly syntax requires parallelism or, to borrow an expression from mathematics, 'like terms' in the phrases and clauses that go with correlatives. 'To reach the end of the pier *you can either walk or ride* (or *either you can walk or you can ride,* but not *either you can walk or ride*)'. Nevertheless, as in the position of adverbs, rhythm and intonation may override logical sequence. Here we pass from the domain of *syntax* proper, where we have either limited choice or no choice at all, into the realm of *style*, where we enjoy a greater degree of freedom in making our personal selection.

Sometimes, more frequently perhaps than they themselves

think, speakers may mix up or confuse two constructions by a process called *contamination*, since the term *blend* is reserved for morphology (Chapter 5) and *contagion* for semantics (Chapter 11). If such syntactic contamination becomes very common and is subsequently accepted by a whole community, it then develops into an *idiom* (French *idiotisme*, German *Spracheigentümlichkeit*), an expression – phrase, clause, or sentence – peculiar to a particular language. Thus 'I am friendly with him' and 'We are friends' have become contaminated and a man may now say idiomatically 'I am friends with him'; or, mixing up 'Things of this sort' with 'These sorts of things', he may find myself saying 'These sort of things'. The French have associated the personal expression *Je me rappelle* 'I recall to myself' with the impersonal *Il me souvient* 'It occurs to me' and so they say *Je me souviens* regularly for 'I remember' and so also *Nous nous en souvenons bien* 'Well do we remember it' and *Autant que je puis m'en souvenir* 'To the best of my recollection'.

Inasmuch as the sentence is the chief unit of speech, the effective speaker is bound to think in whole sentences as he speaks. He carries with him in his mind a certain number of sentence structures, few or many according to his upbringing and training, and into these structures he fits words and phrases to express his immediate thoughts and intentions. In shaping his sentences he trains himself to think ahead of articulation, not too much and not too little, but just that right distance ahead to suit his individual capacity.

CHAPTER 7

THE INDO-EUROPEAN FAMILY

It is indeed a notable fact that about one half of the 3,350 millions of people in the world today speak an Indo-European tongue and that the area covered by this great family of languages is ever increasing. It now includes nearly all Europe and America, a great part of Asia, Australasia, and Oceania, as well as a considerable portion of Africa. Only one other family is increasing, namely Sino-Tibetan. All the remaining families seem to be either stationary or decreasing.

When we speak of a *family* of languages we are obviously using this word in a metaphorical sense. We imply that these forms of speech are demonstrably related and that they come from one earlier form which was common to them all. They may be shown to be similar inasmuch as they share certain common characteristics in phonology, morphology, syntax, and lexicon. Similarity in morphology, especially in flexion and affixation, here counts most of all. Correspondences in sentence structure or syntax come next. Sounds, however, count for less because they may be gradually modified under external influences. Individual words bear uncertain testimony in themselves because they may be adopted or adapted from external sources over long periods of time. The least reliable test is that of meaning, which may shift capriciously and unpredictably.

The nineteenth-century 'comparatists' or comparative philologists – men like Bopp, Grimm, Pott, Schleicher, Brugmann, Osthoff, Paul, and Delbrück – placed the structure of Proto-Indo-European, the language spoken by our ancestors five thousand years ago, upon firm foundations. They laboured assiduously to reconstruct this ancient hypothetical form of speech used by pastoral nomads who lived in South Russia towards the end of the later Stone

Age. They showed, for example, that neither German *Pferd* nor English *horse* had any connexion at all with the original name of the noblest of animals. The former came, like English *palfrey*, from medieval Latin *para-veredus*, a derivative hybrid from Greek *para* 'beside, extra' and Celtic *veraeda* 'light horse'; whereas the latter was related to Classical Latin *currere* 'to run' from older *cursere*, and therefore formerly denoted 'runner, leaper, courser'. They then showed that the original Indo-European form was *ekwos* which became *ikkos* in Greek dialects, but *hippos* in Classical Greek (as in English *hippo-potamus* 'river horse' and *Phil-ip* 'lover of horses'), and which became *equus* in Latin (as in English *equine* 'of, or like, a horse' and *equestrian* 'pertaining to a horseman'). In Old English *ekwos* became first *ehu* and then *eoh*, a form never used in prose and only rarely in poetry, although it actually stood for the letter *e* (written M) in the runic alphabet. The author of *Beowulf* never once used *eoh* although he frequently had occasion to speak of horses, but the poet who wrote *The Battle of Maldon* to commemorate that disastrous encounter between Englishmen and Vikings on the Essex coast in the year 991, did use *eoh* in a well-known dramatic context. Soon after that, however, this ancient word seems to have disappeared altogether from our language. Likewise in Greek itself *hippos* was superseded by other words. In present-day Greek the old word for animal *alogos* 'lacking speech or reason', from privative alpha + *logos* 'word', has been narrowed down to mean 'horse'. So, too, in the neo-Latin languages *equus* has been everywhere ousted by an imported root seen in our word *cavalry*: French *cheval*, Spanish *caballo*, and Italian *cavallo*. Looking further afield among living Indo-European languages, we find Dutch *paard*, Danish *hest*, Czech *kůň*, and Russian *lošad*.

Such simple facts as these illustrate our difficulties in determining family relationships among languages. Because these simple names for the horse are so different in, say, English and Russian, we might naturally suppose that English and Russian are quite unrelated, and, to be sure, we should find plenty of other evidence to support such a seemingly logical supposition. For example, the pattern of Russian verbal inflexions seems strange and complicated to us and the Russian equivalent of simple conversational expressions like 'He isn't here' or 'I don't feel well' have entirely different syntactic structures. Nevertheless, because we have adequate records of early forms, we can prove that English and Russian do belong to one family. We can prove that English *wheel* and Russian *koleso* are cognate since they both go back to Indo-European *kwelos*, with its gradational variant *kwolos* and its reduplicated by-form *kwekwlos*. Indeed, these are both cognate with English *cycle* from Greek *kuklos*. Similarly we can demonstrate irrefragably that *beef* and *cow* are ultimately akin since they both go back to Indo-European *gwous*, the one through Latin *bōs, bovis*, and the other through Old English *cū*. Suppose, on the other hand, that no records had survived to furnish us with links in these long chains of evidence. We should be completely baffled. No expert knowledge and no ingenuity would be of the least avail. We know that related languages are recognized as related for only a limited period after their separation. Even when the same word is preserved in two kindred tongues, it may be so changed in the course of a few thousand years that, without records to guide us, we can discern no essential likeness whatever between the two resultant forms. That is why we are so much less dogmatic today than scholars were a century ago about the precise ordering of language families over the face of the globe. As a working hypothesis we may fairly assume that some twenty families, of which Indo-European is one, may be differentiated in the Old World.

The most ancient of all languages was Sumerian, a non-Indo-European language spoken in Mesopotamia or Iraq at least six thousand years ago. The Sumerians used cuneiform or wedge-shaped writing and, although their language was no longer spoken after 1939 B.C. in the third dynasty of Ur, ancient texts were copied for religious and educational purposes until the Christian era. Sumerian is thus the oldest *recorded* language on earth, more ancient in this respect than

Chinese, Akkadian (Assyrian and Babylonian), Egyptian, Hebrew, or Hittite.

The latter was the most ancient of all Indo-European languages, spoken in Anatolia or Asia Minor until the thirteenth century before Christ when it seems to have become extinct. Two varieties of recorded Hittite may now be distinguished, the first being cuneiform like Sumerian and the second pictographic or hieroglyphic like ancient Egyptian. Extensive collections of cuneiform tablets were unearthed in 1905 at Boghazköy on the site of the prehistoric capital Hattusas about eighty miles east of Ankara, and in 1917 the Prague scholar Bedřich Hrozný proved their linguistic affinity with Indo-European. A revolution was also effected in early Greek studies by the discovery in 1939 of clay tablets at Pylos in Messenia and their subsequent decipherment as Mycenaean Greek by Michael Ventris in 1952. This meant putting back the beginnings of recorded Greek to a time long before Homer, perhaps to a date as early as 1500 B.C.

Two other extinct Indo-European languages, Agnean and Kuchean (sometimes called Tokharian A and B), were also re-discovered in Chinese Turkestan early in the present century. Among other well-attested defunct languages may be mentioned Phrygian in Asia Minor and Illyrian on the shores of the Adriatic (familiar to us from Shakespeare's *Twelfth Night*). Doubtless many new facts relating to the earlier histories of the Indo-European peoples will be revealed by archaeologists and epigraphists in the not distant future and fresh light will be thrown on the paths taken by migrating nations after their dispersion. More information will probably be gleaned about the structure and vocabulary of the parent language itself. It is already known that nearly all the descended languages have common words for natural phenomena like *night, star, dew, snow, wind, thunder,* and *fire*; for animals like *hound, goat, ewe, ox, steer,* and *sow*; for parts of a house like *door, timber,* and *thatch*; for parts of the human body like *ear, eye, tooth, heart, nail, knee,* and *foot*; and, most significant of all, for primary family relationships like *father*, *mother*, *brother*, and *sister*. Sometimes, of course, we require special knowledge to trace these affinities. Take, for instance, the first common form just mentioned, English *night*. It corresponds to German and Dutch *nacht*. Obviously these are closely related, but which is nearer the oldest known form? We can answer this simple question correctly only if we happen to know that this particular noun belonged in Old English to the group of monosyllabic consonant stems and that it was therefore subject, like *tooth* and *foot* in the above list, to a sound change called front mutation. Thus German *Nacht* (familiar to us from the Christmas hymn *Stille Nacht, heilige Nacht*) is in fact nearer Common Germanic *nahti-* deriving regularly from Indo-European *nokti-* exactly as in Latin *noctis* 'of night', genitive of *nox*, whence the Latin adjective *nocturnus* and English *nocturnal*. From *night*-ly to *noct*-urnal we pass back through three or four thousand years of linguistic history. As we shall see later (in Chapter 9), it is the joy of recognition – the joy of recognizing something old and well known in what seems at first to be new and unknown – that endows these comparative studies with such intellectual pleasure and satisfaction.

Proto-Indo-European was a highly inflected language. Substantives and verbs were richly varied in their paradigms. The former had no fewer than eight case-forms in daily use – nominative, vocative, accusative, genitive, dative, locative, ablative, and instrumental. Verbs employed numerous and extensive suffixes. Both substantives and verbs had distinctive forms for dual number. The forms of the pronouns already showed different roots like *I*, *me* and *we*, *us* in English. There were no separate inflexions for the passive, but only for the middle voice, which expressed the notion that the speaker was specially interested in the action denoted by the verb. Forms for the passive voice therefore developed later in various ways in derivative languages. As for word order, it was free as in Greek and Latin. Subject, verb, object, or adjunct might stand first, since superabundant inflexions showed syntactic relationships clearly. Generally, however, attribute preceded substantive as in *good man*. Counting was based on ten and not on twelve as in ancient Babylon: nevertheless traces of the duodecimal system remained, as indeed they still do in our *dozen* and *gross* and in our *eleven* and *twelve*, 'one' and 'two left', that is, 'left over after counting ten on the fingers of both hands'. Whereas the numerals one to four were felt to function as adjectives, those above four were taken as nouns. There was a word for 'hundred', *kmtóm*, an aphetic abbreviation of *dekmtóm* 'decade of tens', or, quite simply, 'ten tens'; but there was no one form for 'thousand', which was accordingly denoted in various ways in the derived languages. Incidentally, this form *kmtóm* showed divergent developments in its initial plosive, becoming a sibilant in the four eastern branches (Indo-Iranian, Armenian, Balto-Slavonic, and Albanian), but remaining a plosive in the four western ones (Greek, Italic, Celtic, and Germanic). The former are sometimes described as the *satem*-group (from Avestan *satem*), and the latter as the *centum*-group (from Latin *centum* pronounced *kentum*).

It has not proved practicable to introduce maps into this little book, and it might therefore be advisable at this point to open our atlases at a map of Europe or at least to visualize such a map with our 'mind's eye'. Let us imagine, then, that round about the year 2000 B.C. our ancestors began to migrate in all directions from their homes in South Russia and that these waves of migration went on for the next three thousand years including in their final phases such well-known historical events as the Great Invasion of England by the Norsemen in A.D. 865 and the Norman Conquest by their kinsmen in 1066. We may picture the Hittites entering Anatolia or Asia Minor quite early in pre-history and the Vedic Indians passing between the Caspian and Aral Seas across the Persian uplands and through the mountain defiles of Afghanistan down into the Indus and Ganges valleys. The Illyrians may well have been the first to turn south-west and their form of speech may have provided the underlying basis or substratum for Italic and Celtic, the tongues of later invaders. The Greeks moved south-east into their peninsula in two main waves: first the Achaeans who passed into Thessaly and the coastal islands and who later made raids into the south-west corner of Anatolia, and then the Dorians who surged along the spine of the Balkan peninsula into Morea and Crete. Leaving the middle Danube, Italic migrants then advanced into Illyria and crossed the Adriatic into the future Italy. They had long had Celts as neighbours, whose speech was so close to theirs that we may rightly postulate an original Celto-Italic language. The Celts gave permanent names to many rivers throughout Western Europe. They moved in successive waves into France, Spain, and Portugal. Some crossed the narrow seas into Britain: others made their way into Italy and Greece, and even beyond Greece into Asia Minor. The Galatians, who were visited by St Paul on his first and third missionary journeys, were the 'Gauls of the East'. To them the Apostle addressed his famous Epistle in A.D. 50. Writing at the beginning of the fifth century, St Jerome rightly observed that the Galatians of Angora used essentially the same speech as the Gauls of Trier.

The Slavs and the Germans seem to have been the last to move. The Baltic Slavs – Letts (or Latvians) and Lithuanians – hardly moved at all. They still have their homes where they lived four thousand years ago. But the subsequent Russian expansion west to the Elbe and east across plain and steppe to the Amur proved in many ways the most imposing of all. No less impressive were the sweeping migrations of the Goths into Spain, Italy, and the Balkans, and the disastrous incursions of the Vandals into Northern Africa. The Germanic Franks poured into Gaul. Angles, Saxons, Jutes, and Frisians crossed into England, followed a few centuries later by the Norsemen of the Viking Age (A.D. 750–1050) who found new homes in England, Scotland, Ireland, the Western Isles, Iceland, and Greenland, and even explored America as far south as Massachusetts.

As we now turn from this rapid survey of the Indo-European peoples in the past to their positions and relative importance in the present, we naturally begin with India in the east where Sanskrit or Old Indian still survives as the sacred language of the Hindus in much the same way as Latin lives in the west, and indeed throughout the world, as the liturgical language of the Roman Church. Indian languages descending from Sanskrit are now spoken in a fairly compact region in northern India and Pakistan, bounded by Persian (a related Indo-European language) on the north-west, Tibetan on the north and north-east, Munda on the south-east, and Dravidian south of a line running obliquely from Goa to Puri. An Indo-European language called Sinhalese is spoken in southern and central Ceylon. Hindi and Urdu are now the official languages of India and Pakistan respectively. They may be described as dialectal varieties of Modern Indian or Hindustani, but unfortunately they are written in divergent scripts. Whereas Hindi is recorded in Devanagari or 'sacred refined' characters inherited from Sanskrit, Urdu is written in a Persian form of Arabic. At the same time it must be emphasized that these are not just two ways of representing one language, like Serbian and Croatian (page 101). If Urdu is transcribed into Devanagari, it remains recognizably Urdu. The two dialects still differ in structure and vocabulary, since they have been subjected to different influences over a long period of time. The other related languages employed in the sub-continent are Bengali in and around Calcutta, Bihari in the Ganges basin around Patna and Benares, Oriya in Orissa south-west of Calcutta, Marathi in the Bombay region, Rajasthani in an extensive area round Jodhpur, and Punjabi in the 'Land of the Five Rivers'. It has been computed that well over four hundred millions speak Indo-European languages in the sub-continent as against one hundred million who use Dravidian tongues – Tamil, Telugu, Kanarese, and Malayalam – in southern India. Nor should we forget that Romany, or *Romani chiv* 'gipsy tongue', is basically Indian, although it now contains numerous borrowed words. It is still a living lingo used by these 'spoilt children of nature' all over the world.

Persian is not only the language spoken throughout a large part of Iran but also an important secondary speech among Moslems in Pakistan and India. Avestan, the language of the Zoroastrian scriptures, is a form of Old Persian that has left no direct descendants, but related to Modern Persian are Kurdish, heard in the mountains of eastern Turkey, Iraq, and western Iran; Balochi, the main language of Baluchistan; and Pushtu, the chief means of communication in Afghanistan.

Although it is now spoken by less than four million souls in the southern Caucasus and eastern Turkey, Armenian stands alone as a separate branch of the Indo-European family. Throughout their long and troubled history the Armenians have preserved their individuality and have not allowed themselves to be absorbed by the imperial rulers of Media, Persia, Rome, Byzantium, Turkey in the past, or of Russia in the present. Today, it is true, Armenia forms a constituent republic of the Soviet Union, bounded by Georgia on the north, Soviet Azerbaijan on the east, Persian Azerbaijan on the south, and Turkey on the west, but her language remains active and vigorous. It possesses French loan-words dating from the Crusades, and it continues to incorporate Persian words in abundance as well as Russian terms in the fields of administration and technology.

It is a notable fact that Old Prussian, which became extinct in the sixteenth century, was a Slavonic and not a Germanic tongue. It belonged to the Baltic division of Slavonic and was therefore akin to present-day Lithuanian and Lettish. As we have already observed (page 64), Lithuanian is the most conservative of European languages in both phonology and morphology, and especially in the forms of its inflexions. Its vowel-system, like that of Classical Greek, is nearer to Indo-European than is that of Vedic Sanskrit itself. The Lithuanians are still pastoral and agricultural people, long secluded by dense forests from industrial changes. In their well-preserved language they illustrate the simple principle that linguistic stability rests upon continuity of culture and way of life, and upon isolation from external disturbances and foreign impacts. Today the Lithuanian Republic, with its population of only three millions, is subjected to high pressure from Russian and to a lesser extent from Polish and German. As for the sister Republic of Latvia, it is smaller still and it has long been influenced by its neighbour Estonia whose language, closely related to Finnish, is therefore non-Indo-European.

Turning from this interesting Baltic group to the nine Slavonic languages proper, we note at once that we may conveniently classify them geographically into three groups of three: Great Russian, Byelorussian, and Ukrainian in the centre, north, and east; Polish, Czech, and Slovak in the west; and Slovene, Serbo-Croatian, and Bulgarian in the south. Great or Muscovite Russian is now the established language of the Union of Soviet Socialist Republics (abbreviated CCCP, where C stands for our S and P for R, the official title being Soyuz Sovietskikh Socialisticheskikh Respublik), extending across the Eurasian plain to Vladivostok 'rule the east'. This vast expansion did not begin until the sixth century of our era. Indeed, the city of Moscow was founded later than Kiev and Minsk, the ancient capitals of the Ukraine and White Russia respectively. Until the twelfth century Moscow was a small village hidden away among forests and marshes. Two centuries later, however, it rose to become the cultural centre of the great central plain. Its linguistic pre-eminence was assured in the year 1755 when the University of Moscow was founded at the instigation of Mikhail Vasilyevich Lomonosov. Moscow is now the meeting-place of the Supreme Soviet or Praesidium to which delegates are sent from subsidiary soviets throughout the Union including those republics like Lithuania, Latvia, Georgia, and Armenia where second languages are duly recognized. Ukrainian is spoken by about forty million people and Byelorussian or White Russian by about seven. These are so closely akin to Muscovite and to each other that they might almost be regarded as dialects rather than languages. This applies to a certain extent to other juxtaposed Slavonic tongues. As you journey westward, say, from Moscow to Minsk in White Russia, and so on to Warsaw and Lodz in Poland, and then to Prague in Czechoslovakia, so the forms of words and the patterns of phrases and clauses change gradually by stages like the colours of the spectrum. Neighbouring languages are mutually intelligible to a large extent, but distant ones are unmistakably divergent in phonology and morphology no less than in syntax and lexicon. All the Slavonic languages, however, share some things in common. They are all rich in consonant sounds, sometimes using unusual initial clusters, and often showing pairs of consonants as binary oppositions of palatal and non-palatal, like the two varieties of initial dental plosives in English *due* [dju:] and *do* [du:]. Substantives have seven cases and three genders. Verbs have forms for both *tense* expressing *time* and *aspect* expressing *manner* of action. The actions or states denoted by verbs are viewed from the standpoint of *time* as past, present, and future, and from the standpoint of *manner* of action as completed or perfective, as progressive or imperfective, as instantaneous or momentary, as iterative or frequentative, and so on. On the whole the scheme of the verb is essentially aspectual. The speaker shows an attitude of mind in which the continuation or completion of an action is of greater importance to him than its reference to past, present, or future time. On the other hand, the Slavonic languages differ among themselves in the position of stress. Whereas Czech and Slovak words, probably influenced by neighbouring Hungarian, carry stress rigidly on the first syllable, or on the governing preposition in a phrase, Polish words normally bear stress on the penultimate or last syllable but one, whereas in Russian words the fall of stress is shifting and unpredictable. It may even move about within the declension of one and the same substantive. This is true of Serbo-Croatian also, but speakers of that language avoid placing the stress on the last syllable. Moreover, the Slavonic languages differ among themselves in their ways of writing and printing. Those peoples who received Christianity from the Orthodox Church – Russians, Byelorussians, Ukrainians, Serbs, and Bulgars – have adopted the Cyrillic script, whereas those who were converted by Roman evangelists – Czechs, Slovaks, Poles, Croats, and Slovenes – have naturally appropriated the Latin alphabet. Thus we may rightly describe Serbo-Croatian as one language with two scripts, as we are reminded in Belgrade every day by duplicated street signs, public notices, and even national newspapers. It is regrettable that further discrepancies arise within both Cyrillic and Roman groups of scripts because one sound is not always denoted by the same symbol: for example, the affricate [tʃ] (which occurs initially and finally in English *church*) is written *cz* in Polish, but č in Croatian and Czech, and [nj] the palatalized nasal (which appears medially in English *canyon*) is written ń in Polish, *nj* in Croatian, but ň in Czech, and so on. The oldest Slavonic literature is recorded in Bulgarian. Old Bulgarian or Church Slavonic dates from the ninth century. It still lives as a sacred liturgical language. Just as serious students of Germanic philology read Gothic, so Slavonic specialists read Old Bulgarian. Today Bulgarian is spoken not only by the six and a half million inhabitants of Bulgaria itself, but also by many communities in Greek Macedonia, Rumanian Dobruja, and southern Bessarabia.

Albanian is by far the smallest of the eight living branches of Indo-European since it is spoken by only one and a half million people. It certainly comprises a branch in itself for it has no close relationship with either Serbian or Greek. Some would associate it with extinct Illyrian, but in so doing they proceed from the little known to the unknown. As André Martinet once observed (in *Word II* 126), fashionable researchers into Proto-Indo-European favour either the Illyrians or the laryngeals, and we really know precious little about either! Albanian has two dialects: Gheg in the north and Tosk in the south. As the result of successful domination by Venetians and Turks, its vocabulary is mixed. Unfortunately we know little about its history because, apart from legal documents, no literature survives that is older than the seventeenth century.

In this respect Albanian presents a marked contrast to Greek or Hellenic which vies with Hittite and Sanskrit for first place as the most antique of all Indo-European tongues. Recent decipherment of Linear B Mycenean script (page 93) has antedated the beginnings of Greek by three centuries and more, carrying them back to a time long before the sack of Troy (1183 B.C.) described by Homer in his *Iliad*. We are particularly fortunate in possessing not only an abundant literature but also a large mass of inscriptions in many dialects extending over a long period and covering a wide area. Hellenistic Greek, or Koiné, became the general language of the Mediterranean countries after the death of Alexander the Great (323 B.C.). It was, to be sure, the first language of the Antonines who ruled the Roman Empire at the time of its greatest extent in the second century after Christ. Today, however, Modern Greek has only ten million speakers. Its forms have changed remarkably little in three millennia. It has two varieties, literary and colloquial or Demotiké, and a classical scholar can read either without difficulty. He needs some training to understand spoken Demotiké which shows wholesale monophthongizations of inherited diphthongs, a too generous relaxation of grammatical standards, and a considerable importation of foreign words from Italian and Turkish. There are no longer any differences in vowel-length, all vowels being of similar duration and clearly enunciated, whether stressed or unstressed. Apart from such modifications of pronunciation, it is indeed surprising how many common expressions have remained unchanged, substantives like *anthropos* 'man', *arithmos* 'number', *dromos* 'road, way', *khronos* 'time', *nomos* 'law', *ouranos* 'sky', *philos* 'friend', *polis* 'city', *potamos* 'river', *pragma* 'thing', *prosopon* 'face', *thalassa* 'sea', and *topos* 'place', as well as adjectives like *makros* 'long', *mikros* 'small', *monos* 'alone', *oligoi* 'few', *palaios* 'old', *protos* 'first', and scores of others. The numerals, too, are remarkably well preserved in spite of a few simple and reasonable shortenings like *trianta* 'thirty' for older *triakonta* and *saranta* 'forty' for *tessarakonta*. A classical scholar may read his Plato and feel quite at home in modern Athens, but at the same time he can hardly fail to reflect on that capricious turn in fortune's wheel whereby the Greek language has so shrunk from its former spaciousness to its present narrow confines in Greece itself and yet, by way of compensation, it has expanded immeasurably as the inexhaustible source of supply for the new scientific and technological vocabulary which is fast becoming international and worldwide.

The modern descendants of Latin, on the other hand, include no fewer than five great national languages – French, Spanish, Portuguese, Italian, and Rumanian – and five regional languages with important distinctive features – Provençal in southern France; Catalan in north-eastern Spain, so like the former that many would class the two together as one; Rumansch, or Rhaeto-Romanic, made one of the four recognized languages of Switzerland (page 34) as recently as 1938; Galician, or Gallego (its Spanish name), spoken in north-western Spain, but more closely related to Portuguese; Sardinian spoken on the island of Sardinia; and Dalmatian, recently heard on the eastern shores of the Adriatic, but dying with Antonio Udina in 1898. All these ethnic and regional languages have descended not so much from the literary language of Cicero and Virgil as from the speech of the Empire before its disintegration in the fifth century, called Vulgar Latin, the speech of the *vulgus* or 'common men' and of the legionaries in distant outposts of empire, many of whom were born, lived their lives, and died without ever once setting eyes on the Eternal City The records linking up Vulgar Latin (before 500) with the various derivative Romance languages are seldom continuous. Our first linguistic entity in French, for instance, is the text of the Strasbourg Oaths of 842, which may be regarded as marking the transition from Gallo-Roman (500–842) to Old French. On historical and documentary grounds we may similarly place the beginning of Italian at 964, Castilian at 1145, Catalan at 1171, Portuguese at 1192, and Rumanian much later, at some date, perhaps, in the sixteenth century. All in all, the Romance languages present a longer and larger collection of recorded evidence than any other branch of Indo-European, or indeed than any other group of languages anywhere in the world. Beyond Europe their expansion has even rivalled that of the Germanic branch. French has found a home in the province of Quebec, in parts of Louisiana, in French Guiana, and in Algeria; Spanish in Mexico, Cuba, Central and South America outside Brazil, and Rio de Oro in north-western Africa; Portuguese in Brazil, as well as in Angola and Mozambique in Africa; Italian in considerable areas in north-eastern Africa, including Tunisia, Libya, Egypt, Eritrea, Ethiopia, and Italian Somaliland. The area of most rapid growth in population is Latin America where the percentage of annual increase is now 2·5 as compared with 1·7 for the world as a whole.

Of the once extensive Celtic languages four still live: Breton and Welsh, which belong to the Brythonic or P-Celtic division; and Irish and Scots Gaelic, which are Goidelic or Q-Celtic. Breton is not a survival of Gaulish, as one might naturally suppose, but an overspill from Cornish, which became extinct as late as the nineteenth century. Cornish Celts migrated from south-western Britain to Armorica under pressure from the westward-driving Saxons in the fifth and sixth centuries of our era and founded the duchy of Little Britain or Brittany which from the end of the tenth century to the middle of the fifteenth was practically independent of the French kings. Modern Breton is spoken by about a million people living west of a line from Saint-Brieuc to Saint-Nazaire. Welsh is likewise spoken by about a million people, but its speech area is far less compact. Over half the Welsh-speaking population, it is true, lives in Glamorgan, which contains both Cardiff, the recently created capital of Wales, and Swansea. Elsewhere Welsh is still heard in Anglesey and the upland counties of Caernarvon and Merioneth, in the cosmopolitan city of Liverpool, and in the lowlands and coastal plains of

Cardigan and Carmarthen. Welsh literature vies with Irish in antiquity and knowledge of this rich inheritance is fostered and encouraged by annual poetic and musical 'sessions' or *eisteddfodau* which attract enthusiastic competitors from all parts of the principality and even from far beyond its borders. The literature of Ireland or Eire is also of high intrinsic merit and interest, going back to the ogam inscriptions of the fifth century. In their earnest endeavours to reinstate the old national language, patriotic government officials have chosen the dialect of Munster to serve as the foundation for present-day standard Irish, but the natives of Dublin go on speaking a particularly attractive and euphonious variety of modern English the same as ever. Only in the western and south-western counties of Mayo and Galway, Kerry and Cork, is Irish now heard in free conversation to any large extent. Nevertheless it still possesses a vigorous offshoot in Scots Gaelic. Just as Breton is not, as we have already noted, the ancient language of Little Britain or Brittany, but was carried there across the sea from Cornwall, so Gaelic is not the autochthonous speech of the Highlands and the Western Isles, but was imported thither across the North Channel from Ulster from the fifth century onwards. Scots Gaelic is now spoken by about one hundred thousand Highlanders and it is cherished by many thousands more who have emigrated to Nova Scotia and Cape Breton Island. Closely related to both Irish and Scots Gaelic is Manx which until 1960 was still spoken by a few bilingual elderly folk in the Isle of Man and which is permanently enshrined in a notable translation of the Book of Common Prayer made in the third decade of the seventeenth century.

Since the final disappearance of East Germanic with Gothic as a spoken tongue in the eighteenth century, the Teutonic languages have been represented by two divisions only, North and West, the former consisting of Icelandic, Norwegian, Swedish, and Danish, and the latter including German, Plattdeutsch, Flemish, Dutch, Frisian, and English.

Icelandic has a rich literature of sagas and poetry dating from the twelfth century and as a language it is intrinsically archaic. Having changed so very little during the last thousand years, it is now nearer than Modern English is to the speech of King Alfred the Great. Students of Anglo-Saxon do well to spend a long vacation working on Icelandic farms and listening to everyday conversation that has changed relatively little since the Viking Age (750–1050). The Old Norse tongue that was spoken throughout Scandinavia about the year 1000 has changed least in Iceland owing to its geographical isolation and the persistence of a strong literary tradition. An Icelander today can read the sagas fluently without special training although, like a modern Greek reading Homer, he will pronounce many vowels differently. Unlike the latter, however, he will encounter no serious difficulty in respect of vocabulary. Icelandic has a remarkably pure lexicon. Many Danish words, admitted during the period of Danish rule, have since been deliberately extruded. Icelandic agrees with the other North Germanic languages in using a suffixed definite article in substantives and a suffixed reflexive -s termination in the passive forms of verbs.

Norwegian, as we have already observed, now consists of two competing varieties, bokmål (riksmål) and nynorsk (landsmål). The former is based on literary Danish inasmuch as Norway was united with Denmark politically for many centuries (1380–1814) and in the sixteenth century Danish became the written language to the exclusion of Norwegian through the austere influence of the Reformation, the complete monopoly of the printing press, and the intellectual hegemony of the University of Copenhagen. The Norwegians had no university of their own before the foundation of the University of Christiania (now Oslo) in 1811. When, three years later, Norway achieved independence, there soon followed a revival of interest in dialect. Ivar Aasen investigated his home dialect of Sunnmøre and then proceeded to construct a kind of synthetic standard for landsmål on the basis of the living speech of Vestlandet, Hardanger, Sogn, and Voss. Meantime Henrik Ibsen and Björnstjerne Björnson were writing in classical Dano-

Norwegian and this *bokmål* in a slightly modified form is generally preferred by the people of Oslo who now comprise one eighth of Norway's population of nearly four millions.

Swedish, spoken by eight and a half million people, is used not only in Sweden but also very extensively in Finland or Suomi, as well as in the United States. Paradoxical as it may seem, the earliest known forms of Swedish are preserved in one hundred Russian loan-words introduced by the Swedes who actually founded the Russian Empire in 862. These included proper names made famous in literature, like *Igor* from *Ingwar* and *Olga* from *Helga*. Modern Swedish is clearly the most important North Germanic tongue, sensibly guided and controlled by the Swedish Academy, founded in 1786, through its grammar (1836), its still unfinished dictionary (begun in 1893), and its spelling reform (1906). Danish likewise has continued to standardize its official language on the basis of common usage, more especially in the city of Copenhagen where one quarter of the population of four and a half millions now lives. Inevitably Danish has been strongly influenced by German in many ways, including morphology. Its numerous derivatives ending in *-selskab* and *-videnskab*, for instance, are obviously modelled on their German counterparts in *-gesellschaft* and *-wissenschaft*.

We may divide the West Germanic group of six into three national languages, German, Dutch, and English; and three regional tongues, Plattdeutsch, Frisian, and Flemish. Taking the regional ones first, we may note that Plattdeutsch is a collection of Low German dialects descending from Old Saxon and retaining many linguistic features, like *st-* pronounced as in English, which distinguish it from Neuhochdeutsch or New High German. Frisian is still spoken in Friesland in the Netherlands by the Ijsselmeer as well as along the northern shores of Germany beyond the Ems and Weser, on the Schleswig coast beyond the Elbe, and, with dialectal divergences, on the islands of Sylt, Föhr, and Amrun. Frisian is the nearest akin to English of all living tongues. Indeed, Old Frisian and Old English were so nearly allied that they constituted one language called Anglo-Frisian, marking the transitional or intermediate stage in the story of our language between West Germanic and Old English in the centuries immediately preceding the settlement of Angles and Saxons in England.

Flemish, Vlaams, or Belgian Dutch is the language of Flanders spoken by about four and a half million persons in a thickly populated industrial and agricultural region in and around Ghent. Officially it has equal rights with French, and public documents are required to be published in both languages. Actually there is considerable friction between the two and Flemish-speaking Belgians have to assert themselves from time to time against their more powerful neighbours.

That Dutch stands midway between German and English may be shown quite simply by comparing such forms as German *Baum* 'tree', Dutch *boom* (borrowed as a nautical term into English), and English *beam* (as in *hornbeam*); *Auge* 'eye', *oog* (as in English *ogle* 'to eye amorously'), and *ee* (dialectal); *Traum*, *droom*, and *dream*; *Zaum* 'rein, bridle', *toom*, and *team*; or, showing a different vowel harmony, *Heim*, *heem*, and *home*; *Speiche*, *spaak*, *spoke* (of a wheel); *Seife* 'soap', *zeep*, and *soap*; and so forth. If you know German, you will encounter no great difficulty in mastering Dutch, but you will often be reminded that it is indeed a great national language in its own right with its own well-preserved traditions. European Dutch or Netherlandish is now spoken as a 'language of colonization' in various parts of the world, especially in Indonesia, and as a creolized dialect in Ceylon and in both the East and West Indies. Cape Dutch or Afrikaans is based upon the speech of migrants from 1652 onwards and it has developed simplified forms as the result of isolation from Europe and through contact with Hottentots, Malayo-Portuguese from the East Indies, French Huguenots, Germans, and British. The definite article has become invariable as in English, the conjugations of verbs have been simplified, and parts of speech are interchanged. Afrikaans, now fully standardized, is one of the official languages of South Africa. Its vocabulary remains ninety-five per cent Dutch in spite of isolation and in the face of all those external contacts just mentioned.

German is the most conservative of the West Germanic group and its structure is more rigid and orderly than that of English. It is the language of the German and Austrian Republics and of part of Switzerland. As both first and second language it is widely used in Central Europe on the one hand and in Scandinavia on the other. It is also employed as a means of communication in many parts of Africa and Oceania. Moreover, it is used by millions of German immigrants and their descendants in the New World – in Ohio and Pennsylvania, as well as in Latin America, more particularly in Argentina, Chile, and South Brazil.

The wide range of the Indo-European family throughout the world is indeed so impressive that we are sometimes led almost to forget that there remain not a few languages in Europe itself which are quite as certainly non-Indo-European – Basque, for example, spoken by about one million people in the Western Pyrenees and having no demonstrable kinship with any other speech on earth; Maltese, a Semitic dialect related to Arabic and Hebrew; Finnish, Estonian, and Hungarian, all three belonging to the Finno-Ugrian division of Ural-Altaic and therefore related to Turkish, which is also partly in Europe; various other Ural-Altaic tongues in North Russia such as Lapp, Karelian, and Permian; and finally North and South Caucasian which show neither affiliations with any Indo-European language nor connexions with each other. A survey of these and other non-Indo-European tongues will engage our attention in the next chapter.

CHAPTER 8

NON-INDO-EUROPEAN TONGUES

THE mention of Basque towards the close of the previous chapter reminds us rather forcibly that our knowledge of the history of the world's languages is still quite elementary. Here we find an ancient language spoken by a million people living on the very threshold of such ancient civilizations as those of France and Spain, and yet showing no discernible kinship with any other tongue on earth. The name *Gascony* is Basque and therefore indicates that this language was spoken farther north. But what is it? Is it Iberian, the ancient speech of the Peninsula, or is it pre-Iberian? Or does it belong to that extensive pre-Roman Aquitanian tongue which may have affinities with North Caucasian? Its native speakers call it Euskara 'clear-speaking': its structure is essentially agglutinative. Its syntax is intricate, partly because its verb has no active voice. A man cannot say 'John cuts the hedge' in Basque, but only 'By John the hedge is cut'.

The Caucasian languages present as many problems as Basque itself and their relationships with one another are far from clear. Indeed, the term Caucasian is more geographical than linguistic and in any case these languages may be divided into two distinct groups, North and South. The North Caucasian group consists of many separate units, including Abkaz, Chechen, and Avar, the latter showing features of exceptional interest. Avar is remarkably rich in consonants, having no fewer than forty-three, but all consonant groups or clusters, except the simplest, are avoided. On the other hand, Avar has few vowels. The substantive shows thirty cases and there is a resulting dearth of prepositions. The South Caucasian group also comprises many units, including Laz, Mingrelian, and Georgian, the latter spoken by one million people and boasting an important and ancient literature beginning with a fifth-century translation of the Bible. Georgian is the official language of the Soviet Republic of Georgia and the recognized medium of instruction in the renowned University of Tiflis. A Soviet philologist, Nikolai Yakovlevich Marr (1864–1934), son of a Scottish geologist and his Georgian wife, recently formulated the notorious theory that the Caucasian languages were of Japhetic origin and were therefore related to the pre-Indo-European or Mediterranean tongues of remote antiquity. Japheth, you may remember, was younger brother to Shem and Ham, children of Noah, to whom 'sons were born after the flood' (*Gen.* x:i). It is now generally agreed that the Shemitic or Semitic and Hamitic languages belong to one family called Hamito-Semitic, and, because the term Japhetic has been used in more senses than one, it is now usually discarded by linguists. But Marr boldly asserted that the Japhetic, Nostratic, or Alarodian language was the ancestor of both North and South Caucasian, which were demonstrably akin to Basque and Etruscan and probably related to ancient Sumerian. Such a bold assertion has little scientific validity because it rests on uncertain foundations, but it is not altogether unattractive. As we now survey the languages of the world outside Indo-European, we shall be better advised, however, to ignore such irresponsible hypotheses and see the world as it now is. We shall do well to proceed geographically. If we have no maps available, we can visualize continents and countries in the mind's eye, knowing that mental visualization is the secret of much successful study. Even maps and diagrams convey only limited information in themselves. I have all the elaborate maps of Father Wilhelm Schmidt (1926) and Professors Antoine Meillet and Marcel Cohen (1952) around me as I write, and yet I find that I must use my imagination at every turn. Languages overlap and come into daily contact in a hundred ways. Seldom do they present fixed divisions like political boundaries.

Nevertheless, without undue simplification, we can distinguish ten outstanding families of languages in the Old

World besides Indo-European: Hamito-Semitic in south-west Asia and north Africa; Ural-Altaic in east Europe and central Asia, with important offshoots in northern and central Europe; Japanese-Korean in Japan and Korea; Sino-Tibetan in China, Tibet, Burma, Thailand, Indo-China, and Manchukuo; Dravidian in central and southern India and northern Ceylon; Austro-Asian or Mon-Khmer in south-east Asia; Malayo-Polynesian in an island world extending from Formosa to New Zealand and from Madagascar to Easter Island; Sudanese-Guinean in a wide belt across the Sudan from Gambia to Kenya; Bantu in central and southern Africa; and finally Khoin, or Hottentot-Bushman, in various regions of south-west Africa.

We may profitably base our report – and, after all, it is only a kind of interim report and nothing more – on the supposition that these ten families are separate groups without historical relationships, but we should not forget that this is no more than a convenient assumption and that modifications may have to be made from time to time in future as knowledge increases.

The Hamito-Semitic languages straddle the continents of Africa and Asia, and include Egyptian, Berber, and Cushite in the Hamitic sub-family, and Hebrew and Arabic on the Semitic side. Egyptian once vied with Sumerian in antiquity, but, like Sumerian, it is now a dead language apart from Coptic which survives solely in the sacred liturgy of the African Christians called Copts. It is customary to divide the history of Egyptian into three periods: Old or hieroglyphic, Middle or hieratic, and New or demotic. The latter became extinct in the third century of our era. Etymologically a *Copt* (Arabic *Qibt*) is merely an E-*gypt*-ian (Greek Ai-*gupt*-ios), but now the word has an entirely ecclesiastical reference and denotes a Christian. Today the Copts number under one million. They use an alphabet of twenty-four letters based on Greek with seven supplementary ones borrowed from demotic Egyptian. Their language shows a drastic modification of demotic, but it is invaluable to Egyptologists. The hieroglyphs of Old Egyptian number about six hundred, representing consonants only, and they were first deciphered in 1822 by Jean François Champollion with the aid of the famous Rosetta Stone which bears a text in both hieroglyphic and demotic script, together with a version in Greek.

The Berber languages of northern Africa are descended from the speech of the ancient Numidians who helped Rome in her struggle with Carthage. They include Tuareg, spoken by the Bedouins of the Sahara Desert; Shluh, the vernacular of southern Morocco; and Kabyl, heard in the mountains of Algiers and Tunis. The Berbers call themselves Imazighen 'freemen, nobles' and they show laudable independence in maintaining their inherited dialects in the face of Arabic opposition. So, too, do the Cushites of Ethiopia and of the eastern horn of Africa between the Nile and the Red Sea. Somali, Galla, and Beja are still spoken by large populations over wide areas. It is interesting to observe that these Cushite languages contain words of two consonants like Old Egyptian. They may well preserve a structure more ancient than the now universal triconsonantal pattern of the Semitic sub-family.

The most ancient Semitic language was Akkadian, also called Assyrian or Babylonian, spoken in Mesopotamia in prehistoric times and recorded in cuneiform literature. Later it was succeeded as the language of administration by Aramaic and by its closely related dialect known as Syriac. One form of Aramaic is still important as the medium of much Rabbinical Jewish literature, while Syriac is used in eastern liturgies and in early Christian literature. The language of Christ was Western Aramaic, as in *Talitha kumi* 'maiden, arise' (Mark v:41) and *Ephphatha* 'be opened' (Mark vii:34). Even some small parts of the Old Testament (Gen. xxxi:47, Jeremiah x:11, Daniel ii:46–vii:28, and Ezra iv:8–vi:18, vii:12–26) were recorded in Aramaic, whereas all the rest was written in Hebrew, the speech of ancient Canaan 'low region'. Hebrew was indeed largely superseded by Aramaic in everyday usage in the second century B.C., but it continued unperturbed as a liturgical language. As the national language of Israel, Palestinian Hebrew has taken new life in the twentieth century. Phoenician, the language of commerce throughout the Mediterranean Sea from the fifth to the second centuries B.C., was closely akin to Hebrew and in its later form, known as Punic, it lived on as the language of the Carthaginian Empire. It came to an end with the destruction of Dido's famous city by the Romans in 146 B.C.

Today Hebrew and Arabic are the two living Semitic tongues, the one so extremely ancient that theologians long assumed it to have been used in the garden of Eden, and the other so relatively recent that, search where we will, we can find no inscription earlier than A.D. 328. Arabic began to expand rapidly in the seventh century when it became the voice of the new world religion of *Islam* or 'resignation'. On the thirteenth day of September in the year of grace 622, Mohammed 'the praised' made his *hegira* or 'departure' from Mecca, fleeing for safety to the city of Medina, and this therefore stands as zero year in Moslem chronology. Mohammed spoke the dialect of Mecca and in that dialect the sacred books of the *Qur'an* or 'reading' were subsequently recorded. The Moslem Arabs took their language and religion with them wherever they went on their wars of conquest, ranging from Iran to Spain. Arabic superseded Egyptian in Cairo itself and it influenced many neighbouring languages like Persian, Hindustani, Turkish, Malay, Hausa, and Swahili not only in vocabulary but also to a certain extent in phonology and syntax. Literary Arabic has become standardized throughout the entire Arabic world and it remains strongly conservative. Its rich and varied literature can be understood by all who can read its script. Arabic is now spoken all the way across North Africa from Casablanca to Cairo, and far south into the Sahara as well as in Arabia itself and in Syria, Jordan, Lebanon, and Iraq. Being so widely diffused, it has an importance out of proportion to the number of its speakers. The modern world owes its numerals to the Arabs. You will speedily realize the measure of this debt if you try keeping your banking account in Roman figures! As a matter of fact the Arabs did not invent these symbols, which had their origin in India, reaching Baghdad in the eighth century and Venice some three or four centuries later.

Arabic and Hebrew are both characterized by *triliterals* or triconsonantal roots. *Islam*, for instance, is based on the three consonants *s – l – m* as in Arabic *salam* 'peace' and *mu-slim*, active participle, 'resigning one'. Nominal and verbal forms are distinguished by vowel modifications which are unrecorded, but are readily supplied by the reader himself. In the spoken language of Cairo *ye-kteb* means 'to write', based on the *k – t – b* triliteral. Hence are formed such expressions as *kataba* 'he has written', *ya-ktubu* 'he will write', *yu-ktabu* 'it will be written', *el-kateb* 'the clerk', *kitab-un* 'the writing, book', and so on.

The next great family of languages on our list is, like Hamito-Semitic, also bipartite, its two divisions being named after well-known mountain ranges, the Urals on Europe's eastern fringe and the Altai Mountains rising north of the Gobi Desert in the heart of Asia. It is therefore called Ural-Altaic and it is divided into two sub-families: Finno-Ugrian (or simply Uralian) and Turco-Tartar (or simply Altaic). Now *Ugrian* is merely a reduced form of *Hungarian* (from *Hungari*, *Ungari*, *Ungri*, or *Ugri*) and so the name of the first sub-family reminds us that Finns and Hungarians or Magyars are related and that they forced their way into northern and central Europe from the east. Finnish, spoken by some three millions, and Estonian, spoken by about one million, are not isolated, however, like Hungarian. They have a near relative in Lapp, the language of thirty thousand hardy folk inhabiting the mountain slopes and valleys of northern Finland, Sweden, and Norway in the 'lands of the midnight sun'; and they have more distant relatives in Cheremiss and Mordvin in the basin of the River Volga, countless linguistic islands around the Ural Mountains in the Russian area, and yet farther east in Permian and Ostyak, languages still spoken by an unascertainable number of people from the Sverdlovsk Gap to the Kara Sea and in the wild Siberian tundra of the basin of the River Ob. In contrast to these widely scattered speech communities of thousands or hundreds or even less, Hungary with its population of twelve million stands as a solid block in impressive isolation. As late as the ninth century of our era the Magyars made their way across south Russia from their homes somewhere on the great bend of the Volga between Gorki and Saratov. Late-comers to central Europe, the Hungarians have never fully settled down.

The languages of the Altaic or Turco-Tartaric sub-family fall into three main groups, represented by Turkish, Mongol, and Manchu, spoken in Turkey, in European Russia east of the Volga, and throughout Asian Russia, Chinese Turkistan, Mongolia, and Manchukuo, as well as parts of north-west Iran and north Afghanistan. Turkish proper, or Osmanli, is the only Altaic tongue possessing a really great literature. We rightly associate these majestic Altai Mountains with fierce conquerors like Genghis Khan and his grandson Kublai, founder of the Mongol dynasty of China, who revelled in that oriental magnificence which Marco Polo described in such vivid language; or the ruthless despot Timur, born in Samarkand, dramatized by Christopher Marlowe in *Tamburlaine*; or Akbar, who subsequently became the most tolerant and enlightened of all the Mogul emperors. No longer now do intrepid leaders issue forth from these Asian heights to conquer the world, but, in their stead, peaceful nomads follow the ordered rhythm of the seasons in their lives – spring on the open steppe, summer on high pastures, and winter in low valleys. Linguistically, then, we may fairly regard Finnish, Hungarian, and Turkish as three spearheads of advance, now widely separated, projected from central Asia into the west.

Osmanli is spoken by eighteen millions of people and it now has Kemal's Roman alphabet of twenty-nine letters in full use. The letters *q*, *w*, and *x* are omitted: *c* is pronounced [dʒ], *ç* [tʃ], *ğ* [x], *j* [ʒ], and *ş* [ʃ]. Undotted *ı* [ə], *ö* [ø], and *ü* [y] have these particular qualities, and they play an essential part in the operation of *vowel harmony* which is a notable feature of Altaic, by which front vowels are followed by front-vowel endings and back vowels by back-vowel endings, and by which the vowel of a first suffix always harmonizes with that of the root to which it is attached, and each succeeding suffix with the one before. The front vowels are *e*, *i*, *ö*, *ü*; the back ones *a*, *o*, *u*; and undotted *ı* [ə] is neutral. For instance, the plural inflexion of nouns has two forms *-ler*: *-lar* and the infinitive ending of verbs has likewise two forms *-mek*: *-mak*. Thus *ev* 'house' has as its plural *evler* 'houses', but *oda* 'room' gives *odalar* 'rooms': *vermek* 'to give', but *almak* 'to take', and so forth. The Altaic languages show a high degree of agglutination. In Turkish the root is generally monosyllabic and remains unchanged, but it may acquire numerous additional morphemes expressing the most complex grammatical relationships. Thus the root *sev* means 'love', *sev-mek* 'to love', *sev-dir-mek* 'to make to love', *sev-il-mek* 'to be loved', *sev-me-mek* 'not to love', and *sev-il-me-mek* 'not to be loved'. Verbs and substantives may have as many as eight affixes added to one root and this means that Turkish has nothing corresponding to prepositions and no genuine relative clauses. Verbs stand at the end of the sentence. Through the centuries Turkish has preserved its structure with tenacity. It has, however, borrowed words freely, especially from Arabic. Its near relatives, showing similar features, stretch far across northern Asia: Azerbaijani, heard in north-west Iran and the Caucasus; and Uzbek, Kirghiz, and Kazakh, spoken in central Asia. The more distantly related Mongol languages are used by some three million people in Mongolia itself and by many scattered communities in various parts of Asia and even in European Russia. No less scattered are the speakers of Manchu, a rapidly diminishing language which cannot compete with Chinese on equal terms. Finally, we should not forget Yakut, still a living tongue in the far north of Siberia, detached, but undoubtedly Altaic in both structure and distinctive features.

The relationship of Japanese and Korean to each other and to the other tongues of Asia remains highly conjectural.

Proof of kinship with Korean rests upon similarity of structure. Both languages are agglutinative in type and use suffixes in a precise order. Both ignore gender, number, and person in declension and conjugation, and both have the same verbal structure as well as other common features. On the whole, however, the evidence is inadequate. Japanese script conceals, or renders imperfectly, the early stages of linguistic history. Japanese, to be sure, has used Chinese ideograms or pictograms since the fourth century of our era, but, unlike modern Chinese, it employs inflexions and therefore requires phonetic symbols to record them. That is why long ago the Japanese devised the *kana* characters, representing definite syllables like *mu* or *ru* with fixed pronunciations. These may be added to ideograms in order to supply inflexions and suffixes or, especially in popular magazines and newspapers, to help less educated readers to understand more readily, as when you write (for a different reason, of course) '£5 five pounds' in English. Consonants and vowels usually alternate as in *hara-kiri* and *mikado*, syllables being normally open and words therefore ending in a vowel, whereas one-syllable words in Chinese often end in *-n* or *-ng* and in Cantonese even in *-p*, *-t*, or *-k*. The influence of the Chinese vocabulary on Japanese has been steady and continuous for many centuries past.

The history of Korean before the fifteenth century is completely unknown and no full descriptive analysis of the present language is yet available. It would nevertheless seem to be highly plausible that Korean is related to Japanese and that both are ultimately Ural-Altaic, and so distantly connected with Finnish, Hungarian, and Turkish. As we should expect, a very large part of the Korean lexicon comes from Chinese. The name *Korea* stands for Japanese *Korai* which itself represents Chinese *kao li* 'lofty (and) beautiful'. The Koreans call their country *Hankuk*.

This epithet *li* in *kao li* just mentioned may serve to remind us that the traditional standard writing of China is called *wen li* 'literature beautiful'. It is the precious inheritance of all who can read in China and Japan alike. It goes back to at least the middle of the second millennium before Christ so that its earliest extant records are contemporaneous with Sanskrit. Indeed, the golden age of Chinese literature was roughly coeval with that of Greek. Meng-tse (372–288), or *Mencius*, was born in Shantung only twelve years after Aristotle (384–322) was born at Stagirus in Chalcidice. These two distinguished philosophers lived all their long lives and died with no glimmer of knowledge of each other's existence.

Chinese belongs with Thai or Siamese and Tibeto-Burmese to the great Sino-Tibetan family whose outstanding characteristics are monosyllabism and significant tonality. Chinese is autochthonous, since its old home is the great southern bend of the Hwang Ho or Yellow River. It is now spoken throughout the Chinese People's Republic and also by large groups of colonists in Malaya, Indo-China, Siam, and the East Indies. It has served as a medium of culture for Koreans, Japanese, and Annamese, and it has provided the source from which those peoples have enriched their vocabularies continuously, even as modern European tongues have constantly drawn on Latin and Greek. The written language still serves as the bond of union among spoken dialects whose speakers are less intelligible to one another than Danes and Swedes or Portuguese and Spaniards. The northern dialect in its Peking variety has been chosen by Hu Shih and his helpers as the *kuo yü* or 'national language' of the future. It is spoken in all China as far south as the Yangtse valley, except in its lower part, and now, by the edict of Mao Tse-tung, it is taught in schools throughout the republic. The Wu dialects prevail in Suchow, Ningpo, Shanghai, and the Yangtse delta; the Min dialects in Fukien, with well-marked varieties in Foochow and Amoy, encroaching on Kwangtung with Swatow and Hainanese; Cantonese in the greater commercial cities of the south; and Hakka, largely a rural patois, is used in Kwangtung and parts of the adjacent provinces. If we agree that the distinction between a language and a dialect rests solely on mutual intelligibility, we must conclude that these are indeed languages rather than dialects. The traditional symbols are therefore very important. They may be likened to the Arabic numerals in daily use throughout Europe. Where for 87 an Englishman says 'eighty-seven', a Frenchman reads 'quatre-vingt-sept', an Italian 'ottantasette', and a Spaniard 'ochenta y siete'.

Not only are Chinese words monosyllabic, but they remain unaltered in form. Substantives never change to show case or number (like our *home, home's, homes* or *foot, foot's, feet*): verbs never change to show person or tense (like our *do, does, did* or *come, comes, came*). Thus every concept or relation is expressed by one syllable, definite in both form and meaning, and quite fixed. Two or more words may be juxtaposed as in *steam-ship* or *tea-pot*, or as in *self-go-cart*, the new word for *automobile*. Two or more words may even be associated in such a way as to give a meaning common to both or resulting from their common factors. Thus the symbols for two bright objects, sun and moon, are joined in *ming*² 'bright'. Further, *ming*² 'bright' and *pai*² 'clear, white' combine to form the verbal notion 'to understand'.

These index-figures attached to *ming*² and *pai*² indicate rising word-tone in accordance with the system devised by Sir Thomas Francis Wade (1818–95) who taught Chinese at Cambridge after retiring from the post of minister plenipotentiary at Peking. Significant tonality implies that tone conveys meaning. The suprasegmental prosodeme of tone or pitch of the word has *objective reference*, altering its significance just as much as the substitution of a different segmental phoneme would change it. Ancient Chinese probably had a level, a rising, and a falling tone in each of two series, upper and lower. It therefore had a set of six tones altogether, one more than modern Siamese and two more than standard Pekingese. So, for example, in Pekingese *ma*¹ with level tone, like a clock ticking, or as in counting one, two, three, means 'mother'; *ma*² with rising tone, as if asking a question, means 'flax'; *ma*³ with end-rising tone, as in making an apology or implying a concession, means 'horse'; whereas *ma*⁴ with falling tone, as in naming the word, means 'to rebuke, scold'. How on earth, you may ask, do people manage to remember each distinctive form? The simple answer is that for them the tone forms an integral part of the memory-picture of the word which is stored in the mind from earliest childhood.

Siamese or Thai is spoken by twenty million people in and around Thailand. Tibetan includes Balti, the standard literary language of Tibet, as well as a multitude of dialects. Burmese is the language of administration in Burma, spoken and understood by more than ten million souls. Other interesting Sino-Tibetan languages include Bodo, Naga, and Lolo.

No less interesting than these remote tone languages of northern India and Pakistan are the Dravidian tongues of the Dekkan or 'South', notably four important literary languages now spoken by over one hundred millions altogether – Telugu, Tamil, Kanarese, and Malayalam, as well as a considerable variety of unrecorded dialects dispersed throughout central India, of which Gondi, Kurukh, and Kui are noteworthy. The latter may be described as shrunken enclaves – linguistic 'pockets' or 'islands' – persisting somewhat precariously among alien communities in the spacious hills of the Central Provinces. To these must be added the Brahui language, a solitary survivor on the mountains of Baluchistan, reminding us that Dravidian languages covered the sub-continent before the invasion of the Indo-Europeans through the mountain passes of the north-west. Doubtless the Dravidians themselves had been similar invaders, reaching India by those same paths many centuries earlier in the dark backward and abysm of time. In our present picture of the great languages of the world we must continue to regard Dravidian and Ural-Altaic as separate families, but is it so very surprising that we do find points of resemblance between the structure of Tamil and that of, say, Finnish? Both are moderately agglutinative, using few prefixes but abundant suffixation, and possessing a simple consonantal pattern. Tamil has fewer speakers than Telegu, but it is the most important of the Dravidian languages by virtue of its rich and abundant literature dating back to the second century. It is still spoken by thirty-seven million people living in the southern half of the Madras presidency, in the north and east of Ceylon, and by emigrants in the Malay peninsula. Tamil preserves a very copious native Dravidian vocabulary. It has given us *curry*, *coolie*, *pariah*, *cheroot*, *corundum*, and *mulligatawny* 'pepper-water'.

Telugu is spoken by forty-two millions of people living in the northern part of the Madras presidency and in adjacent regions of Hyderabad, whereas Kanarese is the speech of seventeen million persons inhabiting Mysore and the south-western part of the Nizam's dominions, as well as western coastal districts from Karvar to Mangalore. In the states of Cochin and Travancore, Malayalam is spoken by some fifteen millions. It may be regarded as a late dialectal development of Tamil to which it is still fairly closely allied.

Scattered far and wide over south-east Asia we find another distinct linguistic family known as Austro-Asian, Mon-Khmer, or Kolarian. The first designation is, of course, a geographical one and on the whole it is the best. These Austro-Asian languages, Munda, Mon, and Khmer, were not committed to writing until recent times and it is impossible to tell how many tribesmen speak and understand them. Munda is in use among nomads wandering over the north-eastern plateaus of central India, Mon among the tribes of Burma, and Khmer among those of Cambodia or southern Indo-China. In all these strange tongues prefixes and infixes play a large part in the making of words, and not suffixes as in Dravidian.

Before leaving India we should certainly mention one very remarkable language called Burushaski, spoken in the inaccessible valleys of the extreme north-west in the states of Hunza and Nagir. Like Basque, it is completely isolated. All kinds of conjectures and speculations have been suggested about Burushaski. Perhaps it is the sole surviving remnant of a substratal language covering a wide area of Asia in remote antiquity.

We move into an entirely different but no less wonderful region when we pass on to consider the Malayo-Polynesian family, subdivided into an impressive number of languages and an almost infinite variety of dialects. This family extends far and wide over coastal plains, peninsulas, islands, and archipelagos from Formosa in the north to New Zealand in the south and from Madagascar in the the west to Easter Island in the east, but excluding Australia, Tasmania, and central New Guinea. The speakers of Malayo-Polynesian languages number over one hundred millions and they are scattered over an area almost as extensive as that covered by Indo-European. For convenience it is customary to divide this group into four sub-families with names all ending in *-nesian* (*nesos* means 'island' in Greek): Indonesian, Melanesian, Micronesian, and Polynesian.

The most important member of the Indonesian sub-family is Malay, which has its home on the north coast of Sumatra, and which now ranks twelfth among the world's languages. It is clearly destined to hold a position of importance in the commerce and government of the Far East. Under the name *Bahasa Indonesia* it has been publicly adopted as the official language of that extensive region, whereas Pidgin or Bazaar Malay performs a useful function as an indispensable medium of trade and as a provisional means of communication in the Pacific area. In their own books and newspapers the Malays have long employed an adapted Arabic alphabet, but they are now using Roman letters more and more. Malay has been described as 'the world's easiest language', with no harsh consonant clusters, no difficult morphology, and no involved syntax. Many Malay words have already found their way into our language: *sago, bamboo, gong, cockatoo, bantam, caddy* (for tea), *gutta-percha, raffia,* and *launch* in the sense of 'pinnace' (from the Malay adjective *lanchar* 'speedy, swift').

Near akin to Malay are the other languages of the Indonesian sub-family spoken on Java, Borneo, Celebes, Bali, Molucca Islands, Philippines, Formosa, and Madagascar. Javanese possesses a notable literature dating from the ninth century and inspired by Sanskrit models. Tagalog (stressed on the second syllable) has been made the national language of the Philippine Islands by decree. Malagasy is spoken by some five million people on the large island of Madagascar off the east African coast.

The Melanesian sub-family includes about thirty-five near and distantly related languages spoken in the Solomon, Santa Cruz, Torres, Banks, New Hebrides, and Loyalty archipelagos, as well as in Rotuma and the Fiji islands. Fijian is doubtless the best known of these.

Micronesian embraces some eight tongues spoken in the Gilbert, Marshall, Caroline, and Marianne archipelagos and on the island of Yap. Polynesian comprises about twenty tongues including Maori in New Zealand and the picturesque languages of the more easterly Pacific islands, such as Samoa, Tahiti, Hawaii, and even Easter Island itself.

However varied and changeful these Malayo-Polynesian forms of speech may appear to be on first acquaintance, deeper study reveals that they have many linguistic features in common. Their phonemic patterns bear strong resemblances. Substantives often consist of disyllables with the first syllable stressed, since they are generally composed of root plus determinative, and they bear no marks of inflexion for number or gender. Verbs are distinguished by numerous affixes as transitive, intransitive, passive, causative, reflexive, reciprocal, frequentative, or iterative. Consonant clusters and final closed syllables are rare, so rare, in fact, that consonant sounds tend to become eliminated altogether.

The Papuan languages of New Guinea and the aboriginal languages of Australia are gradually vanishing before competent linguists can find time to subject them to scientific analysis. In this respect they differ from the Negro tongues of Africa, to which we now direct our attention, for these have been carefully examined by teams of specialists in recent years. These African Negro tongues, numbering over five hundred, are now spoken by at least one hundred million black people south of the Sahara Desert and the Tropic of Cancer, and they fall into three groups – Sudanese-Guinean, Bantu, and Khoin.

The first group covers a wide belt across the Sudan from Gambia to Kenya, presenting a veritable chaos of speech forms among which may be mentioned Ewe, Ibo, Hausa, Efik, Mandingo, Mende, Nubian, Twi, and Yoruba. Ewe is spoken in Togoland and in part of Ghana, and it also serves as a lingua franca over a wide area. Ibo is used in south-eastern Nigeria. But by far the most important of all Sudanese-Guinean languages is Hausa, spoken in central Sudan and northern Nigeria, for it has become one of the most important languages of Africa in recent years as an international medium of trade.

The Bantu languages present a fairly homogeneous collection spoken by some fifty millions in central and southern Africa on the other side of the so-called 'Bantu line' which crosses the Congo jungles obliquely from the gulf of Cameroons in the west to Mombasa in the east. The immediate neighbours of the Bantu (i.e. *ba-ntu* 'human beings, people', plural of *mu-ntu* 'man'), so named for the first time by the famous linguist Wilhelm Bleek (1827–75), are the Sudanese in the west and centre and the Hamitic peoples in the east. According to native tradition, the Bantu moved south from homes on the Upper Nile and occupied the centre and south-east of the continent, but they had failed to conquer the south-west region peopled by Hottentots and Bushmen when the first Europeans arrived at the Cape of Good Hope. The members of the Bantu family are still numerous: among the better known are Swahili, Luganda, Kaffir, Zulu, Luba-Lulua, Subiya, and Herero. By far the most important is Swahili (from Arabic *suahiliyi* 'of the coasts, coastal') originally the speech of the people of Zanzibar and of the coasts of the adjacent mainland. Like Hausa in the Sudanese-Guinean group, Swahili has long served as the general medium of trade throughout central Africa. Before the advent of railways and automobiles, much exploration and development depended on the services of Swahili carriers. Today Swahili has acquired further prestige as the recognized language of instruction in the primary schools of Kenya, Tanganyika, and many provinces of the Belgian Congo. It is written in an adapted form of Arabic script and its vocabulary has been greatly enriched from Arabic sources. The other Bantu languages are oral. Indeed, to write them down is to give them a rigidity as unknown to their speakers as to the sweet bird-songsters of the forest. The Bantu languages have similar structures of fascinating interest, characterized by euphonious open syllables, prefixal concord, and sensory ideophones. An open syllable ends in a vowel. The only consonant groups accepted are nasals followed by homorganic plosives (i.e. plosives formed in the same part of the mouth as the nasal concerned, like the *t* in the *nt* of *Bantu*), and single consonants followed by semi-vowels (i.e. [w] or [j] like the *sw* of *Swahili* or the *ny* of *Kenya*). All words, whether pronouns, adjectives, or verbs, which stand in agreement with a substantive, bear added prefixes accordingly. These mobile prefixes therefore vary from sentence to sentence and endow even proper names with delightful variations. The name is Ganda, to be sure, but we may properly say that Luganda is spoken by the Baganda who inhabit Uganda. Ideophones are not so much words conveying meanings as qualifiers suggesting the total impressions made upon the speaker by such actions as, say, pressing something soft, sneaking about stealthily, laughing inwardly, or appearing unexpectedly.

In the sparsely populated desert and scrub of south-west Africa a quarter of a million aboriginal pygmies speak Khoin with its two branches large and small, Nama or Hottentot 'stutterer' in the north and San or Bushman in the south, both distinguished phonologically by clicks or suction sounds produced by rapid and violent intakes of breath. These clicks are distinctive sounds or phonemes, of which Nama has four and San seven.

As we now cross the Atlantic to the New World, we are reminded that it has more open spaces and fewer people than the Old and yet, surprisingly, it has more languages. Apart from the European languages of immigration – English, Spanish, Portuguese, French (with its notable offshoot, Haitian Creole), Dutch, German, Danish, Norwegian, Italian, Czech, and Polish – America is the abode of numerous aboriginal tongues: Eskimo-Aleut, 24; North American, 351; Mexican and Central American, 96; Antillean and South American, 783. The number of languages is thus very large indeed, but their living speakers are in some instances scarce – a few thousand perhaps, or only a few hundred. For the most part neglected by the comparative philologists of the nineteenth century, these fascinating oral systems have been studied and analysed by the American linguists and anthropologists of the twentieth – Franz Boas, Edward Sapir, Leonard Bloomfield, Benjamin Lee Whorf, Kenneth Lee Pike, Harry Hoijer, and Charles Francis Hockett, to name no others. Even so, it seems that many of these 1,254 Amerindian tongues are destined to vanish unrecorded and unremembered from our quickly changing world.

Anthropologists are generally agreed that man entered America from Asia by way of the Alaskan bridge and the Bering Strait. Before the emergence of the great apes, the Atlantic was an impassable barrier. America was probably unoccupied during that long period between the rise of the higher mammals and the appearance of man. Man therefore first entered America as man from Asia, and not from Europe or Africa. When this particular specimen of Homo sapiens made his first entry, he had already learnt to tame dogs but not yet horses or oxen, nor had he hit upon the notion of the wheel from his casual log-rolling. He bore Mongolian features. As we might well expect, the present-day speech of the Hyperboreans of the extreme north-east corner of Russian Siberia is distantly related to that Eskimo-Aleut of Arctic Canada which extends from the Aleutian Islands and Alaska to Labrador and Greenland with wide southern sweeps on either side of Hudson Bay. It would seem that no centres of civilization developed in North

America to be compared with the three ancient cultures of the Aztecs of Mexico, the Mayas of Yucatan, and the Incas of Peru. Their languages, Nahuatl, Mayan, and Kechuan, still show great vitality and bid fair to outlive all the aboriginal tongues of the north – Athapaskan in northwestern Canada from Alaska to Hudson Bay; Algonquian in western and central Canada, Alberta, Saskatchewan, Manitoba, Ontario, and Quebec, in the states of Minnesota, Wisconsin, and Michigan, as well as in New Brunswick, Nova Scotia, and the New England states; and Iroquoian around Lakes Erie and Ontario and in detached areas adjoining Blue Ridge. Many dialects of these and other Amerindian languages may be familiar to you from the novels of James Fenimore Cooper (1789–1851). Their speakers in the whole of North America now number less than half a million. In Mexico, however, and in the republics of Central America they number four millions, since many people still speak only Indian tongues, their vocabularies being enlarged and reinforced, as life becomes more sophisticated, by numerous expressions borrowed from Spanish. As for South America, with its ten republics and three Guianas (British, Dutch, and French) it abounds in native tongues. Eight millions or more still use them every day, but their mutual relationships have never been satisfactorily determined. Mention may here be made of Arawak and Carib, brought south from the West Indies; Tupi-Guarani spoken in the Amazon basin and along the coast of Brazil; Araucanian in Chile; and Kechuan, the language of the Incas already mentioned, spoken by at least four million persons over a wide area reaching from Equador through Bolivia and Peru to northern Argentina.

The more interested we may become for one reason or another in these picturesque languages, the more respect we have for those enterprising and energetic pioneers in modern linguistics who have made synchronic study of unwritten forms of speech a scientific possibility. In some ways South America is still the linguist's happiest hunting-ground. Although the languages of civilization are ever increasing,

Spanish (mainly Andalusian) and Portuguese (in Brazil) having about forty-five million speakers each, the inherited tongues are remarkably viable in the second half of the twentieth century. They furnish linguists with invaluable material for observation and experiment. How utterly and completely they disprove the assumption that primitive peoples are incapable of creating and controlling elaborate linguistic structures! It would be no exaggeration to say that the empirical investigation of these obscure aboriginal languages has effected a salutary revolution in our methods of linguistic analysis and has shed new light on the very foundations of language itself.

CHAPTER 9

THE PRACTICAL STUDY
OF LANGUAGES

PEOPLE may decide to study foreign languages for various reasons. They may do so for the immediate purpose of satisfying the requirements of some public examination or of getting greater fun and enjoyment out of a holiday abroad. Men of business may have to deal directly or indirectly with foreign correspondence and research workers may realize the importance of being able to read the latest accounts of advances made in their subject as soon as they are published in foreign journals, without waiting for a translator, who may or may not be competent to present a precise rendering with one hundred per cent accuracy. People may be keenly interested in the activities of a foreign nation for political reasons and they may need to acquire that close knowledge of current affairs which travel abroad and the reading of foreign newspapers and journals alone can supply. Students of literature must surely be able to read the masters at first hand – Montaigne, Pascal, Rousseau; Calderón, San Juan de la Cruz, Cervantes; Dante, Leopardi, Croce; Goethe, Schiller, Rilke; or perhaps Dostoyevsky, Tolstoy, and Chehov. Learning a new language implies approaching a new world and it inevitably leads to a widening of intellectual experience, since indeed

> all experience is an arch wherethro'
> Gleams that untravell'd world, whose margin fades
> For ever and for ever when I move.

Learning a new language well enough to be able to understand it when heard, to speak it, read it, and write it, is such an arduous discipline that we certainly need some strong urge to drive us on. The four distinct and separable *activities* just mentioned – listening, speaking, reading, and writing –

two *receptive* (listening and reading) and two *expressive* (speaking and writing) – call for constant, preferably daily, exercise. These activities are concerned in varying degrees with four *aspects* of language study – pronunciation, grammar, vocabulary, and idiom. It is profitable to keep these four *activities* and four *aspects* clearly in mind rather than to dwell unduly on the relative values of the spoken and written forms of language, both of which, in broad and general terms, may be said to be equally important in the modern world.

Learning a new language calls for no great originality of mind or critical faculty, but it does demand an eager intellectual curiosity and a constant and lively interest in the endless ways in which human ideas may be expressed. It demands quick observation first of all, reasonable ability to mimic and imitate, good powers of association and generalization, and a retentive memory. It gives healthy exercise to our mental faculties, enlivening attentiveness, quickening alertness, and heightening sensitivity. Does it increase our powers of expression in our mother tongue? Only to a limited extent, perhaps, and this depends very much upon our previous upbringing and training. Certainly it increases our appreciation of the intrinsic qualities of English. Only by having some basis of comparison can we examine our own language from without and gain some notion of its peculiarities. After all,

> What do they know of *English*
> Who only *English* know?

We may, it is true, make equally useful comparisons by studying the great languages of classical antiquity, Greek and Latin. To gain the greatest possible insight into the nature of language itself, we should take up the investigation of at least one non-Indo-European tongue, like Chinese, Tamil, or Malay. We should not allow ourselves to be deterred from attempting to learn anything at all about a language on the ground that we cannot hope to master it completely within the time at our disposal, since in some measure all linguistic knowledge, even that of our native tongue, is imperfect and fragmentary. Nor should we suffer ourselves to be deterred on the ground that the language of our need or choice is difficult. The difficulty may be more apparent than real. Russian presents a serious initial difficulty because it uses Cyrillic and not Latin letters. Hindi is written in the ancient Devanagari characters inherited from Sanskrit: Urdu is recorded in the Arabic alphabet imported by the Muslim Mogul conquerors. Oriental languages seem to be difficult not only in their written forms but also in their morphological and syntactic structures, which differ fundamentally from those of Indo-European. Moreover, as we have already noted, some languages are more highly organized than others and learners therefore require long training to write them correctly and stylistically, while encountering no grievous obstacles in speaking them simply and effectively. This is largely true of French, and for this reason French is not so good a language for children as many educationists would claim. The pronunciation of French is exceptionally difficult for English-speaking children, for whom Spanish or Italian would offer easier beginnings.

From some points of view it might be submitted that hard and easy features, at least in the spoken language, cancel one another out in the end and that therefore all languages may be mastered equally well. Every language, even a quite primitive one, holds within itself a well-adjusted system, complete in itself and adequate for all needs. There is no such thing as an incomplete language in active use.

To master a language we need to make a full and practical study of the four main aspects or features named above – pronunciation, grammar, vocabulary, and idiom. Let us examine each of these in turn in the light of the present-day science of linguistics.

A good pronunciation is acquired by attentive listening to the language well spoken, preferably by native speakers, by full understanding of the movements made by the organs of speech in articulation, and by accurate observation of the parts played by the dynamic prosodemes of length and stress, pitch and juncture. Learning by ear in the country itself may have positive disadvantages at the beginning. Visits abroad should be reserved for a later stage when the pattern of phonemes and prosodemes has already been grasped by systematic study and daily drill. In the meantime, every opportunity should be taken of hearing the language spoken well by educated native speakers who show no eccentricities of utterance and who are willing to speak with a clear and unhurried enunciation. Modern science offers valuable facilities to the learner even in his own home in the form of accessible foreign broadcast programmes which include all the official languages of the United Nations with the sole exception of Chinese. Both the beginner and the more advanced student can derive much profit also from the formal lessons broadcast from British stations, which are generally lively and entertaining, combining genuine instruction with light-hearted pleasantry. From time to time a teacher of genius will send forth innocent vibrations through the ether with such zest and zeal that he succeeds in convincing his hearers that, with only a little bit of extra effort, they can gain access to a veritable El Dorado of linguistic treasures for the first time in their lives, even though, in sober fact, they have been bored to death by French or Spanish or German at school and university for years. Nor should we underrate the usefulness of gramophone records which we can put on at any time we please, even while dressing or doing household chores. Excellent recordings can now be procured of all the better-known languages, consisting of 'situational' descriptions and conversations, clarified by accompanying handbooks with their topical illustrations.

No serious student should ever be content with 'imitated pronunciation', however carefully presented, but he should learn to read and write the symbols of the International Phonetic Association as a matter of course. It is surprising, if not deplorable, that so many British and American publishing firms should rely upon other amateurish methods, even those enterprising publishers who have issued comprehensive series of linguistic manuals that are most useful and competent in other respects. They do so partly for typographical reasons, but partly, too, to avoid frightening the general reader. Henry Cecil Wyld got over this difficulty in *The Universal Dictionary of the English Language* by using two modes of transcription, the first a popular one for the untrained reader and the second a phonetic one for the professional student. In his *English Pronouncing Dictionary*, first published in 1917, Daniel Jones adhered faithfully to broad phonetic or phonemic script from the outset, preferring precision and accuracy to popular approval, and he set the same good example in the London Phonetic Readers which were prepared by members of the Phonetics Department of University College in collaboration with native speakers for French, Italian, Welsh, Danish, Dutch, Czech, Polish, Bengali, Burmese, Cantonese, Punjabi, Sechuana, and other languages. Whatever our purpose may be in approaching the study of a new tongue, we should get at once a clear picture of its phonemic pattern – high, mid, low vowels, front and back; diphthongs and semi-vowels; with lip-rounding and without; bilabial, labiodental, interdental, postdental, palato-alveolar, palatal, velar, and glottal consonants (classified according to place of articulation); plosive, affricate, nasal, lateral, rolled, and fricative consonants (classified according to manner of articulation); consonants voiced and unvoiced. The number and distribution of these sounds or phones will vary in interesting ways from language to language. For instance, most languages have alike six plosives, voiceless and voiced – p, b, t, d, k, g – but some have more fricatives or more affricates than others. Some prefer syllables to be open, ending in a vowel: others have no objection to consonant clusters, but at the beginning of the syllable rather than at the end; or perhaps the other way round; and so forth. Such observations greatly help towards a good general idea of the phonological structure of the language concerned.

No less significant for us in our mastery of pronunciation

are the speech attributes or prosodic features of duration, stress, pitch, and juncture, which endow discourse with life and force. The very word *articulation* 'action or process of jointing' implies not only the enunciation of individual sounds but also the mode of their combination in the flow of speech. Sounds are isolable for the purpose of analysis and description. In living utterance they are joined. Over-insistence on precise production of single phones may therefore do more harm than good. However exactly you may produce them, you will fail to use them effectively and attractively if you have not schooled yourself to set them in motion and link them all together rhythmically and harmoniously. On the other hand, if you have caught the accepted rhythms and harmonies, you may speak agreeably and intelligibly, even though your formulation of individual sounds is imperfect. Good teachers accordingly demand right prosodemes from the beginning and they themselves try hard to set a good example by using correct stresses and tunes in all that they themselves say throughout their courses of instruction.

It is often urged that the learner of a foreign language should imitate the ways of an infant in the gradual acquisition of its mother tongue. The word *infant* 'not speaking' (from the Latin present participle *infant-em*) reflects the significance of speech-learning in the daily life of the child. Indeed, the infant's acquisition of language is a unique process, which has rightly engaged the attention of linguists down the ages. A child has little else to do than babble and chatter, and it receives every encouragement to learn to make the appropriate noises. It has formed no set habits that may interfere with this central activity. Delighting in mimicry and repetition, it proceeds by trial and error to emit more and more precisely the noises heard from adults and it gains glimpses of meaning by associating these noises with things and goings-on in the world around. Such conditions cannot really be reproduced for the grown child or adult who finds himself in a position having by comparison both advantages and disadvantages. His advantages over an infant lie in the fact that he has more mature intelligence and almost limitless powers of symbolization, abstraction, extrapolation, and generalization: he suffers from disadvantages in that he has many other things to do with his time and that his native speech habits conflict continually with the new ones he seeks to acquire. Learning a second language is largely an artificial process and it can never be anything more than a modification, greater or smaller according to circumstances, of the child's more natural way of learning its first language. Intelligibility and reasonable efficiency should be the chief aims of the adult student. He should be well content if he can speak French in Paris or Spanish in Madrid or Italian in Florence with such good enunciation and rhythm that he never has to repeat a sentence. Whether he is ever mistaken for a native – even for a native from some obscure place up country – should not be regarded as a prime consideration.

By the term *grammar* we mean *morphology* and *syntax*, considered in Chapters 5 and 6 of this book, taken together as one combined object of investigation. It is obviously profitable to keep them on different levels for the purpose of linguistic analysis, but we may conveniently bring them together again in practical study where it is our aim to establish a workable theory well supported by abundant examples. Morphology, as we have already observed, includes the study of inflexions, as well as affixation and composition, and it is quite clear that we cannot speak and write grammatically without a complete mastery of these often very complicated modifications. Must we then devote much time to the purely mechanical recitation of paradigms? Certainly we should give some time to parrotlike memorizing, but exactly how much will largely depend upon our mental attitude. Some people derive much pleasure from learning by heart and rattling off the names of the nine muses, the twelve minor prophets of the Old Testament, the twelve Roman Caesars, or the twelve signs of the zodiac; but others find these psittacine enumerations utterly irksome. No German, they say, bothers about committing to memory *der die das, den die das,* etc., and no Frenchman recites aloud *je sais, que je sache,* etc., or *je vais, que j'aille,* etc. That is true enough, but then, as we have just seen, the native learns his mother tongue when young as a full-time job. On the whole it may be said that a certain amount of rote memorizing is essential for speedy progress in learning a highly inflected language, but that it should never be entirely divorced from the study of syntactic structure and function.

The sentence is the unit of speech. In the Second World War, when thousands of British and American servicemen were required to learn foreign languages at top speed in highly intensive courses organized by the London School of Oriental and African Studies and the American Council of Learned Societies, new techniques were devised, which involved little or no repetition of detached declensions and conjugations, but plenty of clause and sentence drill on the basis of 'graded structures'. Courses were arranged not only in French, Spanish, Italian, German, and Russian, but also in Chinese, Japanese, Korean, Thai, Burmese, Fanti, and Hausa. Instructors were supplied with phonographic recordings of graded material accompanied by printed texts. Native teachers were generally available for checking and consultation. Study was concentrated into four months of arduous training given to small groups of ten or twelve throughout the day. This training was directed towards the control of actual situations that had already arisen and that might at any time recur. On the assumption that any proposition in real life is, in the well-known words of Bronislaw Malinowski, 'never detached from the situation in which it is uttered', all sentences were framed in living contexts. Grammar was taught by variation and substitution. For example, in a simple sentence like *Today we meet at three o'clock* there are four variables: the adverb of time, the personal pronoun, the tense-form of the verb, and the numeral denoting the hour. All four may be varied within the same sentence pattern and such variation implies the manipulation of 'formal grammar'. Again, to give another example, I may modify a simple statement like *This road through the mountains is suitable for normal vehicular traffic* by all kinds of parenthical expressions, such as *according to reports just received, so far as we know, to the best of our knowledge, as shown on the map inclosed,* and these may be varied endlessly. In ordinary discourse parenthetical expressions serve as useful conversational lubricants and an easy command of them will stand us in good stead in any language: *to be brief, to cut a long story short, to tell you the truth, of course, naturally, as was to be expected, as you may well believe, you see, between ourselves,* and so on. They give the speaker a little extra time to think without disturbing the main structure of the sentence which remains unimpaired. They are useful adjuncts to the speech of courtesy, and, as Harold Goad has so wisely observed (in *Language in History,* page 12), 'In our intercourse with others the emotional approach is in the first instance most significant. ... There are no more important expressions in any tongue than "Please", "Thank you", "Excuse me", "I am sorry", "Good morning", "Good-bye", "Look out!", "Help! help!", and similar appeals, addresses, warnings, or exclamations, varying not only according to circumstances, but also with the persons addressed.' Every effort should be made, before visiting a foreign country, to learn the forms of salutations and greetings, leave-takings, expressions of thanks, apologies, and acknowledgements of apologies from others. It is surely a mark of social grace to be a good and patient listener, but this does not mean to keep prolonged silence. If someone offers you a piece of information or takes the trouble to warn you of possible difficulties, courtesy demands that you should always make suitable acknowledgement. After all, what would you say in English on such occasions? *I see. Quite. I agree. I am not altogether surprised. How very annoying! Only too true. Is that so? You don't say so! Never mind! Well, well! Thank you so much! Very kind of you to tell me!* Such responses and observations may be merely formal, but they are preferable to grim silence. At least they show that you are paying due attention to the speaker and that you are well disposed towards him. The appropriate expressions can best be gleaned from experience. To win your way through to the attainment of social and conversational ease in a linguistic medium not your own is surely the art of arts.

The fundamental vocabulary required for ordinary purposes is probably similar for most languages. Pronouns, or other forms of address and reference, are utterly essential; and so, too, are prepositions. The numerals – cardinal, ordinal, adverbial, distributive, and fractional – are most important, followed close in order of priority by names of coins and money values, weights and measures, days of the week, months of the year, seasons of the year, and parts of the day. Some fifty or sixty verbs are necessary, and perhaps a slightly smaller number of adverbs and adjectives. Modern phrase-books generally give good selected vocabularies based on statistical computations of word frequency, but very often the long lists of substantives contain much redundant material, such as lists of minerals, metals, animals, birds, fishes, insects, old-fashioned articles of furniture, minor parts of the human anatomy, and obscure diseases, which one might have no occasion to mention from one year's end to another.

Whereas command of sentence structures must be certain and complete for all essential requirements, the building up of a vocabulary can be more casual and incidental. The ready speaker who finds himself at a loss for a word may exercise his skill by substituting an unambiguous periphrasis. If he can increase his working vocabulary by an average of twenty words a day, he may be satisfied. We English-speaking people should appreciate, more fully than we usually do, the unparalleled advantages we enjoy in approaching the vocabulary of a foreign tongue just because our language has been so receptive and hospitable throughout its long history and because it continues to welcome to its store any new word that serves an immediate purpose. We find plenty of Italian and Spanish even in Shakespeare. Every day of our lives, in radio and television programmes, in newspapers and journals, in addresses and lectures, and in conversation with our friends, we hear such French expressions as *bonhomie* 'good nature, geniality, pleasantness of manner', *cachet* 'distinguishing mark of excellence or authenticity', *contretemps* 'hitch in the proceedings, slight mishap', and *dénouement* 'unravelling of a plot, final solution'; or noun phrases with *de* such as *chef d'œuvre*, *coup d'état*, *esprit de corps*, *fin de siècle*, and *pièce de résistance*; or miscellaneous noun phrases like *mise au point* 'focusing, re-statement of facts in their right proportions', *mise en scène* 'setting, scenery, and properties of a play', *pied à terre* 'temporary lodging, somewhere to stay', *tête-à-tête* 'private chat', *tout ensemble* 'general effect', and *un mauvais quart d'heure* 'an unpleasant experience'. We hear a person referring to something quite indescribable as a *je ne sais quoi*, or to something in the best taste as *comme il faut*. If it is self-evident, *cela saute aux yeux*; if it is only too obvious, *cela va sans dire*. We are told to do our duty whatever the consequences, or *fais ce que dois advienne que pourra*; better late than never *mieux vaut tard que jamais*; and *voilà tout* no more need be said! Without opening a grammar book we learn the three inflected forms of the past participle in *chose jugée* 'something quite settled, no longer *sub judice*', *fait accompli* 'thing done beyond recall', and *bien entendu* 'naturally, of course'. We may then be reminded that French *chose jugée* is Spanish *cosa juzgada* where -*ada* is the feminine inflexion of the past participle so familiar to us as children in King Philip's *Armada* of 1588. *Armada* still means 'armed force at sea' or 'fleet' in Spanish, whereas *armata*, its Italian counterpart, may refer to either 'navy' or 'army'. We may compare other familiar words, like Spanish *plaza*, Italian *piazza*, and French *place* in *Place de la Concorde*; or Spanish *pueblo*, used especially of native Indian villages in Mexico and Arizona (as described by D. H. Lawrence in his novels), cognate with Italian *popolo*, French *peuple*, and our own *people*. We recognize many geographical names in the New World and elsewhere as of Spanish origin: *Los Angeles* 'the angels', *Buenos Aires* 'good airs' in the sense of 'fair winds', *Ecuador* (equator), *Trinidad* '(Holy) Trinity', *Tierra del Fuego* 'land of (the) fire', *Rio Grande* (great river) with the attribute following, as so often in the Romance and Celtic languages, to be compared with our *court martial* and *Mount Pleasant*, not to mention other Spanish names like *Sierra Nevada* (in both Spain and California) 'snowed saw' that is 'craggy ridge of mountains covered with snow,' and *Casablanca* (in Morocco) 'white house'.

Besides *piazza* just noted, we hear other architectural terms adoped straight from Italian like *belvedere* 'beautiful view' in the sense of 'look-out tower', *cupola* 'little cup', *pergola*, *portico*, and *rotunda*; terms belonging to art like *madonna*, *pietà*, *virtuoso*, and *vista*; to poetry like *canto* and *stanza*; names of musical instruments like *pianoforte*, *piccolo*, and *violoncello*; of musical compositions like *cantata*, *opera*, *oratorio*, *solo*, and *sonata*; and of musical directions, which, like mathematical and pharmaceutical symbols, are universal – *adagio*, *allegro*, *andante*, *forte*, *piano*, *rallentando*, *staccato*, and so many others.

Whereas the French alluded to the Russian earth satellite launched in 1957 as *bébé lune*, 'baby moon', the British were content to retain the Russian *sputnik* 'fellow-traveller, satellite', a trimorphemic derivative composed of the preposition *s-* 'together, with', the substantive *-put-* 'journey, way', and the agent suffix *-nik* 'doer'. For a long time this characteristic Russian word was on everyone's lips. Other familiar Russian words are *duma* 'deliberative assembly', *samovar* 'self-boiler' in the sense of 'tea-urn', *soviet* 'council, committee', *troika* 'three-horse sledge or carriage', and *vodka* 'dear little water', diminutive form of *voda*.

From Arabic we have borrowed the greatest number of eastern loan-words, such as *alcohol*, *alembic*, *algebra*, *alkali*, *almanac*, *azimuth*, *cipher*, *nadir*, *zenith*, and *zero*. As we have already had occasion to note (page 115), we could learn very much about Arabic morphology by comparing the well-known forms *salaam* (Arabic *salam*), *Islam*, and *Muslim*. Even to Chinese the gate stands for us just a little ajar. We readily recall from our schooldays names like *Hwang Ho* 'yellow river' and *Hwang Hai* 'yellow sea'. We can easily deduce the designations of the four compass directions if we bear in mind that the native forms of Peking and Nanking, namely *pek king* and *nan king*, mean 'north capital' and 'south capital'; while *Kwang-si* and *Kwang-tung* signify 'spacious west' and 'spacious east'. A Chinese would always say *nan, pek, si, tung* 'south, north, west, east', an order fixed for him by tradition from ancient times. *Kuomintang* 'people's nationalist party' is a recent trimorphemic compound from *kuo* 'kingdom, nation', *min* 'people', and *tang* 'party'. Geographers now speak of a *tsunami* or 'storm wave' (Japanese) produced by submarine earthquake or volcanic eruption. How interesting it is, and how evocative of the joy of recognition, to detect a Hebrew plural in *cherubim* and *seraphim*, an Arabic plural in *fellaheen*, a French diminutive in *motet*, a Spanish diminutive in *peccadillo*, an Italian superlative in *fortissimo* and *pianissimo*, and a Russian comparative in *Bolshevik* and *Menshevik*, to mention no others!

Languages vary considerably in their use of idioms or 'private turns of phrase' – *idiotisms* as they were called in seventeenth-century English, French *idiotismes*, German *Spracheigentümlichkeiten* 'language peculiarities'. Idioms are forms of expression approved by usage, but often ungrammatical and illogical. Some have been inherited from older periods of the language, like *to take to wife*, where *to* retains its old meaning of 'as, in the capacity of', as also in *to call to witness*. Others arise from contamination of two syntactic structures, as when *Don't cough if you can help it* becomes associated with *Don't cough more than you must* and so produces *Don't cough more than you can help*. Others again result from ellipsis of some phrase or clause, however unmindful the speaker may be of anything omitted or suppressed, as when he says that the lawns in Lakeland are *as green as green*, that is 'as green as the colour green can ever be'; or that his neighbours are all *well to do*, that is 'well able to do for themselves in the world'; or that someone *gave him to understand*, that is 'gave him information to lead him to understand'. Many idioms have their beginnings in picturesque metaphors, like *to be at a loose end* (said of a horse whose tether has broken or slipped) or *to play to the gallery* (said of an actor who seeks to win popular applause). Many idioms, too, express a different way of viewing a situation, as when the French ask *Depuis quand demeurez-vous à Paris?* 'Since when do you dwell at Paris? rather than 'How long have you been living in Paris?'; or when they say *Vous avez raison* 'You have reason' instead of 'You are right'. They ask *Qu'est-ce que cela fait?* 'What is it that that does?' whereas we say 'What does it matter?' where our denominative verb *matter* is highly idiomatic. I have often wondered why the French say *C'est bien aimable à vous* 'very kind *to* you' and not '*of* you', but perhaps they are here more logical than we are *after all* (another elliptic idiom for 'after all has been said') since *à vous* means 'on your side, on your part'.

Obviously you must take idioms as separate linguistic units and learn them as distinct entities. It is useful to regard them as part of your receptive equipment for listening and reading, not as absolutely necessary for your expressive activities in speaking and writing. Ineluctably your receptive knowledge will always surpass your expressive faculty. It follows that in listening and reading you should do your utmost to appreciate and understand every conceivable kind of idiom, but in speaking and writing you should be somewhat cautious. Foreign idioms may be very tricky in use. You should aim, first of all, at mastering a sound, straightforward, all-purpose style. In friendly conversation and intimate correspondence, perhaps, you may 'show off' your knowledge of idiom, but in formal discussions and conferences you should make it your first aim to state what you have to say simply and effectively, and then, if required to do so by the secretary, to write an informative summary without effort as a matter of course. It is surely not unreasonable to hope that the day is not far distant when, by virtue of improved techniques, all professional students, including scientists and technologists, will be able to speak and write at least one second language with competence and clarity.

CHAPTER 10

COMPARATIVE LINGUISTICS

ANYONE who has taken the trouble to master a foreign language will naturally find himself comparing that language with his own in the range of its vocabulary, in the diversity of its sounds, in the variety of its inflexions, in the complexity of its compound words, in the structure of its sentences, and in many other ways. For a very long time in the history of linguistics men were content to compare merely the written forms of words. Indeed, it would be hardly an exaggeration to say that little progress was made in comparative philology from Pāṇini's treatise on Sanskrit or Old Indian grammar, which he compiled some time towards the end of the fourth century before Christ, to Friedrich von Schlegel's monograph on a similar theme, namely 'On the Language and Wisdom of the Indians' (*Über die Sprache und Weisheit der Indier*), written over two thousand years later. Now Pāṇini proceeded on the rational assumption that the verbal root was the basis of Sanskrit speech, upon which nouns and adjectives were built by means of suffixes. His painstaking description of the sacred language of India was more detailed and discriminating than any other attempted in antiquity. It was more scientific than anything produced by the Greeks, who had already shown considerable interest in the relation of language to logic and philosophy. Plato (427–347 B.C.) had touched upon the origins of words in his *Cratylus*, and Aristotle (384–322 B.C.) had gone much further than his master in his well-known tripartition of words on a logical basis into *onómata* 'nouns', *rhḗmata* 'verbs', and *súndesmoi* 'conjunctions' (in a wide sense including what we now call 'functors', 'operators', or 'structure-words'). Richly endowed with the gift of intellectual curiosity, the Greeks had a way of wondering at things that other people took for granted.

Few of them, however, studied any other form of speech than their own and they were all too prone to assume that the structure of their own language embodied the universal shapes of human thought on a background of cosmic order. Later the Alexandrians, Dionysius Thrax in the first century B.C. and Apollonius Dyscolus in the second century of our era, wrote competent grammars that came to be well known and used throughout the Greek-speaking lands of the Mediterranean. Meantime Roman grammarians like Varro, who dedicated his *De Lingua Latina* to Cicero, and Quintilian, who taught Pliny the Younger, had followed Greek traditions fairly closely. They were imitated in their turn by Donatus in the fourth century and by Priscian in the sixth. Greek names of word-classes or parts of speech were translated into Latin and it was in their Latin forms that they were subsequently adopted by the grammarians of medieval and modern Europe. Priscian's complete grammar, of which over a thousand manuscripts survive, was a favourite textbook throughout the Middle Ages. It probably came into the hands of the first English grammarian, Ælfric, Abbot of Eynsham, who played the scholar's part in that Benedictine revival of learning in tenth-century Wessex which we usually associate with the names of Dunstan, Oswald, and Æthelwold. Priscian provided a model for Alexander de Villa Dei (that is, of Villedieu in Normandy) who put together the comprehensive school-book *Doctrinale Puerorum* at the close of the twelfth century, and he also influenced Antoine Arnauld and the other brothers of Port Royal des Champs when they came to prepare their *Grammaire générale et raisonnée* in the assured belief that the Latin tongue embodied in itself canons of logic which were universally valid and that Latin grammar was grammar proper. Such views prevailed well into the nineteenth century and they are by no means without adherents even today.

The dawn of modern linguistics came late in the eighteenth century and, most appropriately, it came as the immediate result of the rediscovery of the language of Pāṇini. On 27 September 1786, Sir William Jones (1746–94), Chief Justice at Fort William in Bengal, communicated his third paper to the Asiatic Society at Calcutta, which contained the famous declaration: 'The Sanscrit language, whatever be its antiquity, is of a wonderful structure; more perfect than the Greek, more copious than the Latin, and more exquisitely refined than either; yet bearing to both of them a stronger affinity, both in the roots of verbs and in the forms of grammar, than could possibly have been produced by accident; so strong, indeed, that no philologer could examine all three without believing them to have sprung from some common source which, perhaps, no longer exists. There is a similar reason, though not quite so forcible, for supposing that both the Gothick and the Celtick, though blended with a very different idiom, had the same origin with the Sanscrit; and the old Persian might be added to the same family, if this were the place for discussing any question concerning the antiquities of Persia.' Thus in these oft-quoted sentences Sir William announced clearly and unequivocally the relationship between three of the great languages of antiquity – Sanskrit, Greek, and Latin – and at the same time he anticipated the reconstruction of that 'common source which, perhaps, no longer exists' – the parent Indo-European language itself. By 'Gothick' he meant Teutonic or Germanic. His 'not quite so forcible' reasons for admitting the latter to full relationship were soon strengthened, but his hesitation to recognize Celtic as a genuine member was long reflected in the term *Indo-Germanic* or *Indogermanisch* which was first used by those philologists who continued to regard Indian and Germanic as the extreme east and west branches of the family.

Sir William's discovery was not wholly new. Even in the sixteenth century an Italian missionary, Filippo Sassetti, had noted the correspondence between the Italian numerals from six to nine *sei, sette, otto, nove* and their Sanskrit counterparts *ṣáṣ, saptá, aṣṭá, náva*, and other missionaries managed to acquire a good working knowledge of Sanskrit. In 1768 the French Father Cœurdoux compared words like *dàna-* 'gift' and *vidhávā* 'widow' with Latin *dōnum* and *vidua*.

Alexander Hamilton, who had earlier been a member of the Asiatic Society at Calcutta, found himself interned in Paris after the Napoleonic War, and he there spent his time listing the manuscripts in the national library and teaching Friedrich von Schlegel, the author of the above-mentioned treatise 'On the Language and Wisdom of the Indians' which appeared in 1808.

Comparative studies now made rapid progress. Only six years later, in 1814, the Danish scholar Rasmus Christian Rask (1787–1832) finished his *Investigation into the Origin of the Old Norse or Icelandic Language* which he wrote for a prize competition organized by the Danish Academy of Science at Copenhagen. This remarkable essay, published in 1818, really offered a comparative Indo-European grammar in embryo. It may be taken as a landmark in the recent history of linguistics which, for our present purpose, we may conveniently divide into three periods: first, from Rask to the Neo-grammarians; second, from Brugmann to Bloomfield; and third, from Bloomfield to the present day.

Rask's scheme of linguistic affinities was surprisingly accurate and he set an excellent example to future linguists by adducing illustrative evidence at every step. In a general way, if somewhat incompletely, he here formulated that law of the Germanic consonant shift by which the original voiceless plosives *p t k* became the voiceless fricatives *f θ h*; the voiced plosives *b d g* became unvoiced to *p t k*; and the aspirated voiced plosives *bh dh gh* became unaspirated to *b d g*. Thus, limiting our examples to English, we may compare Latin-derived *p*aternal, *t*rinity, and *c*entury with native *f*atherly, *th*ree, and *h*undred; rever*b*erate, cor*d*ial, and a*g*riculture with war*p*, hear*t*y, and a*c*re; *f*raternal (Latin *f*rāter from **bh*rātar), *r*u*f*ous (Latin rūfus from **rudh*os), and *h*ost (Latin *h*ostis from **gh*ostis) with *b*rotherly, re*d*, and *g*uest. Being a Dane, Rask applied his brilliant discovery mainly to the Scandinavian languages. It was left to his German contemporary Jakob Grimm (1787–1863) to extend these principles to the Germanic languages as a whole, formulating the law in wider terms in the second edition of his *Deutsche Grammatik* in 1822. He was here using the epithet *deutsch*, modern 'German', in the sense of 'Teutonic' or 'Germanic'. His book, therefore, presented a comparative grammar of Gothic, Scandinavian, English, Frisian, and Dutch as well as German. This particular series of changes, which took place in Common Germanic from about 600 to 100 B.C., came to be known as *die erste Lautverschiebung* 'the first sound-shifting' in order to distinguish it from *die zweite Lautverschiebung* which affected Old High German alone much later, probably from about 600 to 800 A.D. This was a further modification of the second stage of the Germanic shift just mentioned by which *b d g* were unvoiced to *p t k*. Initially, and medially after consonants, these resultant voiceless plosives *p t k* became *pf ts* (now written *z*) and *kh* (now written *k* and so neutralized), thus giving Modern German *Pf*und, *Pf*effer, *Pf*eife, *Pf*laume, and *Pf*licht 'duty' for English *p*ound, *p*epper, *p*ipe, *p*lum, and *p*light; *Z*ahl, *Z*agel, *Z*ahn, *z*wei, *z*wanzig, and *z*wölf for English *t*ale (formerly 'number' as in 'Every shepherd tells his tale' Milton *L'Allegro* 67), *t*ail, *t*ooth, *t*wo, *t*wenty, and *t*welve; *K*alb, *k*alt, *K*orn, *K*inn, and *K*irche for English *c*alf, *c*old, *c*orn, *ch*in, and *ch*urch. After vowels, however, these same voiceless plosives *p t k* became *ff zz* (now written *ss*) and *hh* (now written *ch*), thus giving Modern German o*ff*en, Se*ss*el, and Zei*ch*en for English o*p*en, se*tt*le 'bench', and to*k*en.

Grimm's Law and the High German Consonant Shift, as we now usually call these changes, were soon confirmed by later investigators, especially Franz Bopp (1791–1867) and August Friedrich Pott (1802–87). In 1833 Bopp began to publish a comprehensive treatise on Indo-European grammar and in the same year Pott issued the opening instalment of his *Etymological Investigations*. The etymology of a speech-form is simply its 'true' history, ascertained by comparing its oldest recorded forms with those in related languages and by 'reconstructing' the parent form on the basis of that comparison. Thus English *mother* appears as *mōdor* in *Beowulf* and as *mōðer* or *mōðir* in the Old Norse sagas. It corresponds to Old Frisian *mōder*, Old Saxon *mōdar*, and Old High German *muoter*. All these forms together point back unmistakably to a Common Germanic word **mōder* (marked thus with a star or asterisk to denote that it is nowhere actually recorded). This Common Germanic form is in its turn related to or cognate with Sanskrit *mātar*, Greek *mḗtēr*, and Latin *māter*, which point back conclusively to a Proto-Indo-European **māter-*. Beyond or behind this form, to be sure, we pass into the more shadowy realm of conjecture, but we may fairly surmise that *ma*, like *pa* and *ba*, and also like their doubled or reduplicated forms *mama*, *papa*, and *baba*, had its origin in the easiest of all syllables that might be babbled by a toothless child. All three simple forms, *ma*, *pa*, and *ba*, consist of a bilabial plosive consonant, articulated by the lips alone, followed by that low back vowel sound made with the tongue lying as flat and lax as possible. Pronounced with level tone, *ma* means 'mother' in Chinese. *Ma* and *pa* seem to have the stable significations 'mother' and 'father', but *ba* has shown some interesting semantic shifts. For instance, the reduplicated form *baba* gives our *babe*, the only form in the King James Bible (as in 'Out of the mouth of babes and sucklings hast thou ordained strength', Psalm 8:2): modern *baby* is a diminutive. Now Italian *babbo*, a pet-form used much like our 'daddy', is threatening to supersede *padre* altogether in familiar conversation, whereas Spanish *padre* (whence our *padre* 'chaplain, clergyman') knows no such rival. In Old Church Slavonic *baba* changed its sex-reference and became the regular word for 'grandmother', whence, by the addition of diverse hypocoristic suffixes, have evolved Russian *babuška*, Polish *babka*, and Czech *babička*. It is clear that in the parent language the words for 'father' and 'mother' were both formed by suffixing to *pā-* and *mā-* the contrasting element *-ter* denoting 'the other member of the pair', as in Latin al*ter* ego 'one's other self', literally 'second I', and as in dex*ter* and sinis*ter* 'right' and 'left'. Very early the stress in *'pā-ter* was shifted to the second syllable with consequential reduction of the root vowel to *pə'ter*. That is why the forms for 'father' and 'mother' no longer rhymed in the recorded languages of antiquity: Sanskrit *pitar-* but *mātar-*, Greek *patèr* but *mèter*, Latin *pater* but *māter*. That is why, too, they no longer rhymed in Old English *fæder* and *mōdor*, and why they do not rhyme in present-day English or in Swedish and Danish *fader* and *moder*, Dutch *vader* and *moeder*, or German *Vater* and *Mutter*. Curiously enough, this difference has been levelled out in the Romance languages as the outcome of that prolongation of the short vowels in the open stressed syllables of disyllabic words in fourth-century Latin by which *pater* became *pāter* and so rhymed once more with *māter*, and thus we have today French *père* and *mère*, Spanish and Italian *padre* and *madre*.

We can confidently reconstruct the words in the parent language for 'brother' and 'sister' as **bhrāter* and **swesor*. In the former the first element *bhrā-* was a gradational variant of the verbal root **bher-* 'to bear, carry', the brother being presumably the 'sustainer' or 'protector' of his sisters in that nomadic society. The second morpheme was, of course, the same *-ter* as in **pā-ter* and **mā-ter* discussed above. In **swe-sor* the first component was the reflexive element meaning 'one's own' and the second one signified 'female', seen also in Latin *uxor* (whence our *uxorious*) or *uk-sor* 'wife'. Thence derived by explicable sound-changes Common Germanic **brōper* and **swestr*, Old English *brōðor* and *sweostor*, Modern English *brother* and *sister*, the latter by way of Scandinavian. Thence, too, have derived Sanskrit *bhrātar-* and *svasar-*, Latin *frāter* and *soror*, but not Greek: Swedish *broder* and *syster*, Dutch *broeder* and *zuster*, German *Bruder* and *Schwester*, Russian *brat* and *sestra*, but not Spanish. It so happens that both Greek and Spanish have abandoned inherited forms in favour of the defining attributes **hadelphos* and **ghermanos* with which they came to be early associated. Greek *adelphós phràtēr* signified 'brother of the same womb' (older *ha-delphos*), but the attribute then came to be used alone and *phràtēr* survived only in the sense of 'member of a clan'. The feminine attribute *adelphê* likewise came to signify 'sister'. The *Adelphi* Terrace in London was built by the brothers Robert and James Adam in 1770, and *Philadelphia*, capital of Pennsylvania and third city in the United States, was intended by its Puritan founders to be an abode of 'brotherly love' (*Epistle to the Hebrews* xiii:1). Similarly Spanish has substituted *hermano* 'brother' and *hermana* 'sister' from Latin *germānus* 'genuine, of the same germ' (as in our own legal expressions *brother-* and *sister-german*) for the old inherited forms *fradre* and *soror*. French shows the development of the traditional forms into *frère and sœur*, whereas Italian prefers to use the euphonious diminutives *fratello* and *sorella*.

These short etymological excursions may suffice to show how alluring such studies can be. It would be too much to say that all this information may be gleaned from the writings of Bopp, Pott, and the other mid-nineteenth-century philologists. After all, they made many mistakes. Bopp was obsessed with the fallacious notion that every verb-form contained within it the morpheme 'to be'. Pott sometimes took a breezy view of etymologizing, but he was seldom so daring in his reconstruction of difficult forms as his younger contemporary, August Schleicher of Prague (1823–68). Schleicher's 'Compendium of the Comparative Grammar of the Indo-European Languages' appeared in 1861 and achieved instant recognition. He undoubtedly relied too exclusively upon Sanskrit and upon what he regarded as the impressive simplicity of the parent language. His work was important because it was much used by the so-called Junggrammatiker or Neo-grammarians who made such notable advances in the eighteen-seventies.

The regularity of phonemic changes caught the imagination of men at this time. Exceptions to general changes taking place in the speech of a whole community were thought to be only apparent. It was incumbent upon trained linguists to find rational explanations for these apparent exceptions. Such a rational explanation of a seeming irregularity in the development of the original voiceless plosives *p t k* into Sanskrit and Greek was offered by a professional mathematician, Hermann Grassmann of Stettin, in 1862. According to Grassmann's Law of the dissimilation of aspirates, the speakers of these ancient languages could not tolerate the aspirated plosives *ph th kh* at the beginning of two successive syllables. Wherever such a sequence of sounds developed, they just de-aspirated one of them, generally the first. Thus, for example, the Greek verb 'to run' was not *thrékhein* but *trékhein*, although its aorist was *éthreksa* (side by side with suppletive *édramon*). We ourselves now say *trichology* 'study of the hair' and *trichopathy* 'treatment of the diseases of the hair', and not *thrichology* and *thrichopathy*, because, although the Greek nominative was *thríks* 'hair', the genitive was *trichós*. What more do you want? Grassmann's Law cannot fail to warm the heart of every true-born philologist.

Not many years later, in 1875, a rational explanation was found for a whole series of apparent exceptions to Grimm's Law by Karl Verner of Copenhagen (1846–96). In his famous article entitled 'An Exception to the First Soundshifting' (*Eine Ausnahme der ersten Lautverschiebung*) published in 1877, Verner showed that the voiceless fricatives *f θ h*, which developed from original *p t k* in the first stage of Grimm's Law, became voiced to *v ð g* when the stress in Indo-European did not immediately precede them, and that the unshifted sibilant *s* was voiced to *z*. In Old English ð was further modified to *d*, and *z* to *r*. Whereas **'bhrāter* became Old English *brōðor* by Grimm's Law, **pə'ter* became *fæder* in accordance with Verner's Law. Such divergences were most apparent in the tense-forms of strong verbs which have been mostly levelled out again by the operation of analogy in the later history of English, but we may still detect interesting survivals in such contrasted forms as dea*th*: dea*d*, see*the*: so*dd*en, wa*s*: we*r*e, ri*s*e, and lo*s*e: (for)lo*r*n.

The Junggrammatiker – August Leskien, Karl Brugmann, Hermann Osthoff, Berthold Delbrück, Hermann Paul, and others – opened our second period of linguistic history in the 1870s. August Leskien of Leipzig (1840–1916) was at this time inaugurating a new era in Slavonic scholarship. His university colleague Karl Brugmann (1849–1919) was collaborating with Berthold Delbrück of Jena (1842–1922) in the production of an ambitious 'Outline of the Comparative Grammar of the Indogermanic Languages' (*Grundriss der vergleichenden Grammatik der indogermanischen Sprachen*) whose first edition eventually appeared in several volumes from 1886 to 1900 and whose second edition (1897–1916) is still valid for general principles. Hermann Paul of Munich (1846–1921) was writing his 'Principles of Linguistic History' (*Prinzipien der Sprachgeschichte*) which subsequently appeared in five editions from 1880 to 1920, each one showing some advance on its predecessor. In some ways, however, the most enterprising and forward-looking of all the linguists at work in the seventies was a young student named Ferdinand de Saussure (1857–1913) who made a remarkable contribution to our knowledge of Indo-European ablaut in 1878 at the early age of twenty-one. Strangely enough, after this brilliant start, he published very little, but he taught with distinction at Paris and Geneva and his invigorating and provocative lectures on general linguistics were recorded and published post-humously in Paris in 1916 under the title *Cours de linguistique générale* by two of his pupils, Charles Bally and Albert Sechehaye. This book has had a powerful and salutary influence on the range and direction of European linguistics ever since, although it must be admitted that de Saussure's insistence on a rigid distinction between *langue* (language as a traditional structure or code of signals) and *parole* (speech as a means of communication in daily use) is no longer everywhere in favour.

De Saussure certainly adopted a new attitude to speech and language. He showed that speech is not merely a chain of phonemes and morphemes following one another in linear sequence like beads on a string. He demonstrated that language is a structure with different levels. One modification of part of the structure immediately affected the whole. A linguistic change was like a move in a game of chess. De Saussure included among his pupils two good men – Charles

Bally (1865–1947), already mentioned, and Antoine Meillet (1866–1936). Bally continued his master's teaching at Geneva, expounding stylistics as a science and defining the tasks and functions of descriptive or synchronic linguistics. Meillet taught in Paris and distinguished himself in many fields, including Greek, Latin, Tokharian, Germanic, and Slavonic. Endowed with the gift of lucid exposition, Meillet became a prolific writer. In addition to many other achievements, he corrected and supplemented Brugmann's work on Indo-European comparative philology and he provided students with admirable introductions to Greek, Armenian, Persian, and Common Slavonic. 'A language,' he averred (in his review of the third edition of Michel Bréal's *Essai de Sémantique* contributed to *Année sociologique* 8 (1903–4) (page 641), 'forms a very delicate and complicated system in which everything is held together rigorously and which does not allow arbitrary and capricious changes ...' (... *un langage forme un système très délicat et très compliqué où tout se tient rigoureusement et qui n'admet pas de modifications arbitraires et capricieuses* ...). This notion of language as *un système* or *un ensemble où tout se tient* was expressed elsewhere in Meillet's books and it would be no exaggeration to say that this simple statement, often quoted at congresses and in periodicals, has become the watchword of twentieth-century structuralists.

Meantime linguistic studies had made great strides in the New World where William Dwight Whitney had anticipated Paul's *Prinzipien* by some thirteen years when he published his *Language and the Study of Language* in 1867. American linguists were not slow to realize that a superabundance of accessible material lay just beyond their thresholds in the unrecorded languages of Red Indian aborigines. From first-hand observation and analysis of Amerindian tongues whose structural systems were unlike Indo-European and also unlike one another, field-workers like Franz Boas (1858–1942), Edward Sapir (1884–1939), and Leonard Bloomfield (1887–1949) collected valuable material and acquired unique experience. Throughout his long life Boas gathered facts about a very wide range of aboriginal dialects. Sapir specialized in that Pacific dialect of Athapaskan which is still spoken in Oregon and California. Bloomfield worked intensively on Menomini, a branch of Central Algonquian surviving in Wisconsin and around the Great Lakes; he also mastered Tagalog, now the official language of the Philippine Islands. Thus these pioneers trained themselves and their pupils to think empirically and to make patient analysis of speech-systems that had served whole communities long and well but had never been committed to any form of writing. Both Sapir and Bloomfield wrote books on language in general. Sapir's short but profound study appeared in 1921 and Bloomfield's comprehensive treatise was given to the world in 1933 – just one third of the way through this century of rapid change. This period was indeed fruitful in the production of quite outstanding studies in general linguistics by Otto Jespersen of Copenhagen, Eduard Sievers of Leipzig, as well as Henri Delacroix and Joseph Vendryès of Paris. Bloomfield's *Language* may well be regarded as opening the third period in our historic sketch because it has probably had a more powerful influence on the direction of linguistic studies than any other single book published in this century. It has served as the starting-point for almost all work done since 1933.

Bloomfield was a behaviourist. His professed disciples in America – Bloch, Trager, Harris, Hoijer, and Hockett – have all continued to work empirically in non-Indo-European fields and to improve the techniques of linguistic analysis. Just at the time when Bloomfield was writing *Language*, the principle of the phoneme was taking shape. Notable contributions to this important phonological theory were being made by men as widely separated geographically as Sapir and Bloomfield in North America, Trubetzkoy and Jakobson in Central Europe, and Yuen Ren Chao in China. The phoneme proved itself a fruitful topic for discussion at the first and second International Congresses of Linguists meeting at The Hague in 1928 and at Geneva in 1932. It has become indispensable in devising techniques of comparison and analysis for those languages which have no history, no written document of the past, and even no script. Different schools of thought now emphasize different aspects of general linguistics but in the second half of the twentieth century they are all agreed in regarding each individual language as a complete structure or system amenable to analysis and they are all engaged in attempting to improve the techniques of that analysis.

For anyone who knows two foreign languages fairly well it is surely a stimulating and profitable exercise to spend a few hours comparing them structurally along the lines suggested by recent text-books of applied linguistics. We may, for example, compare and contrast the phonological patterns of French and German, each with its thirty-five or so phonemes, alike in number but unlike in quality. French has four nasal vowels which function as distinctive phonemes, but it shows no phonemic opposition between vowels long and short. In final stressed syllables all four nasal vowels (as in *un bon vin blanc* 'a good white wine') and two buccal vowels [ø] and [o] (as in *deux mots* 'two words') are long. The remaining vowels are long only if the final consonant is *j*, *r*, *v*, *vr*, *z*, or ʒ (as in *feuille* [fœ:j] 'leaf', *sœur* [sœ:r] 'sister', *preuve* [prœ:v] 'proof', *suivre* [sɥi:vr] 'to follow', *aise* [ɛ:z] 'ease', and *rouge* [ru:ʒ] 'red'. In German, as in English, long and short vowels – there are just eight of each – constitute distinct phonemes, and therefore differences in length are far greater than in French. We have only to compare, say, German *Beet* 'flower-bed' with *Bett* 'bed', *kam* 'came' with *Kamm* 'comb', *Sohn* 'son' with *Sonne* 'sun', or *Fuss* 'foot' with *Nuss* 'nut'. Moreover, whereas in French the vowel-sound standing final in a monosyllable must be short, as in *beau* [bo] 'beautiful', *cou* [ku] 'neck' and *thé* [te] 'tea'; in German it must be long in this position as in *roh* [ro:] 'raw', *Kuh* [ku:] 'cow' and *Tee* [te:] 'tea'. Apart from *ja*, *nu*, and *da*, all German monosyllables end in long vowels, diphthongs, consonants, and consonant clusters, but they do not end in short vowels. German has just three diphthongs as phonemes, as in *Bein* [bain] 'bone', *Baum* [baum] 'tree', and *Bäume* [bɔymə] 'trees'; whereas French has none. A Frenchman may, it is true, make diphthong sounds in rapid speech as when he pronounces *paysan* 'peasant' as [peizɑ̃], or *aérer* 'to ventilate' as [aere], or *réussir* 'to succeed' as [reysir]. Old French had falling diphthongs which later became rising, with the almost inevitable consequence (as in Italian) that the first element has become a semi-vowel as in *roi* [rwa] 'king', *ouaille* [wɑj] 'sheep', and *bien* [bjɛ̃] 'well'. Henry Sweet once observed that, if English had shed so many of its final consonants in pronunciation as French has, many utterances would now be completely unintelligible. Listen carefully to people talking French and notice how the syllable-structures are essentially vocalic. Most syllables, in fact, end in vowels or single consonants: *ami* [ami] 'friend', *eau* [o] 'water', *yeux* [jø] 'eyes', *œuf* [œf] 'egg'. In German syllables often begin with three consonants (as in *Strahl* [ʃtrɑ:l] 'ray') and end with four (as in *Herbst* [hɛrbst] 'autumn'). A limited number of technical and learned words like *stratégique* and *strophe* do, in fact, begin with *str-* in French, but they are late borrowings from Latin and Greek. Had they been borrowed sufficiently early to have conformed to the phonemic pattern of French, they would surely have been pronounced with a prosthetic vowel like *estreindre* 'to embrace' from Latin *stringere* or *estroit* 'narrow' from Latin *strictus*, now duly simplified to *étreindre* and *étroit*.

French and German present a contrast in their use of stress. Indeed, in this respect French stands alone. Whereas Spanish and Italian generally carry the main lexical stress on the penultimate or next-last syllable, French bears a light stress, accompanied by a slight rise in pitch, on the last syllable of all in word, word-group, and sentence. German carries a much more forceful stress and it resembles English and Dutch in bearing stress on various syllables in word and phrase. In exceptional circumstances a Frenchman may use forceful stress to express strong emotion and he may then bring it to bear on an earlier syllable in the word: 'A 'bominable!', he may say, or even "Abominable!', or 'Une explosion 'formidable!', but French shows no functional shifting of stress as English does in moving it from *per'fect* verb to *'perfect* adjective, or from *in'sult* verb to *'insult* noun; or as German does in moving it from *um'gehen* 'to avoid' with inseparable prefix to *'umgehen* 'to go around' with separable prefix, or from *unter'halten* 'to entertain' to *'unterhalten* 'to hold under'.

It is now generally agreed among linguists that the word is no more than a conventional or arbitrary segment of utterance and that as a significant unit it is not so structurally important as the morpheme. At the same time the word is more self-contained and autonomous in some languages than in others and that is certainly true of German as compared with French. That is one reason why syllabic liaison is unknown in German but has become so striking a feature of spoken French. A second reason *saute aux yeux* 'strikes us at once': it is that final consonants are invariably articulated in German but seldom pronounced in French. Thus phrases and breath-groups in French come to be linked closely together by the restoration before vowels of consonant-sounds otherwise mute: for instance, linking *z* in *chez autrui, deux heures, pas aujourd'hui*; linking *s* in *vers elle, toujours actif*; linking *t* in *ils sont allemands*; and linking *n* in *bien écrit*, as distinct from *chez moi, deux fois, pas demain; vers lui, toujours paresseux; ils sont français*; and *bien dit*.

French differs from German in retaining no case-flexion for nouns, adjectives, and articles, although it preserved the distinction between *cas sujet* and *cas régime* much longer than the other neo-Latin tongues, and although it still keeps such interesting doublets as *on* from the Latin nominative *homo* beside *homme* from the accusative *hominem*, and *pâtre* from *pastor* beside *pasteur* from *pastorem*. French shows no internal vowel-modifications whether *Umlaute* like German *das Haus*: *die Häuser*, or *Ablaute* like *singen, sang, gesungen*. This lack of regular modifications in French is a noteworthy structural difference because it blurs the patterning of forms semantically related. We may compare German *finden* 'to find': *Fund* 'discovery', *singen* 'to sing': *Sang* 'song', and *kneifen* 'to pinch': *Kniff* 'pinch', which show regular and predictable ablaut relationships, with French *acheter* 'to buy': *achat* 'purchase' (*faire des achats* 'to go shopping'), *jouer* 'to play': *jeu* 'game' (*jouer gros jeu* 'to play for high stakes'), *soigner* 'to take care of': *soin* 'care, attention', where the vocalic alternations vary from one pair of forms to another.

Prefixes and suffixes perform similar functions in both languages. The former limit the meanings of root elements without affecting syntactic relations, whereas the latter tend to affect these relations and to determine word-class. We may equate, morpheme for morpheme, French *sur-hum-ain* with German *über-mensch-lich*, and French *in-hum-an-ité* with German *Un-mensch-lich-keit*. French makes far less use of affixation and composition than German does, and even less than do its sister-languages Spanish and Italian. Take, for instance, the Latin suffix *-issimus* forming the superlative degree of adjectives. In Spanish it survives as *-ísimo* and in Italian as *-issimo*, but in French (apart from rare forms like *richissime*) it has disappeared. Spanish *fortísimo* 'strongest' is Italian *fortissimo* (abbreviated to *ff* as a musical direction), but in French we can say only *le plus fort*.

In its employment of diminutive and agent suffixes French shows much greater variety than German. Each substantive in French seems to have its own unforeseeable diminutive suffix which a foreigner must learn in order to speak correctly: *jardin-et* 'little garden', *fort-in* 'small fort', *mon frér-ot* 'my little brother', *négr-illon* 'negro-boy', and so on. In German the suffixes *-chen* and *-lein* may be added to any noun you like, even if the diminutive so formed is not listed in any dictionary. They are general-purpose living suffixes. Instead of *kleine Feder* 'little feather' you may say either *Federchen* or *Federlein* for 'featherlet'. In German, as in Greek, all diminutives are neuter: *die Frau* 'the (married) woman', *das Fräulein* 'the young (unmarried) woman'. In French, as in Latin, diminutives follow the genders of their originals: *le tour* 'the turn', *le touret* 'the spinning-wheel'; *la tour* 'the tower', *la tourelle* 'the turret'. Again, whereas in French the forms of the agent suffix are many and various: *écrivain* 'writer', *fabricant* 'manufacturer', *forgeron* 'blacksmith', *juge* 'judge', *locataire* 'tenant', *peintre* 'painter', *tisserand* 'weaver', and so on, in German the common agent suffix is *-er*, corresponding to French *-eur*. Curiously enough, French *friseur* 'curler' is now the regular word in German for the 'hairdresser' who is *le coiffeur* in French. Our own *connoisseur*, the 'expert judge' who is a 'knowing' fellow, came into English in the eighteenth century and has retained its older spelling, while in French it has been modernized to *connaisseur* [kɔnɛsœr]. Before the invention of the internal combustion engine a *chauffeur* was a 'stoker' or 'fireman', literally 'one who heats' (Latin *cale-facere* 'to make hot'), but today the word *chauffeur* in the sense of 'car-driver' is in general use throughout the world. It has, however, only recently assumed this international use in French itself and some purists still insist on the use of *mécanicien* in this sense.

As we pass from the morphological process of affixation to that of composition, we observe a yet more striking contrast between the two languages. French seems reluctant to form new compounds and therefore has recourse to various kinds of phrase: German shows astounding vitality in its proliferation of compound words. French speakers seek openness and clarity: Germans prefer compactness and precision. For 'labour-saving' a German can say *arbeitsparend* but a Frenchman is not allowed by the peculiar genius of his language to say anything like *labeur-épargnant*. He must say *une invention qui économise le travail* or use some other circumlocution to express the notion of 'labour-saving device'. For 'old-fashioned', German *altmodisch*, he must use some such phrase as *à l'ancienne mode*, or *de forme antique*, or, with a nostalgic undertone, *de la vieille roche*. Very often, of course, he will find a derivative to serve his turn: *pélerinage* 'pilgrimage' for *Pilgerfahrt*, *prêtrise* 'priesthood' for *Priesterstand*, *oreiller* 'pillow' for *Kopfkissen*, *pommier* 'apple-tree' for *Apfelbaum*, and hundreds of others. Often, too, he will find a simple word for a German transparent or self-explanatory compound: *dé* 'thimble' for *Fingerhut* 'finger-hat', *gant* 'glove' for *Handschuh* 'hand-shoe', *patin* 'skate' for *Schlittschuh* 'slide-' or 'sledge-shoe', *famine* 'famine' for *Hungersnot* 'hunger's need', *vivres* or *denrées* 'victuals' for *Lebensmittel* 'life's means', and many more. A Frenchman avoids all those long compounds in which a German seems to take delight. In ordinary conversation we hear a German using such expressions as *Hauptverkehrszeit* 'rush hour', *Verkehrsknotenpunkt* 'traffic junction' and *Umgehungsstrasse* 'by-pass'. He may even have recourse to serial compounding and may refer to his *Feuer- und Lebensversicherungsgesellschaft* which a Frenchman would have to denote by some such phrase as *Compagnie d'assurances contre l'incendie et sur la vie.*

With these somewhat desultory points of comparison between the French and German languages we must now bring this chapter to a close. We have touched only on the fringe of a very great theme and yet we have gone far enough to realize that a full-scale comparison of two language systems might well demand some years of hard work. It has been truly said that 'no *complete* structural analysis of any language has so far been achieved by any linguist'.

LANGUAGE AND THOUGHT

'CAN a man think without using some form of words?' This is a very old question to which the short and simple answer is 'Yes, he can'. A man can think in images alone, without words; in diagrams and models; in gestures, as in using the deaf and dumb alphabet; and even rarely in muscular movements. If, while completely absorbed in some task, you hear the clanging bell of a fire engine in the distance, you may perhaps see the image of a house ablaze with the mind's 'inward eye' without ever thinking or enunciating the vocable 'Fire!' and without allowing yourself to be deflected for one split second from what you are doing. If you catch sight of a small child tripping off the kerb in a busy thoroughfare, your action is instinctive and 'as swift as thought': you have no time to think or shout 'Stop!' On such occasions seeing is the stimulus: prompt movement is the response. Nevertheless, in spite of all that the 'behaviourists' may say, a human being is never a purely sensitive creature. For one thing, an entirely sensitive being cannot err. 'Only thinkers are capable of so distinguished an achievement as making a mistake.'

A man can think in more ways than one, but thought normally implies the use of verbal symbols. Even so, the process of symbolization may remain surprisingly incomplete. Twentieth-century novelists, like Dorothy Richardson, Virginia Woolf, and James Joyce, have displayed in their different ways that 'stream of consciousness' which flows continuously through our waking minds by day and intermittently through our sleeping brains by night in the strange uncertainty of dreams. On its surface that stream may carry many truncated linguistic structures, immediately expressive, but syntactically inconsequential and incoherent: anacolutha, aposiopeses, and fragmentary predications.

Purposeful and ordered thought, or conceptual cognition, is hard work; and yet 'most men', as Mr T. S. Eliot has recently reminded us, 'are lazy-minded, incurious, absorbed in vanities, tepid in emotion ... and therefore disinclined to think anything out to a conclusion.' To marshal all the available evidence in support of a proposition, to arrange that evidence logically so as to distinguish the main features from the subordinate ones and to select the relevant ones from the irrelevant; to state lucidly the implications of the evidence; to weigh those (perhaps conflicting) implications in the scale of probability; and finally to pronounce the verdict calmly and dispassionately – all this demands a competent manipulation of verbal symbols. Words are symbols and a language is a system of such arbitrary symbols by means of which people communicate with one another. Words in sequence convey meaning or signification. Meaning may be defined as a complex series of relations or correspondences between linguistic symbols and the world of human experience which they represent. These relations or correspondences may be classified in different ways, but for our present purpose in this chapter we shall distinguish three grades of signification, to which we shall assign the terms *semantic value*, *lexical meaning*, and *contextual sense*.

Let us now examine each of these grades or levels of signification in turn. The first belongs to individual sounds or phonemes (Chapter 4), since phonemes clearly distinguish one form, or one set of forms, from another. Take, for instance, the word *set* just mentioned. Its initial sibilant has no independent meaning in itself, and yet it has semantic value inasmuch as it marks off *set* from *bet, debt, get, jet, let, met, net, pet, vet, wet, whet,* and *yet*. By the same token it follows that the vowel of *set* has semantic value, since it separates *set* from *seat, sit, sat, sot, sort* (or *sought*), *soot, sate, site* (*sight* or *cite*). Similarly it is apparent that the final plosive has semantic value, since it differentiates *set* from *said, sedge, sen* (a Japanese coin worth one hundredth part of a *yen*), archaic *saith, sell,* and *cess* (denoting *rate* or *tax* in Scotland and Ireland).

Words and morphemes have lexical meaning, the simplest examples of which are furnished by proper names. If you hear someone mention *York*, you at once think of the cathedral city on the River Ouse situated at the junction of the three ridings. You may even see with the mind's eye an image of York Minster. A proper name offers the clearest example of lexical meaning, especially if it is applicable to one thing only in the world. It may then be regarded as an instance of unique reference or denotation, though, in respect of *York*, we must be careful to say 'unique denotation in this particular context'. There are, to be sure, apart from New York (renamed after James, Duke of York, in 1664), other Yorks in the world – in Nebraska, in Pennsylvania, and in Western Australia. Unique denotation only in a particular context may also apply to personal names. If you hear someone mention Samuel Butler, you cannot tell, without further information, whether he is alluding to the poet of *Hudibras* or the author of *Erewhon*. That is why (in his *Theory of Proper Names*) Sir Alan Henderson Gardiner is careful to insist that only names of unique objects like *Popocatepetl* and *Chicago*, and of unique persons like *Jugurtha* and *Vercingetorix*, can stand as examples of unambiguous denotation because there is, or has been, only one of each in existence. Moreover, such names are mere labels: they have solely deictic significance. To the Mexicans, however, Popocatepetl signifies 'smoking mountain' and Chicago suggests 'wild onions' to the Algonquians. People may or may not associate names with their original meanings and very often memory or oblivion has played a part in the subsequent developments of place-names like *Sutton* 'south town' or *Hampstead* 'home stead' (page 71).

Lexical meaning can be stated in three different ways. Suppose you are working at the bottom of your garden and you ask a boy to bring you a rake from the toolshed. He will at once respond only if he has a correct memory-picture of this particular implement in his mind. If he seems to be dubious about the identity of this tool, you may make a quick sketch of it on the ground with your gardening fork, or you may describe it as 'the thing with a kind of large comb at the end of a pole'. Perhaps, however, the lad is a French guest who has not yet become acquainted with the English name. You then say *râteau*. These are, in fact, the only ways in which lexical meaning can be stated: first, by demonstration; second, by circumlocution; and third, by translation. Demonstration is used by the teacher of a foreign language who has recourse to some form of the 'direct method' in his lessons, and by the lexicographer who includes diagrams and pictures in his dictionary or encyclopedia. Circumlocutions must frequently be used by the editors of unilingual unillustrated dictionaries together with numerous synonyms and near-equivalents. In preparing their two-way dictionaries of foreign languages, the editors must inevitably rely mainly on translations.

Statement of meaning may be fairly simple when instructing a boy to fetch a tool, but it may become rather complex in other situations. Colour names, for instance, present very interesting ramifications of normal references between speech symbols, mental images, and objective realities. Spectroscopists see the colour-spectrum as a continuous scale of light-waves of different lengths ranging from 40 to 72 hundred-thousandths of a millimetre, but speakers of ethnic languages mark off parts of this scale in different ways. The seven colours of the spectrum – red, orange, yellow, green, blue, indigo, and violet – are readily determinable by scientific analysis, but not easily translatable into all languages. The primal opposites, black and white, do not appear in this list of seven, since they lie beyond the confines of ultra-violet on the one side and of infra-red on the other. In a black object the light rays are wholly absorbed, whereas in a white one they are entirely reflected. Black and white became early associated in the mind of man with night and day, darkness and light, evil and good. On the whole, they present no serious divergences, but other colour-names may seem as iridescent as the rainbow itself and as evanescent as the 'uncertain glory of an April day'. Celtic *glas*, for example, may signify 'grey' or 'blue' or 'green'. Our *green*, from the Indo-European root **ghra/* **ghrō*, first designated the colour of plant life, as in the substantive *grass* and the verb *to grow*. So today we find Dutch *groen*, German *grün*, and Swedish *grön*; whereas in the Romance languages we encounter forms deriving from Latin *viridis* 'green', related to *virēre* 'to flourish', as in French *vert*, Spanish and Italian *verde*, and our own *verdant* and *verdure*. In Modern Greek *prásinos*, from the classical word for 'leek', has superseded *chlōrós* (as in our *chloric* and *chlorine*) which is cognate with Latin *helvus* 'bay, yellow' and with our own *yellow* and *gold*. Now the Latin word for 'gold' is *aurum*, whence French *or* and Spanish and Italian *oro*, from the root **aus-* 'reddish' which also gives Latin *aurōra* 'dawn' from a reduplicated form **ausosa*. Virgil applied the epithet *flāvum* 'yellow' to *aurum* 'gold' in the first book of the Aeneid, and, oddly enough, Latin *flāvus* is related to our *blue*, from French *bleu*, which is itself borrowed from Germanic. Is it so very surprising that we should find this instability of reference in colour-names as we chase them down the ages from one language to another? The British Colour Council has devised its catalogue of 240 standard hues, each with a name, a code-number, and a two-surface silk tab appended; but how many of us could both name and describe them all quite accurately without expert guidance? So, too, in referring to features of the landscape, like woodland and pasture, hill and valley, people will naturally think of the scenes and surroundings with which they are most familiar. The Black Forest in Baden on the right bank of the Upper Rhine is the German *Schwarzwald*, whose hardy inhabitants have been immortalized by Berthold Auerbach in his famous *Schwarzwälder Dorfgeschichten*. What has this ancient forest in common with the Cots*wolds* of Gloucestershire, the Yorkshire *Wolds* of the East Riding, the Lincoln *Wolds*, or the *Weald* of Kent? This same Germanic base **walduz* produced Old Norse *vǫllr* which shifted its meaning from 'forest' to 'forest glade', and then to 'untilled field', and subsequently to 'open plain' as in Lancastrian *Wal*thwaite, as in Thing*wall* 'the open field or plain on which the local parliament met' in Lancashire and Cheshire, and as in The Tyn*wald* or Court of the Isle of Man. In Old English the usual word for 'field' was *æcer*, with its old meaning still preserved in Long *Acre* and God's *Acre*, cognate with Latin *ager*, as in *agri*culture: whereas *feld* in Old English meant much the same as present-day Dutch *veld* 'tract of open country, treeless plain'. Indeed, Germanic *field* and Romance *plain* come from the same base $*p(e)l$-, $*p(o)l$-, which also appears in Czech, Polish, and Russian *pole* 'field' and in the name *Poland*. In later Old English *feld* acquired the functional implication 'land for pasture or cultivation'. Only after the ravages of the Black Death in the fourteenth century did it assume its modern sense of 'enclosed or fenced-in plot of land'.

Such simple illustrations as these demonstrate some of the difficulties that those linguists encounter who would attempt to give meaning a *structure* and to systematize these shifting relationships between words and ideas or things. Whence do we derive our knowledge of the external world? What we know about it is based partly on *observation* and partly on *inference* from what we observe. Unfortunately both observation and inference may present us with considerable difficulties. Material objects, the physicist reminds us, are not always what they appear to be, so that observation does not give that degree of certainty which common sense demands. Inferences from what we observe to what we cannot observe – the composition of the moon, for instance, or the structure of the earth's centre – may lead to conclusions that remain only probable even when the premises are true and the reasoning is correct. The modern physicist no longer speaks with that simple clarity which his predecessor displayed only three centuries ago. Newton believed in four fundamental concepts: space, time, matter, and force. For him space and time were solid and independent entities. They have now been replaced by space-time which is not substantial but only a system of relations. Matter has now come to be associated not with Newtonian *force* but with a new concept called *energy*, which is not one thing any more, but comprises a whole range of entities – kinetic, electric, thermal, chemical, atomic, and radiant.

Thus words change their significations with the broadening of knowledge; and semantics, or the science of meaning, cannot be reduced to a rigid system of correspondences. A word may enlarge its notion-sphere by the change sometimes known as *extension*, as when *place* originally 'broad (street)' in Greek comes to signify in English 'any part of space whatever'; or by the change called *specialization*, as when *meat* 'food (of any kind)' comes to be restricted to 'animal flesh'. On the whole, the commoner tendency in most languages is towards specialization which may or may not result from previous *polysemy*. By the acquisition of several different meanings a word may change its reference in the course of time since speakers may select one of these many significations to suit their immediate needs and the others may fall into desuetude. Words may rise or fall in status, they may come to possess new associations by folk etymology, they may be partially displaced, or they may be completely superseded.

Some words carry with them an *emotive colouring* of praise or blame as a close concomitant of their lexical meaning, if not an integral part of it. In a foreign language this affective connotation may be difficult to describe or determine, and it may, of course, be conveyed by other means such as rhythm, intonation, word order, and the use of hypocoristic suffixes. In English we may compare the substantives *scholar* and *statesman* with their near-synonyms *pedant* and *politician*, or the attributes *frugal* and *childlike* with their near-equivalents *niggardly* and *childish*. It might well be argued that all expressions are emotive to some extent. As Henri Delacroix once observed (in *Le Langage et la pensée*), 'All language has an emotive value (*Tout langage a une valeur affective*). If what I say were indifferent to me, I shouldn't say it.' But a man may surely make a purely scientific statement about the velocity of sound or the structure of the atom and in so doing his feelings may be almost unaffected. Almost, perhaps, but never fully one hundred per cent. That is why the philosopher may prefer the colourless signs of symbolic logic and why the mathematician may be more at home with his formulas and equations. The mathematician's symbols are semantically tautologous and his constructions signify in terms of relationship, not of substance. Are you moved to laughter or tears when you learn for the first time that 5 cubed is 125, $(a - b)^2$ is $a^2 - 2ab + b^2$, or that the area of a circle is the square of its radius multiplied by $3 \cdot 14159 \ldots$? Nevertheless even a mathematician may hesitate to buy a house numbered 13 and may go so far as to associate his happy childhood with the fact that he was born in a house numbered 7!

Dictionaries and glossaries, dealing in different ways with the inherent meanings of words, play an ever-increasing part in modern life. Not to mention encyclopedias, gazeteers, directories, and catalogues of all kinds, we have dictionaries on historical principles; dictionaries relating to special periods in the history of a language; dictionaries of contemporary usage, offering guidance and counsel on acceptable and unacceptable expressions; etymological dictionaries giving the histories of words and adducing cognate forms in other languages; pronouncing dictionaries recording the received standard pronunciations of words in phonetic script; dictionaries of synonyms and antonyms, idioms, clichés, phrases, proverbs, and famous quotations; concordances of all the words used by a particular author; dictionaries of regional dialects, slang, cant, school jargon, and underworld lingo; dictionaries of technical terms relating to arts and crafts, science and technology, music, painting, sculpture, architecture; carpentry, ceramics, forestry, weaving; astronomy, aeronautics, anthropology, botany, zoology, entomology, biology, pharmacy, chemistry, physics, electronics, hydraulics, metallurgy, engineering, and shipbuilding; and dictionaries of foreign languages, living and dead. In view of the difficult problems that confront every lexicographer, modern dictionaries and glossaries are extraordinarily efficient in practice. The lexicographer's task is always a difficult one for the simple reason that all his descriptions are approximate. No word (or semantic unit) ever has identical significations in two different utterances. There are no complete synonyms within a language. No exact correspondences occur between words of similar meaning in different languages.

The two most renowned dictionaries of the English-speaking world are *The Oxford English Dictionary* and *Webster's New International Dictionary*. Much can be learnt about our present theme – the relationship between language and thought – by sampling these two great books, that is, by selecting a short series of words and scrutinizing their treatment in the fullest possible detail. *The Oxford English Dictionary* is strictly the 1933 corrected re-issue of *The New English Dictionary on Historical Principles* (1884–1928) together with its First Supplement. It appeared just be.ore the Second Edition unabridged of Webster (1934). It remains far more philological than Webster, which is intended to meet the more practical needs of dwellers in the New World and to serve as a 'key to all the stores of knowledge in the English tongue'. Webster and its derivative dictionaries are therefore factual, encyclopedic, and illustrated. They are, however, not entirely limited to the living language since one of their aims is to help their readers to understand and appreciate the great literature of the past. The third edition of Webster (1961) is an entirely new work. Although its editors claim that it is still a 'citation dictionary', its illustrative quotations are rare and they often consist of brief phrases with no more than a bare mention of the author's name. Now Sir James Murray, who planned *The New English Dictionary* in the first place and who made so good a plan that his fellow-editors never needed subsequently to change it, intended the illustrative quotations to form an integral and prominent part of his scheme. These copious quotations were designed to demonstrate both the uses of words and their various significations particularly, the general principle being to choose one a century for each main sense of a word. These quotations are arranged chronologically within each main paragraph and they are 'left to speak for themselves'. They all consist of complete sentences followed by exact references to their sources, including date, author, book, chapter, and line, so that the reader may place any quotation within its context easily and speedily. The precise edition of the book referred to is given in the bibliography appended to the First Supplement. From the Dictionary itself the reader learns the *lexical meanings*: by studying the quotations in their original settings he ascertains *contextual senses*.

Is it true to say that the signification of a sentence or proposition is the total sum of the lexical meanings of its parts? In general this may hold good, but there are notable exceptions. We may fairly assume that the form-meaning relationship persists at three levels: first, between sounds and semantic values; second, between words and lexical meanings; and third, between sentences and contextual senses. These three levels are not mutually exclusive but cumulative. Together they constitute a structural pattern or hierarchy.

The most notable exceptions to this principle are metaphors and idioms (Chapter 9) which figure far more prominently in some languages than in others. 'It is all up with us' must be taken together as one expression. Like the French 'C'en est fait de nous', it is a *macrosememe*, unanalysable into separate parts. 'I'm from Missouri' says an American, if he regards your story as incredible, just as a Britisher might say in a similar situation 'Tell that to the marines!'

Certain word-classes like conjunctions, prepositions, articles, and pronouns seem also to offer exceptions to this principle. They have necessary functions to perform in the structure of the sentence, but have they lexical meaning within the terms of our definition? What is the precise meaning of *and*? In a phrase like *oranges and lemons* it serves as a link between two meaningful substantives. Nevertheless, it has functional meaning as a marker or sign-post. If we say *oranges or lemons*, or even perhaps *oranges and/or lemons*, we immediately observe vital distinctions in signification. Prepositions are such important structure-words that we could hardly conceive a language without them, and yet, to be sure, Chinese possesses no prepositions at all, but only subordinating conjunctions. Some prepositions may also function as adverbs. English has, in fact, just over twenty of these prepositional adverbs like *across, along, behind, below, down, off,* and *over*. Prepositions have a way of shifting their functional spheres more than other word-classes because they express syntactic relations, and not actions or ideas. This shifting of functional spheres may be well illustrated from the Slavonic languages. For instance, in Russian, Polish, Czech, and Serbian, one preposition may denote four different series of syntactic relations, whether separate or overlapping. Moreover, as a society becomes more highly sophisticated, syntactic relations acquire new subtleties. Thence arise such cumbrous prepositional phrases as *with reference to* and *in respect of* instead of plain *about* or *concerning*, or *anent* borrowed from Scottish courts of law, or even *apropos* and *vis-à-vis* taken straight from French.

Articles define, limit, or modify the signification of substantives; and pronouns are substitutes for nouns. Articles and pronouns have no full lexical meanings in themselves, but only class-meanings. They are certainly not indispensable, seeing that many languages get along very well without either. Articles are parts of the inherited structure of English, but a man could go on speaking intelligibly for quite a long time without using any kind of pronoun. Notice that *I* can refer only to the speaker of the utterance, whereas *we* can have various references. As a 'plural of majesty', or as a journalistic variation, *we* may also refer to the speaker of the utterance. It may stand for 'you and I', for the speaker with the person or persons addressed: but it may refer to a specific group or community assumed by the speaker to be present in the mind of the person or persons addressed. Lastly, *we* may refer to no specific group at all, but to people in general.

Purely verbal thinking – thinking in words without images – is the highest form of conceptual cognition of which a human being is capable. If this is so, may it not follow that a man's outlook on life is in some measure pre-determined for him by the structure of the language he learns as a child? After all, in those formative years between seven and twelve a normal child devotes a very great part of his mental energy to the acquisition and control of a work-ing vocabulary and his whole vision is coloured accordingly. His view of the world becomes his private thought world and, as Edward Sapir observed, 'the thought world is the microcosm that each man carries about within himself, by which he measures and understands what he can of the macrocosm'. This theory was further emphasized and elaborated by that profound American thinker Benjamin Lee Whorf (1897–1941) who made a deep study of Hopi, Shawnee, Nootka, and other aboriginal languages. This so-called Whorfian hypothesis 'that a man's world-outlook is determined by his linguistic upbringing' has probably been exaggerated by its more exuberant proponents, and yet few experienced philologists would gainsay its intrinsic truth.

Meantime these same philologists still feel themselves attracted towards the notion that somehow or other 'mean-ing can be structured'. This notion was indeed discussed at some length by the members of the Eighth Congress of Linguists that assembled at Oslo in 1957, just sixty years after Michel Bréal inaugurated the serious study of meaning with the publication of his *Essai de sémantique, science de significations*. Is this structure of meaning existent in language itself, or is it a kind of frame placed upon language from outside by the investigator? As soon as we abandon form altogether, passing from the certainties of phonology and morphology through the less absolute certainties of syntax and stylistics to that realm of relativities which we call semantics, so we find ourselves studying the universe, all human experience, nothing less. We find ourselves, in fact, in much the same position as Jan Amos Komenský (or Comenius) did in the seventeenth century when he attempted to divide all knowledge into compartments in order to move from ideas and things to forms, instead of (as in conventional dictionaries and encyclopedias) from forms to ideas and things. Long before this the Greeks had tried hard to do so and their endeavours had taken concrete shape in the *Onomasticon* of Pollux of Naucratis in the second century of our era. The original text of this enterprising effort has perished, but from extant secondary sources we gather that it proceeded from the gods to man, man's body, kinship, science, art, hunting, meals, trade, law, administration, and utensils. More recently Comenius's dream of a complete 'picture of the universe of things' (*Theatrum universitatis rerum*) has been partly materialized by Peter Mark Roget and his descendants whose practical *Thesaurus of English Words and Phrases* is now widely used in its revised form in Britain and in its much enlarged version by Sylvester Mawson in America. This universe of ideas is first ordered in six broad classes of abstract relations, space, matter, intellect, will, and affections. These are then divided and subdivided in their turn. But how can the reader steer his course through this uncharted sea of notions? A compass is provided in the shape of an elaborate index which inevitably occupies a large space in the book. A modern Roget has indeed much in common with the subject indexes to library catalogues, especially to those based upon the Dewey Decimal Classification, invented by Melvil Dewey in 1873, and since adopted by the editors of the British National Bibliography. By this scheme all knowledge is divided into ten main sections, each of which is indicated by one of the digits from 0 to 9 – general, philosophy, religion, sociology, philology, science, useful arts, fine arts, literature, and history. Each of these main sections is then further divided into ten subsections, and so on. Philology or linguistics stands in its right place between the social and the physical sciences. Its relationship to human society must now engage our earnest attention.

CHAPTER 12

LANGUAGE AND SOCIETY

LINGUISTICS stands in its right place in the Dewey Decimal Classification between sociology and natural science because it is a social activity on the one hand and a scientific system on the other. It was an outstanding achievement of nineteenth-century philologists (as we have seen in Chapter 10) that they succeeded in establishing the autonomy of their science as an independent discipline in its own right. Now, by a kind of paradox, twentieth-century linguists find themselves more closely associated than ever before with researchers in other fields, not only in history, geography, practical criticism, philosophy, and psychology, but also in mathematics and statistics, physics and electronics, and, above all, in anthropology and the social sciences.

From one point of view language may be regarded, like deportment or etiquette, as a series of actions. Language is an important part of human behaviour, governed by tradition and culture. While we often speak of society as if it were a static structure defined by convention, we should not forget that it is, in a more intimate sense, a highly intricate network of understandings and relationships between the members of organized units of every degree of size and complexity ranging from one human family to an assembly of nations or that ever-growing portion of mankind which can be reached by the press and television through all its transnational ramifications.

The family is the fundamental unit in human society, whether that society is sophisticated or not. As those eminent sociologists Émile Durkheim (1858–1917) and Bronislaw Malinowski (1884–1942) have demonstrated in their different ways, ties of kindred among primitive peoples are strictly observed and sexual laxity is banned. The stability of human society rests on that of the family.

A child's acquisition of language depends largely upon the quality of the family life of which it forms part. Good breeding and upbringing may contribute more to its linguistic development than formal education. The boy or girl who hears lively conversation and discussion among people of all ages within the family circle over a long period of years enjoys untold advantages.

Human society, within the home and without, depends upon constantly operative communication. Deprived of communication, society would cease to exist. Only apparently and externally is it a static sum of social institutions: actually and internally it is revivified and creatively re-affirmed from day to day by particular acts of communication performed by individuals. For example, a political party cannot be said to exist as such, but only to the extent that its tradition is being constantly reinforced and upheld by such simple acts of communication as that John Citizen votes this way or that at elections, thereby communicating a certain message, or that groups of people meet, formally or informally, in order to communicate ideas to one another and eventually to determine what themes of national interest, real or supposed, are to be presented for discussion by members of the party. The political party itself as an historical entity is merely abstracted from thousands upon thousands of such single acts of communication which have in common certain persistent features of reference. If we extend this example into every possible field in which communication has a place, we soon realize that every cultural pattern and every social act involve communication of some kind. Language is a social necessity and the right conduct of discussion is utterly indispensable to every free society, whether political, religious, philosophical, commercial, or economic. The exercise of good and wise chairmanship is of prime importance in all kinds of assembly from parish council to international forum. Numerous meetings are held every day in any civilized society. It is the chairman's responsibility to see that business is conducted in an orderly and expeditious manner; that matters for discussion are presented in such a form that those present will realize at once what they are being asked to consider and what may be expected to result from their decisions; that the decisions reached are relevant, precise, and unambiguous; and that deliberations are not prolonged by the introduction of irrelevant details, pointless repetitions, and unjustified obstructions. An efficient chairman has an easy command of language. He 'senses the feeling' of the meeting, governs it with firmness, and guides it with patience. He encourages discussion and does his best to persuade diffident members to express their views. He knows that freedom of speech is the most precious birthright of every 'open society' and that this freedom can be preserved only by tireless vigilance.

Communication is ever two-way. 'Listening is the other half of talking.' An experienced disputant is ever mindful of the timeless counsel of St Augustine: *Audi alteram partem* 'Hear the other side'. Listening well is no less important than speaking well and it is probably more difficult. Could you listen to a forty-five-minute discourse without once allowing your thoughts to wander? Good listening is an art that demands the concentration of all your mental faculties. In general, people in the western world talk better than they listen. Competition in our way of life encourages 'self-expression' even in those who have little or nothing to express! While ostensibly listening to a discussion, many people are inwardly framing a form of words that will both stun the assembly and lay low their opponents.

In the modern world we see a multiplication of communication techniques. As Stuart Chase has pointed out (in *Power of Words*, Chapter 1), 'the end products of the culture of Western societies are now all around us in Megalopolis, over us in jet airliners, under us in oil wells and bathyspheres. We can travel at twice the speed of sound, communicate at the speed of light, bounce radar beams off the moon. We are controlling plagues, stamping out syphilis, moving in on tuberculosis and polio, eliminating poverty over great areas.' One man can now speak to the whole world: mere physical proximity ceases to be important.

Parts of the world that are geographically remote may, in terms of behaviour, be closer to one another than adjoining regions. As the twentieth century moves on, so the world of learning becomes more closely integrated. Differences between urban and rural societies may long remain, greater or smaller according to circumstances. Within a highly sophisticated community, speech levels may be clearly marked: rhetorical-liturgical-poetical-archaic; literary; common; familiar-conversational-colloquial; and slang. The health and strength of the language will depend, first of all, upon the common speech as it is constantly refreshed and rejuvenated by the best conversation of the day. After all, as Logan Pearsall Smith so well observed (in *Words and Idioms*, Chapter 4), 'human speech is ... a democratic product, the creation, not of scholars and grammarians, but of unschooled and unlettered people. Scholars and men of education may cultivate and enrich it, and make it flower into all the beauty of a literary language; but its rarest blooms are grafted on a wild stock, and its roots are deep-buried in the common soil. From that soil it must still draw its sap and nourishment, if it is not to perish, as the other standard languages of the past have perished, when, in the course of their history, they have been separated and cut off from the popular vernacular – from that vulgar speech which has ultimately replaced their outworn and archaic forms.' Nevertheless, while all levels of speech should enliven and refresh one another in any society that is intellectually vigorous, it is undesirable that there should appear too wide a gap between, say, the diction of poetry and the conversation of every day. Such a gap is more likely to develop in a highly organized language whose forms are prescribed by some overruling authority like the French, Spanish, Italian, or Swedish Academy. An Academy may issue specific decrees regulating literary usage and ordering what must be taught in schools, but it cannot control the gay chatter of the marketplace or the small talk of the household. On the whole, therefore, present-day linguists would refrain altogether from applying the terms *correct* and *incorrect* to any form of expression. They would prefer to say *acceptable* and *unacceptable* and they would regard efficiency as the criterion of this acceptability rather than conformity to any standard or norm. The creative artist needs a sympathetic community around him if his art is to flourish. Initiative comes from within, but fulfilment is best achieved on the background of a living society. The artist's created work – literature, music, painting, or sculpture – is inspired by contemporary society and, if it is to be meaningful, it is handed back to that society again, and, through that society, to the world at large. Dante, Bach, Titian, and Michelangelo drew their strength from a civilization that held one common faith. To understand their work we must either ourselves share that faith or by sympathy and imagination put ourselves in the position of those who hold it. If the language of poetry departs so far from conversational usage that it becomes incomprehensible, then the poet ceases to serve society as one of its 'unacknowledged legislators' and finds himself addressing an esoteric coterie. In this respect Chaucer and Dryden were pre-eminent among English poets since they preserved the tradition of conversational language in poetry in their separate generations. They were among the most intelligible of poets and their influence on our language was both salutary and lasting.

Respect for the language of familiar conversation has induced Charles Carpenter Fries of the University of Michigan to use it as the material for a new kind of grammar. In his text-book called *The Structure of English* he presents a syntactic study in which he shows not how certain authorities think native speakers ought to use their language, but how people actually do use it in natural discourse. Fries, therefore, has taken as his data fifty hours of direct and telephonic conversations by three hundred speakers of standard English who were at the time talking spontaneously and who were quite unaware that their voices were being mechanically recorded. Their talk comprised some quarter of a million running words. The experiment was a notable one because it was in full accord with current views on linguistic rectitude and efficiency.

Effective speech is the product of education and training, even in primitive and unsophisticated societies. People do not learn to speak well by instinct or intuition as they learn to breathe, to eat and drink, or to walk. They learn to speak from the society into which they are born – first the family circle, then the village street or the town quarter, and later the school, the farm, the factory, the workshop, the business house, the professional group, the church, the club, and so on. A British or American child consigned at birth to a Chinese home would learn to speak Chinese with complete normality. A child's educability is almost limitless, and so too are its powers of adjustment.

Good speech is a social convention. It preserves a reasonable balance between discipline and freedom – between the discipline imposed by social convention and the freedom required by the speaker or writer in his endeavour to express himself adequately and effectively. A great poet may scorn prevailing convention and deliberately choose another style, as Milton did in *Paradise Lost* or as Joyce did in *Finnegans Wake*. Both these blind poets were fully prepared to pay the penalty for their departure from convention. Milton chose another tradition – that of classical antiquity. Joyce went the way of his own choosing. As an 'authentic genius out of bounds' he ventured to force communication into a strange channel through which, by its very nature, it could not freely flow. He made an interesting experiment which others have followed, but the ordinary writer is bound by necessity to steer a more even course between discipline and freedom, tradition and novelty, authority and individuality. Well-balanced writing is ineluctably conservative, and yet it needs to be continually revitalized and refreshed by the springing wells of colloquial utterance in all its manifold varieties.

In a time of rapid scientific and technological advance, the need to convey information accurately and unambiguously becomes more and more urgent. Indeed, the problems involved in the presentation of complicated facts are by no means so straightforward as many suppose, nor are their solutions simple. As Reginald Otto Kapp has recently reminded us, the present-day engineer 'can accomplish little except in co-operation with others. His day is crowded with talks, conferences, committees ... Talk and paper are, in these days, among the engineer's most important tools. He must learn to handle them well. The executive engineer has a greater use for them than for the tools that are found in the carpenter's and fitter's shops. So why think that these alone are educative? Why train engineers in the use of tools that they may never have to touch again once they have been launched on their professional career and teach them nothing about the tools that they will have to use?' It goes without saying that every engineer, even a high-ranking executive, must be able to use simple tools in an emergency, but the higher he rises the greater his need of dexterity in using the tools of language. This need is generally realized in industrial communities. In the United States, to be sure, courses in technical and business English are organized in most colleges and universities, and numerous treatises on the writing of reports are published every year. These treatises do, in fact, provide interesting material, but far too many of them have been composed on the assumption that skill in presenting technical and scientific information can be taught as an isolable discipline, standing quite apart from any application that is real to the student. Language is wrongly treated as a separate entity, unrelated to other manifestations of social behaviour. The compilers of these treatises seem to assume that there is such a thing, to use Ludwig Wittgenstein's term, as 'language on holiday', doing nothing in particular but just waiting about for any job that may come along.

Let us imagine, by way of illustration, that an entirely new piece of machinery has just been installed at a motor-car factory and that its place in the assembly line is so important that every senior operative needs to know all about its mechanism without delay. The visiting engineer entrusted with the task of expounding the parts and functions of the new device to these sectional managers has not only to know all that there is to know about it but he has also to be acquainted with the capacities and experiences of the individuals he is addressing. If he is to make his informative talk fully effective, he needs complete technical knowledge, a ready vocabulary, a brisk and businesslike delivery, and a personality that will inspire confidence and overcome unobtrusively any initial prejudices that his hearers may harbour towards the new mechanism. His exposition may or may not be accompanied by diagrams and printed instructions, but in no circumstances should it last more than three-quarters of an hour, because this seems to be man's normal limit of concentrated hearing beyond which attention inevitably flags. Moreover the lecturer must allow plenty of time at the end of his discourse for those searching questions which he will do his best to elicit, answering them cheerfully and briefly, but with great precision and care, adding felicitous illustrations here and there with touches of sparkling wit to keep everyone happy and contented. After question-time he will show no pressing need to scamper off to another engagement, but he will gladly linger with his audience and show no reluctance to continue the discussion in the canteen over friendly cups of coffee.

No two speakers would act in quite the same way in this particular operation, whose successful performance requires, first of all, a good command of language. The more complicated the mechanical change-over and the more involved the human relationships, the greater the linguistic ordeal to which the responsible technician is subjected.

Linguistic dexterity combined with good social sense is also required by the writer of technical reports. It is frequently averred that far too many writers of scientific documents are only semi-literate, when, in fact, their shortcomings are attributable to social causes. A junior technician, say, is called upon to compose a report on some new development without being told for whom the report is intended or how full and detailed it should be. Is it so very surprising that the finished document should give little or no satisfaction? It is dull and formal because it is made to deal with machines and processes which seem to have no connexion with living society. Perhaps a highly qualified man has devoted many precious hours to its composition. Addressed to a remote authority, it evokes no response and it calls forth not a single word of praise or blame. The writer henceforth makes out his reports as an irksome duty which he performs without zest or zeal. Good writing, least of all in practical affairs, is seldom a matter of technique that can be detached and isolated from other facts of human behaviour and experience.

The rendering of technical treatises presents similar problems and these should be faced squarely in these days when exaggerated claims are being made for the use of translation machines. These machines serve many purposes but they have both dangers and limitations. For example, in order to translate a medical dissertation from Russian into his mother tongue, an Englishman needs to possess two capacities and not one. He must know the Russian language and he must be a trained physician. A really competent translation of a scientific treatise is an exacting task. It is best undertaken as a work of close collaboration between author and translator, both of whom know the two languages and both of whom have some acquaintance with the subject concerned.

Notable advances have been made in the teaching of languages in schools by means of projects and consignments and through various laudable attempts to link up literature with life and language with society. In the village schools of Denmark, for instance, the children are taught to see human relationships in ever widening circles – the family; the school; the village itself with its pastor, doctor, dentist, postman, and so on; the countryside; the region or province; then 'little Denmark' once much greater than now and once 'even lording it over England' although at present somewhat circumscribed; and then 'the wide world'.

It is an entirely healthy series of pictures. When the glorious holidays come, the children can see something of this wide world for themselves by cycling south over the frontier into Germany or by taking the ferry east across the Sound into Sweden. Denmark no longer has any desire to 'lord it' over anybody, but she has gifts to offer to 'the wide world' in her literature and songs, her paintings and sculptures. Her most precious possession of all is, of course, her language. Nevertheless these Danish children know very well that they cannot hope to go far in any recognized profession without a good knowledge of at least one language other than their own.

The greater languages tend to extend their domains at the expense of the smaller ones and yet in many parts of the world we see determined efforts to preserve and fortify minority-tongues. After all, language is a symbol of high spiritual worth. When there is any kind of interference with the free speaking of a given language or dialect, or an endeavour to enforce its use, much more than the linguistic factor is at stake. Language then ceases to be a mere means of communication and becomes an emblem or token, tied up with the whole complex problem of personal liberty. In principle, therefore, it is clear that state interference either for or against a particular language is politically unsound except in so far as it becomes necessary for the conduct of government itself. Prohibitions and commands alike arouse resentment. A policy of complete linguistic toleration is both just and expedient. Only when a minority-language is used as a means to stir up subversive violence is state action justified. By the inexorable constitution of society, speakers of minority-languages are liable to certain social and economic disadvantages. Three courses are then open to them: (a) they may, left to themselves, remain as they are and continue to suffer disadvantages; (b) they may, if ambitious, become bilingual; or (c) they may, perhaps in a later generation, discard their inherited speech altogether in favour of the majority-language. Examples of (a) are the Bretons in France, the Catalans in Spain and, to some extent, the Irish in parts of the Gaeltacht along the west coast of Eire; examples of (b) are seen in the French *habitants* in Quebec, the speakers of Rumansch in north-east Italy and Switzerland, and, very largely, the Welsh in Wales; whereas examples of (c) are now furnished by the Scottish Highlanders who are gradually forgetting their Gaelic altogether and following the path already taken by the speakers of Cornish in the nineteenth century and of Manx in the twentieth.

If complete tolerance is the only sane policy for civilized governments to adopt towards minority-tongues, it is no less applicable to great languages also. Their future is quite unpredictable. Will one world language eventually emerge with the gradual spread of one accepted culture? In some measure a world language has already emerged with the rapid advance of science and with the creation of the United Nations Educational Scientific and Cultural Organization, which we call *Unesco*, but which H. G. Wells would doubt-less have christened *World Brain*. Side by side with the development of this new scientific vocabulary, we see considerable progress being made, especially in the cities of Russia and China, in the diffusion of those artificial languages like Esperanto and Interlingua which we have already discussed in our opening chapter.

Unesco is one of the Specialized Agencies of the Economic and Social Council of the United Nations, and so too is that much older organization now known as the Universal Postal Union, inaugurated by the Treaty of Berne in 1874, long before it was incorporated into UNO in 1948. The highest compliment we pay to UPU is that we often forget its very existence. It has functioned so efficiently all these years that we just take it for granted that a letter posted in London will be delivered to its proper destination in Vladivostok or Tierra del Fuego. In recent years UPU has taken a further step forward in world communication by issuing in Roman script a complete list of the post offices in all the five continents. This must surely be regarded as a signal triumph in view of the fact that, apart from numerous lesser ones, there are four other major scripts still in use in the world, namely, Cyrillic, Arabic, Devanagari, and Chinese. Even the Soviet Union and the Chinese People's Republic have been persuaded to accept the Union's stabilized transliterations of the names of their post offices into Roman script. If this process could be extended to other names in Russia and China as well as in the rest of Asia and Africa, one formidable difficulty would be overcome. National governments should now be encouraged to compile gazetteers of all place-names in use within their borders with received pronunciations recorded phonetically as in the pioneer publications of the British and Columbia Broadcasting Corporations. In tasks so important for world peace, many existing institutions should join, such as the Committee of Onomastic Sciences, the International Library Commission, and the International Standards Organization. Inevitably the Universal Postal Union will work in close association with Unesco itself and also with the International Telecommunications Union. Collaboration between these three United Nations Specialized Agencies will surely make substantial contributions towards the advancement of world trade and communication in the coming years.

Meantime universal literacy, nothing less, becomes year by year a pressing necessity. The pace quickens in the race on our planet between education and catastrophe. The problem of illiteracy is not solved by compulsory schooling alone, if, as in Britain, many men's reading is limited to the gutter press, or, as in America, many people assume a 'mucker pose' and shun as affectation anything that suggests conscious refinement or ennoblement of life. Literacy is not a state, but a process: it cannot be finally guaranteed in any society. It involves hard toil in teaching the young and it demands the subsequent enlistment of every conceivable means of enlightening grown-ups – sound radio, television, cinema, theatre, press, museum, art gallery, public library, university extension, and adult education. It is useless to teach the alphabet and the three R's to young people and then turn them back into a society that remains stubbornly uncultured and unlettered. It is essential to fortify them continually against the insidious depravity of soul-destroying slogans; to train them to be wary of all absolutes and oversimplified either-or choices; to show them how to distinguish word from thing, and how to discriminate intelligently between facts and inferences and between inferences and value-judgements; to teach them to see how language really works in action; and to help them to recognize and respect life's fundamental loyalties. In other words, it is essential to create and secure for present-day society a 'climate of literacy' in which alone national democracy is able to function and world government can be achieved.

SELECT BIBLIOGRAPHY

CHAPTER I

THE brief but profound study by Edward Sapir, *Language: An Introduction to the Study of Speech*, New York (Harcourt, Brace), 1921, vii–258 pp., has had a wide influence on twentieth-century linguistic scholarship. It should be read with the *Selected Writings of Edward Sapir in Language, Culture, and Personality*, edited by David Mandelbaum, University of California Press, 1949, xv–617 pp. Even more influential has been Leonard Bloomfield's great book *Language*, New York (Holt), 1933; London (Allen and Unwin), 1935, ix–566 pp., a comprehensive guide to modern linguistics. Louis Herbert Gray, *Foundations of Language*, New York (Macmillan), 1939, xv–530 pp., provides a highly informative introduction to historical method. Two other volumes, one British and one American, provide substantial surveys of the whole field of present-day structural linguistics: Robert Henry Robins, *General Linguistics: An Introductory Survey*, London (Longmans), 1964, xxii–390 pp., and John Paul Hughes, *The Science of Language: An Introduction to Linguistics*, New York (Random House), 1962, xiv–305 pp.

The five books just mentioned are wide and general. Any one of them offers a fairly complete picture and they supplement one another admirably. The next six books by Palmer, Sturtevant, Carroll, Gleason, Potter, and Hockett are methodical and systematic text-books for students. Leonard Robert Palmer, *An Introduction to Modern Linguistics*, London (Macmillan), 1936, xi–216 pp., deals exceptionally well with sound laws and linguistic geography. Edgar Howard Sturtevant, *An Introduction to Linguistic Science*, New Haven (Yale University Press), 1947, 173 pp., is explicitly intended as an introduction to Bloomfield. John Bissell Carroll, *The Study of Language, A Survey of Linguistics and Related Disciplines in America*, Harvard University Press, 1953, xi–289 pp., presents a critical report for educationists on recent teaching and research. Henry Allan Gleason, *An Introduction to Descriptive Linguistics*, New York (Holt), 1961, viii–503 pp., gives a competent and lucid account of present techniques of analysis, accompanied by a *Workbook in Descriptive Linguistics*, 88 pp., containing ingenious exercises (at which anyone can try his hand) in various Asian and African tongues, including Kurdish, Ilocano, Bontoc, Samoan, Dinka, Luganda, Kikuyu, Yoruba, and Swahili. Simeon Potter, *Modern Linguistics*, London (Deutsch), 1957, 192 pp., gives a clear and comprehensive picture of the subject for more advanced students. Charles Francis Hockett, *A Course in Modern Linguistics*, New York (Macmillan), 1958, xi–621 pp., is a university textbook offering a full course of study by the Professor of Linguistics and Anthropology at Cornell University.

Both Gleason and Hockett are mainly concerned with linguistic analysis. It is therefore instructive to compare their textbooks with two brief but important documents produced in America and two discursive volumes of essays published in Britain. The American documents are (1) Bernard Bloch and George Leonard Trager, *Outlines of Linguistic Analysis*, Special Publication of the Linguistic Society of America, Baltimore (Waverly Press), 1942, 82 pp., showing, among other things, the clear distinction between articulatory phonetics and structural phonemics; and (2) Roman Jakobson, Gunnar Fant, and Morris Halle, *Preliminaries to Speech Analysis, The Distinctive Features and their Correlates*, Technical Report No. 13, Acoustics Laboratory, Massachusetts Institute of Technology, second edition 1955, 66 pp. The British volumes are (1) John Rupert Firth, *Papers in Linguistics*, Oxford University Press, 1957, xii–233 pp., emphasizing the importance of the prosodic approach to analysis; and (b) *Studies in Linguistic Analysis*, Special Volume of the Philological Society, Oxford (Blackwell), 1957, 205 pp., consisting of nine essays by Firth and his colleagues at the London School of Oriental and African Studies, and others, further illustrating the functions of the prosodemes of length, stress, pitch, and juncture, and applying prosodemic analysis to various languages.

CHAPTER 2

The relationship between language and nationality was often in the mind of the Danish philologist, Otto Jespersen (1860–1943), and he expressed his views not only in *Mankind, Nation, and Individual from a Linguistic Point of View*, London (Allen and Unwin), 1946, 221 pp., but also in his earlier and more general book *Language, Its Nature, Development and Origin*, London (Allen and Unwin), 1922, 448 pp.

Julian Huxley and A. C. Haddon, *We Europeans, A Survey of Racial Problems*, London (Cape), 1935, 300 pp., was written to refute foreign propaganda: its main thesis is presented with great energy and zest. Other authoritative books on race are William Clouser Boyd, *Genetics and the Races of Man, An Introduction to Modern Physical Anthropology*, Oxford (Blackwell), 1950, xi–453 pp.; Raymond Firth, *Human Types*, London (Nelson), revised edition 1956, 250 pp.; and Conrad Hal Waddington, *An Introduction to Modern Genetics*, London (Allen and Unwin), third impression 1956, 441 pp., especially the second part of Chapter XV on *The Genetic Structure of Human Populations* which gives a succinct exposition of man's racial differences.

CHAPTER 3

The best-known text-books of phonetics on the basis of English are still Daniel Jones, *An Outline of English Phonetics*, Cambridge (Heffer), eighth edition 1956, x–326 pp., and Ida Caroline Ward, *The Phonetics of English*, Cambridge (Heffer), fourth edition 1945, xv–255 pp. For anyone working on African languages Dietrich Westermann and Ida Caroline Ward, *Practical Phonetics for Students of African Languages*, is indispensable. Complete and systematic demonstrations of articulatory phonetics are given by Maurice Grammont, *Traité de Phonétique*, Paris (Librairie Delagrave), third edition 1946, 492 pp.; by Eugen Dieth, *Vademekum der Phonetik*, Berne (Francke), 1950, xv–452 pp.; and by Raymond Herbert Stetson, *Motor Phonetics, A Study in Speech Movements in Action*, Amsterdam (North Holland Publishing Company), 1951, 212 pp. Four other competent American treatises merit special mention: Kenneth Lee Pike, *Phonetics: A Critical Analysis of Phonetic Theory and a Technique for the Practical Description of Sounds*, Ann Arbor (University of Michigan Press), 1943, ix–182 pp.; Roe-Merrill Secrist Heffner, *General Phonetics*, Madison (University of Wisconsin Press), 1949, 253 pp.; Charles Francis Hockett, *A Manual of Phonology*, Baltimore (Waverly Press), 1955, 251 pp.; and Claude Merton Wise, *Applied Phonetics*, Englewood Cliffs (Prentice-Hall), 1957, xii–546 pp.

Nikolai Trubetzkoy's pioneer treatise on structural phonemics, *Grundzüge der Phonologie*, Travaux du Cercle Linguistique de Prague, No. 7, 1939, 271 pp., is probably better known in its French translation by Jean Cantineau under the title *Principes de Phonologie*, Paris (Klincksieck), 1949. Daniel Jones, *The Phoneme: Its Nature and Use*, Cambridge (Heffer), 1950, xvii–267 pp., a sensitive and stimulating study by a mature practitioner, illustrated by examples from many languages, has been supplemented by the same author's *History and Meaning of the Term 'Phoneme'*, London (Department of Phonetics, University College), 1957, 20 pp. A valuable handbook by André Martinet, *Économie des changements phonétiques: Traité de phonologie diachronique*, Berne (Francke), 1955, 396 pp., sums up present-day views on the phoneme with clarity and skill.

A standard work on acoustics is Harvey Fletcher, *Speech and Hearing in Communication*, New York (Van Nostrand), revised edition 1953, 461 pp., and a yet more detailed account of all the complicated processes involved in human hearing will be found in Stanley Smith Stevens and Hallowell Davis, *Hearing, Its Psychology and Physiology*, New York (Wiley); London (Chapman and Hall), 1947, 504 pp. Picturesque descriptions of air-vibrations, harmonies, and the mechanics of audition are offered by Sir James Jeans in *Science and Music*, Cambridge University Press, 1937, 268 pp. An expert account of the invention and use of the acoustic spectrograph is given by Ralph Kimball Potter, George A. Kopp, and Harriet C. Green in *Visible Speech*, New York (Van Nostrand), 1947, xvi–441 pp. Students of cybernetics should first read Claude Elwood Shannon and Warren Weaver, *The Mathematical Theory of Communication*, Urbana (University of Illinois Press), 1949, 117 pp., after which they will certainly find imaginative handbooks in William Ashby Ross, *Design for a Brain*, London (Chapman and Hall), 1952, ix–260 pp., and *Introduction to Cybernetics*, same publisher, 1956, ix–295 pp. Those interested in the application of electronics to language should consult William Nash Locke and Andrew Donald Booth, *Machine Translation of Languages*, Massachusetts Institute of Technology, 1955, 243 pp. An interim report with bibliographies, *Scientific and technical translating and other aspects of the language problem*, 1957, 282 pp., has been printed by Atar at Geneva and published by Unesco. Stimulating reading is provided by *Studies in Communication*, London (Secker and Warburg), 1955, vii–182 pp., the first volume of a series of papers by experts in many fields contributed to the Communication Research Centre, University College, London; followed by a second volume on *Aspects of Translation*, 1958, viii–145 pp.

CHAPTER 4

Ernst Cassirer's life-work *Philosophie der symbolischen Formen* has been translated by Ralph Manheim as *The Philosophy of Symbolic*

Forms, New Haven (Yale University Press); London (Oxford University Press), three volumes 1953–7, entitled (1) *Language*; (2) *Mythical Thought*; and (3) *The Phenomenology of Knowledge*. The first volume gives an original and profound portrayal of linguistic symbolism. Cassirer's famous lecture to the Linguistic Circle of New York on *Structuralism in Modern Linguistics*, which appeared in *Word* 1 (1945), pp. 99–120, was delivered only a few days before his death in that same year. These and his other writings may well be read in conjunction with Carl H. Hamburg's valuable commentary on Cassirer, entitled *Symbol and Reality*, The Hague (Nijhoff), 1956, 180 pp., and Susan Katherina Langer's attractive popularization of Cassirer in *Philosophy in a New Key*, Oxford University Press, 1951, 313 pp. Other notable studies of symbolism are Charles Morris, *Signs, Language and Behaviour*, New York (Prentice-Hall), 1946, xii–365 pp., and Wilbur Marshall Urban, *Language and Reality: The philosophy of language and the principles of symbolism*, London (Allen and Unwin), second edition 1951, 755 pp. The standard text-book is Hans Reichenbach, *Elements of Symbolic Logic*, New York (Macmillan), 1947, xiii–444 pp.

The problems encountered in devising an alphabet for a hitherto unrecorded tongue are discussed at length by Kenneth Lee Pike in *Phonemics: A Technique for Reducing Languages to Writing*, Ann Arbor (Michigan University Press), 1947, 270 pp. The evolution of the world's one and only alphabet is depicted in considerable detail by David Diringer in *The Alphabet, A Key to the History of Mankind*, London (Hutchinson), 1948, xii–607 pp., copiously illustrated by diagrams and plates. A clear account of essential features is given by Ignace Jay Gelb in *A Study of Writing, The Foundations of Grammatology*, London (Routledge), 1952, xv–295 pp., and an erudite description of the cardinal phase in the development of the alphabet is offered by Godfrey Rolles Driver in *Semitic Writing: From Pictograph to Alphabet*, Oxford University Press, revised edition 1954, 254 pp.

CHAPTER 5

We find a systematic explanation of word-structure in Eugene Albert Nida, *Morphology, The Descriptive Analysis of Words*, Ann Arbor (University of Michigan Press), second edition 1949, 342 pp., and a searching demonstration of morphemic analysis in Zellig Harris, *Methods in Structural Linguistics*, Chicago University Press

1952 (also in Phoenix Books, 1960), xv–384 pp. English word-formation has been examined by Otto Jespersen in *A Modern English Grammar on Historical Principles*, Part VI, Copenhagen (Munksgaard); London (Allen and Unwin), 1942, x–570 pp., and by Hans Marchand in *The Categories and Types of English Word-Formation: A Synchronic-Diachronic Approach*, Wiesbaden (Harrassowitz), 1960, xx–379 pp.

Skeat's ten 'canons for etymology', formulated and illustrated in the introduction to his *Etymological Dictionary of the English Language* (final edition 1910) still hold good as sensible and practical principles to be observed. Skeat's canons may be compared with the counsels given by Alan S. C. Ross in Chapter 1 of *Etymology*, London (Deutsch), 1958. In *Origins, A Short Etymological Dictionary of Modern English*, London (Routledge), 1958, xix–970 pp., Eric Partridge has set a new fashion in the old art of etymology by linking together near and distantly related words in chains of discourse, enabling the reader to find his way about by means of a well-devised system of cross-references. Partridge has also supplied a supplement to Henry Cecil Wyld, *The Universal Dictionary of the English Language* (first edition 1932), which contains excellent word-histories. The science of etymology has advanced considerably in the present century. Most Indo-European languages now possess dependable historical dictionaries. For French we have Ernst Gamillscheg, Oscar Bloch in collaboration with Walther von Wartburg, and Albert Dauzat; for Spanish, Joan Corominas; for Italian, Carlo Battisti and Giovanni Alessio; for German, Friedrich Kluge as revised by Alfred Götze and Alfred Schirmer; for Russian, Max Vasmer. A full list of etymological dictionaries will be found in the preface to Carl Darling Buck's *Dictionary of Selected Synonyms in the Principal Indo-European Languages*, Chicago University Press, 1949, xix–1515 pp. A classified list is given by Robert Lewis Collison in *Dictionaries of Foreign Languages, A Bibliographical Guide*, London (Hafner), 1955, 228 pp. The components of place-names are elucidated by Albert Hugh Smith in *English Place-Name Elements*, Volumes xxv and xxvi of the Publications of the English Place-Name Society, Cambridge University Press, 1956.

CHAPTER 6

Otto Jespersen's *Analytic Syntax*, reprinted at Tokyo (Senjo), 1965, 278 pp., is entertaining as a feat of skill in linguistic algebra with multilingual instances. It may best be studied in association with those chapters in the same author's *The Philosophy of Grammar*, London (Allen and Unwin), 1924, 359 pp., which are concerned with 'ranks'. No fewer than five out of the seven parts of *A Modern English Grammar on Historical Principles* are devoted to syntax.

French sentence-structure has been ably expounded by Eugen Lerch in *Der historische französische Syntax*, Leipzig (Reisland), 3 vols., 1934; and that of German by Otto Behaghel in *Der deutsche Syntax*, Heidelberg (Winter), 4 vols., 1923-32. Lovers of French will derive inspiration and pleasure from Albert Sechehaye, *Essai sur la structure logique de la phrase*, Paris (Champion), 1926, 237 pp.; Ferdinand Brunot, *La Pensée et la langue*, Paris (Masson), third edition 1936, 992 pp.; and Charles Bally, *Linguistique générale et linguistique française*, Berne (Francke), 1944, 440 pp.

More recent views on syntax have been expressed by Bloch and Trager in Chapter V of *Outline of Linguistic Analysis*, by Gleason in Chapter 10 of *An Introduction to Descriptive Linguistics*, and by Hockett in Sections 17–24 of *A Course in Modern Linguistics*, all mentioned above. Several articles on immediate, mediate, and ultimate constituents, and on syntactic hierarchy or architectonics, have appeared in the periodical *Language*, of which two deserve special mention here: Kenneth Lee Pike, *Taxemes and Immediate Constituents*, in Vol. 19 (1943), pp. 65–82; and Rulon Wells, *Immediate Constituents*, in Vol. 23 (1947), pp. 81–117. Noam Chomsky has contributed a report on rigorous research to the *Ianua Linguarum* series, entitled *Syntactic Structures*, The Hague (Mouton), 1957, 116 pp., in which he formulates principles relating to syntactic transformations. In *An Introduction to Transformational Grammars*, New York (Holt Rinehart and Winston), 1964, 205 pp., Emmon Bach offers a succinct exposition of subsequent developments in this field.

CHAPTERS 7–8

No complete work on the enumeration and classification of the languages of the world has appeared in English. Willem L. Graff's somewhat sketchy *Language and Languages*, New York 1932, xlvi–487 pp., has been recently reprinted. Mario Pei, *The World's Chief Languages*, formerly *Languages for War and Peace*, London (Allen and Unwin), third (first British) edition 1949, 664 pp., gives sketch-maps, alphabets, word-lists, phrases, and outstanding grammatical features, but, as its title implies, it is concerned with 'chief languages' only. An excellent but quite simple picture of 'other people's languages' is in fact given by Pei in *All About Language*, London (The Bodley Head), 1956, 175 pp. For a really systematic attempt to describe the languages of the world we must therefore go to Father Wilhelm Schmidt, *Die Sprachfamilien und Sprachenkreise der Erde*, Heidelberg (Winter), xvi–595 pp., with a separate atlas of 14 maps; and to Antoine Meillet and Marcel Cohen, *Les Langues du monde*, Paris (Champion), *nouvelle édition* 1952, xlii–1296 pp., with 21 detachable maps in the end-pocket. Excellent short surveys will also be found in many (but not all) books on general linguistics (mentioned under Chapter 1): see Chapter 4 in Bloomfield, Chapter XI in Gray, and Chapter XI in Entwistle. A well-illustrated account of the Hispanic languages in Europe and America is given by Entwistle in *The Spanish Language*, London (Faber), 1936, 367 pp.; of Russian and Russia's minority-languages by William Kleesmann Matthews in *Languages of the U.S.S.R.*, Cambridge University Press, 1951, x–179 pp.; and of the Finno-Ugrian languages by Björn Collinder in *Survey of the Uralic Languages*, Stockholm (Almqvist and Wiksell), 1957, xxii–540 pp. Bernhard Geiger and others have prepared an important synopsis of the Caucasian languages for the *Ianua Linguarum* series, The Hague (Mouton), 1959, 77 pp. Descriptions of less-known languages appear in such periodical publications as the *Bulletin of the London School of Oriental and African Studies*, *Transactions of the Philological Society*, *Lingua*, *Language*, *Word*, and the *International Journal of American Linguistics*. From time to time these journals issue 'special monographs', each one of which is devoted to the scientific description of one obscure language. Such essays and monographs on Amerindian tongues are also published by the lively Summer Institute of Linguistics, Glendale, Los Angeles, California. In *The World's Living Languages*, New York (Frederick Ungar), 1964, xii–212 pp., Siegfried H. Muller gives basic facts about their structure, kinship, location, and number of speakers.

CHAPTER 9

Some of the older approaches to language learning show more common sense than do more recent methods: for example, Henry Sweet, *The Practical Study of Languages*, 1899, xv–280 pp., and Harold Edward Palmer, *The Principles of Language Study*, 1921, 185 pp., both now available as Oxford U.P. Paperbacks. Among the guide-books prepared by skilled practitioners in various fields of teaching, the following are highly recommended: Ida Caroline Ward, *Practical Suggestions for the Learning of an African Language in the Field*, London (Oxford University Press), 1937, 39 pp.; Leonard Bloomfield, *Outline Guide for the Practical Study of a Foreign Language*, Baltimore (Linguistic Society of America), 1942, 16 pp.; Charles Duff, *How to Learn a Language*, Oxford (Blackwell), 1947, 148 pp.; Eugene Albert Nida, *Learning a Foreign Language*, New York (Foreign Missions Conference of North America), 1950, 237 pp.; and Edward Vivian Gatenby, Percival Gurrey, and others, *The Teaching of Modern Languages*, Paris (Unesco), 1955, 295 pp. These books are inexpensive and anyone undertaking the arduous task of learning a new language for some practical purpose in a limited time will be well advised to procure and study them all. A very full bibliography will be found in *The Teaching of Modern Languages* published for the Incorporated Association of Assistant Masters in Secondary Schools, London University Press, 1956, 344 pp.

Wise counsel on the future teaching in British schools and universities of the five chief foreign languages – French, Spanish, Italian, German, and Russian – has been offered by Edgar Allison Peers of Liverpool in '*New*' *Tongues*, London (Pitman), 1945, 142 pp. This counsel may be compared with that given by his Cornell colleague, Robert Anderson Hall, in Chapter 12 of *Leave Your Language Alone!*, Ithaca (Linguistica), 1950. Hall foresees that some eight languages besides English will long remain in full use in the world of literature and science and he is convinced that 'there are good reasons for not regarding it as a curse and trying to get out of it, but, quite the contrary, for accepting it as a blessing and trying to turn it to our best advantage'. To the 'five chief modern languages' just mentioned Hall argues that we must now add Chinese, Malay, and Arabic.

CHAPTER 10

The report of Sir William Jones's third paper addressed to the Asiatic Society of Bengal at Calcutta will be found in Lord Teignmouth's edition of his *Works*, Vol. ii, 1804, p. 268. The whole story of nineteenth-century linguistics has been well told by Holger Pedersen, *Sprogvidenskaben i det Nittende Aarhundrede: Metoder og Resultater*, 1924, translated into English by John Webster

Spargo for the Harvard University Press, 1931. Serious students should not neglect the books of pioneers like Wilhelm von Humboldt, *Über die Verschiedenheit des menschlichen Sprachbaues und ihren Einfluss auf die geistige Entwickelung des Menschengeschlechts*, Berlin (Reimer), 1836, 425 pp.; William Dwight Whitney, *Language and the Study of Language*, New York (Scribner Armstrong), 1867, xi–505 pp.; Hermann Paul, *Prinzipien der Sprachgeschichte*, Halle (Niemeyer), first edition 1880, 288 pp., fifth edition 1920, 444 pp.; and Georg von der Gabelentz, *Die Sprachwissenschaft, ihre Aufgaben, Methoden und bisherigen Ergebnisse*, Leipzig (Weigel), 1891, 522 pp. At the century's close appeared Henry Sweet's highly compact *History of Language*, London (Dent), 1900. In the following year Ferdinand de Saussure (1857–1916) began lecturing at Geneva and the notes made by his pupils, Charles Bally and Albert Sechehaye, published under the title *Cours de linguistique générale*, Paris (Payot), 1916, 331 pp., had an influence on European linguistics comparable with that of Sapir and Bloomfield in America. Antoine Meillet (1866–1936) had been an earlier pupil of de Saussure. Meillet's studies ranged over a wide field and his books on comparative philology were distinguished by profound knowledge and lucid exposition: *La Méthode comparative en linguistique historique*, Oslo (Aschehoug), 1925, viii–116 pp.; *Caractères généraux des langues germaniques*, Paris, fourth edition 1930, xvi–236 pp.; and *Introduction à l'étude comparative des langues indo-européennes*, Paris, eighth edition 1937, xxvi–502 pp.

Another attractive introduction to comparative methods – this time in German – is given by Walter Porzig in Chapter 7 of *Das Wunder der Sprache*, Berne (Francke), 1950, pp. 259–312. My own comparison between French and German is partly based on Charles Bally, *Linguistique générale et linguistique française* (mentioned under Chapter 6).

Robert Seymour Conway, *The Making of Latin, An Introduction to Latin, Greek, and English Etymology*, London (Murray), 1923, ix–146 pp., and Thomas Hudson-Williams, *A Short Introduction to the Study of Comparative Grammar (Indo-European)*, Cardiff (University of Wales Press), 1935, xii–78 pp., are neat and stimulating booklets. An attractive guide to the three chief Romance languages is furnished by Oliver Heatwole in *A Comparative Practical Grammar of French, Spanish, and Italian*, New York (Vanni), 1949, viii–195 pp. Today we find numerous handbooks on the market offering to supply all practical conversational needs in a wide range of living tongues from Afrikaans to Urdu, but too often these handbooks have been compiled according to an unnecessarily rigid plan. The *Teach Yourself* manuals, edited by Leonard Cutts for the English Universities Press, differ widely in competence from one language to another. The more recent volumes set a good style in presentation. *Teach Yourself Norwegian*, by Alf Sommerfelt and I. Marm, deserves special mention. So, too, does Archibald Lyall's *Guide to the Languages of Europe*, London (Sidgwick and Jackson), 1932, 320 pp. Lyall first published this book as a young man and he has since taken pains to improve its general usefulness in subsequent reprints. His twenty-five selected languages include Turkish and Arabic (not to mention Esperanto). Here the learner finds reliable information on matters of etiquette and courtesy as well as a well-tried selection of essential words and phrases.

The volumes in Faber's Great Languages series are studies in depth, professedly historical and comparative. They include Sanskrit, Greek, and Latin as well as all the leading modern tongues. The series will eventually contain historical studies of the Indo-European languages as a whole and of other groups of languages – Romance, Scandinavian, and Celtic.

CHAPTER II

In addition to the philosophical text-books by Cassirer, Morris, Reichenbach, Urban, and Langer, already mentioned under Chapter 4, the reader should peruse some of the books by Bertrand Russell, more especially *The Analysis of Mind*, London (Allen and Unwin), 1921, 310 pp., and *An Inquiry into Meaning and Truth*, London (same publisher), 1940, 352 pp. He should also examine the claims of logical positivism as postulated and modified by Alfred Jules Ayer in *Language, Truth and Logic*, London (Gollancz), 1936, 160 pp., and compare these claims with the author's subsequent inquiry into the foundations of epistemology in *The Problem of Knowledge*, London (Macmillan), 1956, 222 pp. At the same time he will surely derive pleasure and profit from a close study of Henry Habberley Price, *Thinking and Experience*, London (Hutchinson), 1953, 365 pp.

Michel Bréal's *Essai de Sémantique*, Paris (Hachette), 1897, 372 pp., has been translated into English by Mrs Henry Cust, New York, 1900, 408 pp. It is mainly concerned with the ways in which individual words have changed their significations and, in the main, this has formed the topic of later studies by Kristoffer Nyrop and Albert Carnoy in French, and by Karl Otto Erdmann, Hans Sperber, Erik Wellander, and Albert Bachmann in German. A new departure was made by Charles Kay Ogden and Ivor Armstrong Richards in *The Meaning of Meaning*, London (Routledge and Kegan Paul), tenth edition 1949, xxiv–363 pp. This is a challenging, if somewhat one-sided, study and to it is appended a notable essay on *The Problem of Meaning in Primitive Languages* by the anthropologist and sociologist, Bronislaw Malinowski (1884–1942), well known as the author of *Coral Gardens and Their Magic*. Gustaf Stern's *Meaning and Change of Meaning with Special Reference to the English Language*, Göteborg, 1931, 456 pp., is a careful study which has promoted other similar studies in Scandinavia, but the writings of Stern and his pupils are not always easy to read. It is therefore all the more pleasing to turn to the remarkably well-illustrated account of semantic change given by George Leslie Brook in Chapter VIII of *A History of the English Language*, London (Deutsch), 1958, pp. 165–97. A full history of semantic studies and a good summary of present-day views will be found in Stephen Ullmann, *The Principles of Semantics*, Oxford (Blackwell), second edition 1958, 346 pp. Valuable essays on this subject are contributed from time to time to *Lingua*, *Neophilologus*, *Studia Neophilologica*, *Archivum Linguisticum*, *Transactions of the Philological Society*, *Studies in Philology*, *Language*, *Word*, and to the philosophical journals *Analysis*, *Mind*, and *The Philosophical Quarterly*.

CHAPTER 12

Essays on various aspects of social linguistics appear in Part Two of *Selected Writings of Edward Sapir in Language, Culture and Personality*, edited by David Mandelbaum, already mentioned under Chapter 1. Alf Sommerfelt's dissertation *La Langue et la société: caractères sociaux d'une langue de type archaïque*, Oslo, 1938, is based on an examination of the very primitive Australian Aranta. The impacts of one society upon another are described and illustrated by Uriel Weinreich, *Languages in Contact: Findings and Problems*, New York Linguistic Circle, 1953, 148 pp. Marcel Cohen's *Pour une sociologie du langage*, Paris, Albin Michel 1956, 396 pp., contributed to the *Sciences d'aujourd'hui* manuals, is a capable and thoughtful study accompanied by a copious bibliography of recent endeavours in this field.

Some of the problems relating to the future normalization of place nomenclature are discussed by Marcel Aurousseau in *The Rendering of Geographical Names*, London (Hutchinson), 1957, ix–145 pp. The implications of illiteracy and semi-literacy, more especially in relation to British education, are reviewed by Morris Michael Lewis in *Language in Society*, London (Nelson), 1947, 250 pp. Lively and provocative discourses on many features of language as 'the most exact of the social sciences' are given by Stuart Chase in *Power of Words*, London (Phoenix House), 1955, 308 pp.

The first International Congress of Linguists met at The Hague in the spring of 1928 and the published *Proceedings* of that and succeeding Congresses held at Geneva (1931), Rome (1933), Copenhagen (1936), Brussels (1939, only preliminary *rapports* and *résumés*), Paris (1948), London (1952), Oslo (1957), and Cambridge, Massachusetts (1962), provide highly informative reading. The annual *Linguistic Bibliography*, issued by Spectrum (Utrecht and Antwerp), is valuable since it gives full lists of all books, theses, monographs, and reviews having any kind of bearing on language studies. The *Annual Bibliography* of PMLA (Publications of the Modern Language Association of America) comes out in May. Its opening section comprises a complete record of writings on General Linguistics in English, French, Italian, Spanish, German, Scandinavian, and Russian. It will gradually extend its range to include all books and articles published anywhere in the world.

GLOSSARY OF LINGUISTIC TERMS

ablaut, see **gradation**

absolute construction, one completely 'freed' syntactically from the rest of the sentence, e.g. After this, *to cut a long story short,* he went home.

abstraction, philosophical process of stripping an idea of all its concrete accompaniments.

abstract noun, noun denoting a quality or characteristic in general, e.g. *goodness.*

accent, a practical (but not scientific) term used to denote the prosodemes of **pitch** and **stress** taken together.

acoustic phonetics, that branch of phonetics which relates to the production and transmission of sound-waves and their perception by the hearer.

acoustics, 1. science of sound; 2. total properties of audibility and resonance determining the quality of an auditorium in respect of distinct hearing.

active voice, conjugational category of the verb when the subject of the sentence is the performer of the action expressed by that verb, e.g. *John built this house.*

affective connotation, emotive colouring of approval or disapproval acquired by an expression, e.g. *statesman : politician.*

affix, bound morpheme, whether **prefix, infix,** or **suffix.**

affixation, morphological process in which affixes are added to words to form derivatives, e.g. *view : pre-view, home : home-ly.*

affricate, sound articulated as a **plosive** immediately followed by a sharp **fricative** release, e.g. the initial and final sounds in *church* and *judge.*

agglutinative type, morphological classification of those languages which unite diverse elements into single words, e.g. Turkish.

agreement, see **concord.**

allophone, a phone regarded as a positional or contextual variant of those other phones which are also members of one and the same phoneme, e.g. the initial sounds of *keep* and *calm* are allophones of /k/.

anacoluthon, lack of syntactic sequence; beginning a sentence in one way and continuing or ending it in another, e.g. *I know what you – but let us change the subject.*

analogy, process of modifying old forms or creating new ones on the basis of existing patterns.

analytic language, one using few or no inflexions, e.g. Chinese, English.

anomaly, irregularity; deviation from the norm.

antiphony, vowel alteration in the components of echoic compounds, e.g. *ding-dong*, German *bimbam*, Spanish *dindan*.

antonym, word opposite in meaning to another, e.g. *hope* : *despair*.

aphesis, 'sending away' or elimination of an initial unstressed syllable, as in *fence* from *defence*.

apocope, 'cutting off' or omission of a final syllable, e.g. *chap* from *chapman*.

apophony, see **gradation.**

aposiopesis, breaking off or 'becoming silent' in the middle of a sentence, e.g. *If only we could* –

apposition, using a noun attributively with another noun, e.g. *King* Charles; Latin, Carolus *Rex*.

articulation, 'action or process of jointing'; act of uttering sounds by means of the vocal organs.

articulatory phonetics, that branch of phonetics which relates to the formation of sounds by the vocal organs.

aspect, verbal variation indicating whether the action or state is viewed by the speaker as *completed* or *perfective*, *progressive* or *imperfective*, *instantaneous* or *momentary*, *iterative* or *frequentative*, etc.

attribute, see **attributive adjective.**

attributive adjective, adjective modifying a noun directly, in contradistinction to **predicative adjective,** e.g. the *white* house.

back-formation, word-formation in reverse; derivation of a new word, by analogy, from an existing word assumed to be a derivative, e.g. *to edit* from *editor* on the reversed analogy of *actor* from *to act*.

bahuvrihi, Sanskrit '(possessing) much rice', applied to compound words of the *barefoot* type, e.g. *paperback*.

binary opposition, contrast by which every phone in a language is opposed to every other, since a change from one phoneme to another in a chain of discourse gives a new form, e.g. *bit* : *pit*, *bit* : *but*, and *bit* : *bid* stand in binary opposition in regard to their initial, medial, and final phonemes respectively.

blend, coalescence of two free morphemes to form a new word which shares or combines their meanings, e.g. *chortle* from *chuckle* and *snort*.

bound morpheme, one that cannot stand alone as an independent word, e.g. *-ly* in *homely*.

cadence, 1. rise and fall of the voice in speaking; 2. concluding strain (in music).

case, morphological variant of a noun, pronoun, or adjective showing its syntactic relation to other words in the sentence, e.g. He held it at *arm*'s length (genitive case).

category, class into which a word is placed according to its form and function.

chain of discourse, flow of speech regarded as a sequence of phonemes on the phonological level, morphemes on the morphological level, and words on the syntactic plane.

class dialect, variety of speech used by a particular social group within a community.

clause, word-group containing a predicate, e.g. I will do this *as best I can.*

cliché, hackneyed or stereotyped expression, e.g. *grin and bear it.*

click, suction speech-sound, produced by inspiration of breath, characteristic of the Bushman and Hottentot languages.

closed syllable, one ending in a consonant, e.g. in *book-rest* both syllables are closed.

cluster, group of phonemes not necessarily constituting a syllable, e.g. *str-* in *strong*.

code, set of pre-arranged symbols for use in transmitting messages.

cognate, etymologically related; derived from the same root or base, e.g. *mother*, French *mère*, Spanish and Italian *madre*, German *Mutter*.

commutation, see **substitution.**

comparative linguistics, study of related languages with special regard to similarities and differences.

complement, word or words completing the predicate, e.g. The sun is *a star.*

complementary distribution, relationship between two allophones or positional variants of one and the same phoneme, e.g. the initial and final consonant sounds of *lull* are in complementary distribution since in English 'light l' occurs in certain environments in which 'dark l' never appears. Contrast *we learn*: *we'll earn.*

complex sentence, sentence consisting of one principal clause and one or more subordinate clauses, e.g. *The sun brings out the flowers we love.*

complex word, word of two or more morphemes, of which one or more is bound, e.g. *homeliness*.

component, one of the elements or constituents into which any compound speech form can be divided.

composition, morphological process in which two or more free forms are joined to form a **compound.**

compound word, word of two or more free morphemes, e.g. *homework*.

concord, harmony or correspondence between the flexions of nouns and adjectives in respect of number, gender, and case (**nominal concord**), and between those of nouns and verbs in respect of number and person (**verbal concord**).

conjugation, system or **paradigm** of verb inflexions to express tense, mood, voice, person, and number.

connotation, suggested or intensional meaning of an expression, including ideas and associations linked with it.

consonant, 1. voiced or voiceless sound produced by the occlusion or constriction of the air stream passing through the mouth in such a way as to cause plosion or audible friction; 2. letter representing such a sound.

constituent, one of the parts of a complex form.

contagion, semantic **contamination,** e.g. *restive* 'inert, stubbornly resisting' comes to mean 'fidgety' by association with *restless*.

contamination, influence exercised by one syntactic construction on another with which it is habitually or accidentally associated, e.g. *I am friendly with him* becomes associated with *We are friends* and so produces *I am friends with him*.

contextual sense, signification of a sentence in its particular situation or environment.

copula, word, generally a form of the verb *to be*, connecting subject and predicate or complement, e.g. The sun *is* a star.

correlative, expressing a reciprocal relation; applied to certain pairs of forms commonly used together, e.g. *either ... or ...*

decibel, logarithmic unit of sound, one tenth of a bel, recording the minimum difference in power perceptible to the human ear.

declension, system or **paradigm** of inflexions of nouns, pronouns, and adjectives, expressing case, gender, and number.

denotation, expressed or extensional meaning of a word; its direct signification.

determinant, element qualifying or limiting the meaning of another called the **determinatum,** e.g. *rain* in *rainbow*.

determinatum, element qualified or limited in meaning by another called the **determinant,** e.g. *bow* in *rainbow*.

diachronic linguistics, historical study of language and its evolution in the course of time.

dialect, variety of speech used by a particular community either in a specific area (**regional dialect**) or among members of a social group (**class dialect**).

diminutive suffix, formative element denoting smallness in size, e.g. *-let* in *ringlet*.

diphthong, gliding sound, comprising one phoneme, produced by the tongue when it begins at one vowel position and moves in the direction of any other.

dual, grammatical form denoting *two* as distinct from **singular** and **plural,** e.g. Old English *wit* 'we two'.

duration, relative length of time during which the vocal organs remain in the position required for the articulation of a given phoneme or syllable.

echoic word, see **onomatopoetic word.**

elision, omission of a sound or syllable in pronunciation, e.g. *e'er* for *ever*.

ellipsis, omission of such word or words from a construction as will be readily supplied by the hearer, e.g. after all (*has been said*).

emphasis, semantic term used to denote the special importance attaching to a word or phrase, often expressed by higher pitch, or heavier stress, or both.

epithet, see **attributive adjective.**

etymology, branch of linguistics concerned with the origins and histories of words, tracing them back to their earliest determinable forms or *etyma* within the given language group.

etymon, radical or root (Greek *étumon* 'what is true', neuter of *étumos* 'true') from which a word ultimately derives.

euphemism, substitution of a less unpleasant expression for one of disagreeable denotation, e.g. *pass over* for *die*.

euphony, pleasing sound or combination of sounds.

family, group of languages derived from the same parent language.

flexion, see **inflexion.**

flexional type, morphological classification of languages that express syntactic relationships between words by means of inflexions, e.g. Lithuanian.

folk etymology, substitution of a form with familiar components for one of obscure or less obvious origin, e.g. *sparrow-grass* for *asparagus.*

free morpheme, one that can stand alone as an independent form, e.g. both *home* and *work* in *homework.*

frequentative, see **iterative.**

fricative, consonant sound produced by the constriction or narrowing of the air passage at some point in such a way as to cause audible friction, e.g. *f, v* (labiodental); *th* [θ], *th* [ð] (interdental); *s, z* (postdental); *sh* [ʃ] *zh* [ʒ] (palato-alveolar).

function, part played by a speech form in the syntactic structure or architectonics of a sentence.

functor, small word (article, conjunction, or preposition), with little or no lexical meaning, whose function is mainly or entirely syntactic, e.g. *the, but, in.*

government, syntactic process by which one word controls the form of another to which it refers or which is dependent upon it, e.g. He likes *me* and I like *him.*

gradation, alternation of vowel-sounds caused by differences of (a) **pitch** (qualitative gradation) and (b) **stress** (quantitative gradation) in Proto-Indo-European and preserved in the derived languages, e.g. (a) *sit: sat;* (b) *sit: seat.*

grammar, 1. a practical and useful (but not scientific) term applied to cover both morphology and syntax; 2. a treatise on the morphology and syntax of a language.

grammatical category, see **part of speech.**

Grassmann's Law, type of dissimilation occurring in Sanskrit and Greek by which the first of two aspirated plosives in a word lost its aspiration, e.g. Greek *thrékhein* became *trékhein* 'to run' but *éthreksa* 'I ran' remained; *thríks* 'hair' had genitive *trichós* whence our *trichology* and *trichopathy.*

Grimm's Law, series of changes which took place in Common Germanic from about 600 to 100 B.C., by which *p, t, k* became *f, th, h; b, d, g* became *p, t, k;* and *bh, dh, gh* became *b, d, g.*

heterograph, word having the same origin as another, but a divergent meaning and a different spelling, e.g. *metal* 'class of substance': *mettle* 'quality of mind and character'.

heteronym, see **homograph.**

206

homograph, word having the same spelling as another, but a different origin, meaning, and sound, e.g. *lead* 'to guide': *lead* 'base metal'.

homonym, word having the same sound and spelling as another, but a different origin and meaning, e.g. *rest* (from Old English) 'repose': *rest* (from Old French) 'remainder'.

homophone, word having the same sound as another, but a different origin, meaning, and spelling, e.g. *raise: raze: rays*.

hybrid, compound word or derivative with elements from two or more languages, e.g. *television* (Greek and Latin), *bicyclette* (Latin, Greek, and French).

hypocoristic suffix, formative element denoting endearment, e.g. *-nie* in *Johnnie*.

hypotaxis, subordination; syntactic relationship between dependent and independent constructions, e.g. *He who knows can tell us.*

ideophone, modifying element, often onomatopoetic, used in the Bantu languages.

idiolect, variety of speech used by one given individual in its relation to the accepted language system.

idiom, 'private turn of phrase', expression peculiar to a specific language, e.g. *It's all up with us.*

imitative word, see **onomatopoetic word.**

immediate constituent, one of the two or three (next lowest) constituents of which any given construction is formed.

incorporating type, morphological classification of those languages which merge various elements into a composite verb expressing a complete proposition, e.g. Nahuatl.

infix, formative element inserted within a word, e.g. *-n-* in *stand* as contrasted with *stood*.

inflexion, morphological process in which an element is added to a basic form to denote number, person, case, tense, etc., e.g. *home: home-s, wait: wait-ed.*

intersegmental phoneme, see **prosodeme.**

intonation, rise and fall in the **pitch** of the voice in the flow of speech.

intransitive verb, verb used intransitively; verb not governing a direct object, e.g. Somewhere the sun *is shining*.

invariable, having only one form, incapable of inflexion or other change, e.g. *seldom*.

inversion, reversal of normal word order, especially of the order of subject and verb, e.g. *Had I* time, I would gladly go.

isolating type, morphological classification of those languages which use no bound forms, e.g. Chinese.

iterative, verbal **aspect** denoting that the action is repeated, e.g. Latin *clāmitō* 'I keep on shouting'.

jargon, technical expressions used among themselves by members of a particular profession, craft, or trade, not intelligible to the general public.

juncture, an intersegmental prosodeme; manner in which segmental phonemes and syllables are joined together in the flow of speech.

language, a system of arbitrary and conventional vocal symbols by means of which human beings communicate and cooperate with one another.

latent compound, word whose components have become hidden or obscure, e.g. *barn, nest.*

lexical meaning, signification of a morpheme or word considered as part of the total stock of the morphemes or words of a given language.

lexicon, vocabulary, total stock of morphemes in a given language.

liaison, linking together of forms by the pronunciation of an otherwise mute consonant sound before a vowel, e.g. French *sent-il?* [săt il] 'does he feel?' but *il sent* [il sã] 'he feels'.

linear phoneme, see **segmental phoneme.**

linguistics, science of language.

macrosememe, signification of an expression taken as a whole and showing no relation to the meanings or sememes of its parts, e.g. *Tell that to the marines!* signifying 'I am sceptical'.

meaning, complex series of relations or correspondences between linguistic symbols and the world of human experience for which they stand.

metanalysis, misdivision of syllables, e.g. *an apron* for *a napron, a newt* for *an ewt.*

metaphony, see **mutation.**

metathesis, transposition of consonant sounds, e.g. *three*, but *third* from Old English *thridda*.

monophthong, phoneme comprising one phone, e.g. the vowel sound in *bat* as contrasted with the diphthong in *bout* and the triphthong in *bower.*

monosyllable, word comprising one syllable, e.g. *word.*

mood, form of verb indicating whether the action or state is viewed by the speaker as *affirmative, possible, desirable,* etc.

morpheme, minimum meaningful unit of speech, which may be **bound** or **free,** e.g. *home* (one free morpheme): *homely* (two morphemes, one free and one bound): *homework* (two free morphemes): *homeliness* (three morphemes, one free and two bound).

morphemics, see **morphology.**

morphology, study of the morphemes of a language as used in the making of words.

multiple sentence, sentence consisting of two or more co-ordinate clauses, e.g. *The sun warms the earth and brings out the flowers.*

mutation, modification in the quality of a vowel sound through the influence of another vowel in the following syllable, e.g. *tooth: teeth* <* *tōpi.*

nominal concord, harmony or correspondence between the flexions of nouns and adjectives in respect of number, gender, and case, e.g. *this church: these churches.*

nonce-word, word invented for a special occasion and used only once.

obscured compound, see **latent compound.**

occlusive, see **plosive.**

ogam, ancient British and Irish alphabet of twenty letters.

Old High German Consonant Shift, series of changes which took place in Old High German from about A.D. 600 to 800 by which *p, t, k* became *pf, ts* (written *z*), *kh* (written *k* and so neutralized) initially and medially after consonants; but *ff, zz* (written *ss*) and *hh* (written *ch*) after vowels.

onomatopoetic word, one whose sound echoes its sense, e.g. *clack, clang, roar, splash, tinkle.*

open syllable, one ending in a vowel, e.g. in *ba-na-na* all three syllables are open.

operator, see **functor.**

orthography, correct or accepted use of the written characters of a language.

paradigm, system of inflexion, including **declensions** of nouns, pronouns, and adjectives, and **conjugations** of verbs.

parasynthesis, morphological process in which **affixation** and **composition** are joined, e.g. *screw-driv-er* (noun), *web-foot-ed* (adjective).

parataxis, coordination; juxtaposition of independent constructions, e.g. *Who knows? He can tell us.*

parenthesis, phrase or clause inserted into a sentence which is syntactically complete without it, e.g. Here, *as you very well know*, is the end.

parse, 1. to describe a word by classifying it as a **part of speech** and indicating its syntactic relation to the rest of the sentence; 2. to resolve a sentence into its component parts, describing each of these parts in terms of its syntactic function.

part of speech, one of the categories into which words are divided according to their functions.

passive voice, conjugational category of the verb when the subject of the sentence is the object or goal of the action expressed by that verb, e.g. The house *is being built*, Latin domus *aedificātur*.

pejorative suffix, one conveying a disparaging or depreciatory connotation, e.g. *-ish* in *childish*, *-aster* in *poetaster*.

period, 1. pause at the end of a sentence; 2. full stop indicating this pause; 3. periodic sentence.

periodic sentence, sentence in which the most significant part is reserved for the end.

periphrasis, circumlocutory expression.

philology, 1. linguistics; 2. exact and minute interpretation of texts.

phone, sound regarded as a rudimentary member of a phoneme.

phoneme, 1. class or bundle of sounds or phones, no two of which can ever take each other's place in the same environment; 2. minimum distinctive sound-feature into which any given flow of speech can be divided.

phonemics, see **phonology.**

phonetics, science and classification of speech-sounds including their production by the speaker, their transmission as air-vibrations, and their perception by the hearer.

phonology, study of the sounds or phonemes of a language regarded as a system or structure.

phrase, word-group lacking a predicate, e.g. I will do this *to the best of my ability*.

pitch, highness or lowness of tone varying according to the rate of vibration of the vocal cords in uttering a given sound.

plosive, consonant sound made by the occlusion of the air passage at some point: e.g. *p, b* (bilabial), *t, d* (dental or post-dental), *k, g* (palatal or velar).

plural, grammatical form denoting *many* as distinct from **singular** and **dual.**

polysemy, multiple signification; acquisition or possession by one word of several significations, e.g. *head.*

popular etymology, see **folk etymology.**

portmanteau word, see **blend.**

positional variant, see **allophone.**

predicate, that part of a sentence or proposition which expresses something about the subject, e.g. The sun *rises in the east.*

predicative adjective, adjective modifying a noun indirectly and forming part of the predicate, in contradistinction to **attributive adjective,** e.g. the house is *white.*

prefix, formative element placed before a word to make a derivative, e.g. *pre-* in *prefix.*

privative, term applied to prefixes and suffixes indicating the lack or absence of the quality denoted by the main form, e.g. *a-, non-, un-, -less.*

proposition, declarative sentence; expression in which something is predicated.

prosodeme, prosodic feature accompanying linear or segmental phonemes in the flow of speech; one of the suprasegmental prosodemes of **duration, pitch,** and **stress;** or the intersegmental prosodeme of **juncture.**

quantity, see **duration.**

radical element, see **root.**

rection, see **government.**

reduplication, morphological process involving the partial or complete repetition of any formative element or word, e.g. *great-great-grandfather, red red rose,* Latin *cucurrī* 'I ran'.

referend, the thing or idea 'meet to be referred to' by a verbal symbol, e.g. the referend of *honey* is 'the nectar of flowers collected by bees and other insects', and the referend of *courage* is 'that quality of mind which enables a man to face dangers and difficulties without fear'.

regimen, see **government.**

regional dialect, variety of speech used by a particular community in a definite area, e.g. the dialect of Wharfedale in the West Riding of Yorkshire.

root, basic element of a word, common to all cognate forms, to which prefixes and suffixes are added, e.g. **hen* 'grasp' is the root of *in-com-pre-hen-s-ib-il-it-y*.

rune, letter of the Germanic alphabet which consisted of straight strokes based upon Greek and Latin characters suitable for carving on wood and stone.

secondary phoneme, see **prosodeme.**

segmental phoneme, phoneme regarded as the minimum unit of sound in the chain of discourse.

segmentation, linear analysis; dividing the flow of speech into consecutive bits for comparison with bits of other utterances.

semantics, science of meaning; branch of language study concerned with the relationships between **symbols** and **referends.**

semantic value, signification of an individual sound or phoneme as a feature distinguishing the form in which it occurs from certain other forms, e.g. *s-* in *set* has semantic value because it distinguishes *set* from *bet, debt, get, jet, let, met,* etc.

sememe, meaning of a morpheme.

semiotics, science of signs, including sign-signals and sign-symbols.

sentence, minimum complete **utterance;** part of a **chain of discourse** occurring between two periods.

sibilant, consonant with hissing sound [*s, z, ʃ, ʒ*] produced by the tongue on the hard palate.

sign, any mark or gesture, whether **signal** or **symbol,** that conveys information.

signal, special kind of **sign** that gives direct and immediate indication of something.

signification, see **meaning.**

simple sentence, sentence having one predication, e.g. *The sun warms the earth.*

simple word, word of one morpheme, e.g. *home.*

singular, grammatical form denoting *one* as distinct from **dual** and **plural.**

slang, variety of familiar and colloquial speech, often new, picturesque, and striking, but not yet fully recognized and accepted by the community as a permanent part of the common language.

sonority, inherent loudness of a phoneme or group of phonemes.

specialization, restriction of semantic sphere, e.g. *meat* 'food (of any kind)' comes to signify only 'animal flesh'.

stress, relative force of breath with which a syllable or word is uttered.

structural linguistics, study of a language as a coherent structure and homogeneous system.

structure-word, see **functor.**

style, 1. mode of verbal expression; 2. collective characteristics of artistic expression proper to a person or school or period.

stylistics, branch of language study concerned with the free selection of forms.

subject, that part of a sentence or proposition representing the person or thing about which something is predicated, e.g. *John* is engaged in research.

substitution, insertion of one speech-form for another, e.g. To the best of my knowledge (*So far as I know*), this statement is correct.

suffix, formative element placed after a word to make a derivative, e.g. *-ness* in *goodness.*

suppletive, supplying a missing form in a defective paradigm, e.g. go: *went,* Latin fero: *tūlī,* French je *vais*: nous allons.

suprasegmental phoneme, see **prosodeme.**

syllable, group of phonemes uttered with one breath pulse and heard as one unit of sonority.

symbol, special kind of **sign** that represents or stands for something else with which it is made synonymous.

synchronic linguistics, descriptive study of a language at any one point in time.

synonym, word similar to another in meaning, e.g. *freedom*: *liberty.*

syntactic contamination, see **contamination.**

syntax, sentence construction; study of the arrangement and functions of words as members of a sentence.

synthetic language, morphological classification of languages that make abundant use of inflexions, e.g. Finnish.

telescoped form, see **blend.**

tense, verbal form indicating whether the action or state is viewed by the speaker as *past, present,* or *future.*

tone, see **pitch.**

transitive verb, one used transitively; verb governing a direct object, e.g. The sun *warms* the earth.

typology, study of morphological types, e.g. **isolating, flexional, agglutinative,** and **incorporating.**

ultimate constituent, smallest meaningful unit into which any given construction can be broken down, consisting of a morpheme on the morphological level and a word on the syntactic plane.

umlaut, see **mutation.**

utterance, part of a **chain of discourse** occurring between two silences.

verbal concord, harmony or correspondence between the flexions of nouns or pronouns and verbs in respect of number and person.

Verner's Law, modification of the first stage of Grimm's Law by which *f, θ, h* which developed from *p, t, k* became voiced to *v, ð, g* when the stress did not immediately precede.

voice, verbal category denoting whether the subject of the verb is the agent or the goal of the action expressed.

voiced, pronounced with vibration of the vocal cords.

voiceless, not voiced.

vowel, 1. voiced sound produced by the air stream passing through the mouth without plosion or audible friction; 2. letter representing such a sound.

vowel harmony, feature of Turkish and other Ural-Altaic languages according to which front vowels are followed by front vowels and back vowels by back vowels within a word, e.g. *vermek* 'to give' but *almak* 'to take'.

word, minimum free form consisting of one or more morphemes; arbitrary or conventional segment of utterance.

INDEX

This index does not include words used as illustrative examples and it contains no references to the Bibliography.

MORE ABOUT PENGUINS
AND PELICANS

If you have enjoyed reading this book you may wish to know that *Penguin Book News* appears every month. It is an attractively illustrated magazine containing a complete list of books published by Penguins and still in print together with details of the month's new books. A specimen copy will be sent free on request.

Penguin Book News is obtainable from most bookshops; but you may prefer to become a regular subscriber at 3s. for twelve issues. Just write to Dept EP, Penguin Books Ltd, Harmondsworth, Middlesex, enclosing a cheque or postal order, and you will be put on the mailing list.

Another book published by Penguins is described on the following page.

Note: *Penguin Book News* is not
available in the U.S.A.

Also by Simeon Potter

OUR LANGUAGE

Can we ever know too much about the words we use every day of our lives? It is the purpose of this book to present a clear and up-to-date picture of the English language as it is spoken and written in all its amazing variety and complexity. Professor Potter believes that more people today are interested in speech than ever before and that a new spirit of linguistic enterprise and adventure is astir. Can we make the English language of tomorrow yet more effective as a means of communication?

'The author is brilliantly successful in his effort to instruct by delighting. He has only 200 pages at his disposal, yet he contrives not only to give a history of English, but also to talk at his ease on rhyming, slang, names, spelling reform, American English, and much else. The book is admirably clear in its main outlines, but its interest for the common reader derives from the wealth of examples at every point: the chapter on names is particularly well done. Altogether a fascinating book'
– *Higher Education Journal*